INC. YOURSELF

INC. YOURSELF

How to Profit by Setting Up Your Own Corporation

SIXTH EDITION

Judith H. McQuown

MACMILLAN PUBLISHING COMPANY   NEW YORK

COLLIER MACMILLAN PUBLISHERS   LONDON

This book uses 1988 tax rates, with the exception of chapter
13 which uses 1987 tax forms.

Macmillan Publishing Company
866 Third Avenue, New York, NY 10022
Collier Macmillan Canada, Inc.

Library of Congress Cataloging-in-Publication Data
McQuown, Judith H.
Inc. yourself: how to profit by setting up your own corporation/
Judith H. McQuown.
p. cm.
Includes index.
ISBN 0-02-583750-8
1. Corporations—Handbooks, manuals, etc. 2. One-man companies—
Handbooks, manuals, etc. I. Title.
HD2741.M38 1989
658.1'145—dc19   88-15368
CIP

Macmillan books are available at special discounts for bulk purchases
for sales promotions, premiums, fund-raising, or educational use.
For details, contact:

Special Sales Director
Macmillan Publishing Company
866 Third Avenue
New York, NY 10022

10 9 8 7 6 5 4 3

Designed by Jack Meserole

PRINTED IN THE UNITED STATES OF AMERICA

For Harrison Roth

CONTENTS

PREFACE TO THE SIXTH EDITION

Welcome to the sixth edition of *Inc. Yourself: How to Profit by Setting Up Your Own Corporation*. When I first wrote *Inc. Yourself*, eleven years and 250,000 copies ago, the decision to incorporate was a fairly simple one to make.

It isn't anymore.

Nearly every year of the Reagan administration has produced major tax legislation that has impacted the small corporation:

1981   Economic Recovery Tax Act
1982   Tax Equity and Fiscal Responsibility Act (TEFRA)
1982   Subchapter S Revision Act of 1982
1984   Deficit Reduction Act of 1984
1986   Tax Reform Act of 1986
1987   Omnibus Budget Reconciliation Act of 1987 (usually referred to as the Revenue Act of 1987)

Many of the changes have benefited small corporations. Tax rates for most small corporations have been lowered, as shown below:

	1981	1983	1988
Under $25,000	17%	15%	15%
$25,001–$50,000	20	18	15
$50,001–$75,000	30	30	25
$75,001–$100,000	40	40	34
Over $100,000	46	46	34

A corporation whose net income was $50,000 would have paid $9,250 in federal income taxes in 1981, $8,250 in 1983, and $7,500 in 1988.

Only for personal service corporations in the following professions was the corporate rate boosted to a flat 34 percent by the Revenue Act of 1987 late last year:

... health, law, engineering, architecture, accounting, actuarial science, performing arts or consulting. . . .

(Internal Revenue Code §448)

For individuals in these fields, it still may pay to *"Inc. Yourself."* By using a Subchapter S corporation, they can enjoy the legal and business status of a corporation while being taxed at what may be a slightly lower individual rate. Because Subchapter S corporations now work so well for certain professionals, as a result of the Tax Reform Act of 1986 and the Revenue Act of 1987, Subchapter S corporations are the subject of an entire new thirty-seven-page chapter in this edition of *Inc. Yourself.*

Clearly, there are still many compelling business and tax reasons to *Inc. Yourself.* This book will help you make the right decision.

ACKNOWLEDGMENTS

I am grateful to many people who gave so generously of their time—especially during income-tax season.

In particular, I would like to thank: Dean Ridlon of the State Street Bank and Trust Company of Boston; Mary Ellen O'Brien and Jaye Fallar of The Bank of New York; John J. Ryan of the Metropolitan Life Insurance Company; and many people at the Internal Revenue Service in New York City.

Special thanks must go to Todd J. Wolosoff, and to Ranan J. Wichler, Lawrence C. Orenstein, and Stephen A. Baxley of Touche, Ross & Co., who sat patiently for many hours of interviews and helped me with some of the charts and sample tax returns.

At Macmillan I am grateful for the help of Bill Rosen, my editor.

I am especially grateful to John D. Diamond, my lawyer.

And, most of all, my heartfelt thanks to Harrison Roth for all his patience and advice on the fourth, fifth, and sixth editions.

INTRODUCTION

This book is not designed to substitute for your lawyer or accountant, but rather to serve as a guide and enable you to make the most of their professional help. While you *can* incorporate and set up tax shelters yourself, without legal advice, it is far more desirable not to go it alone. Tax laws are complicated and often change from year to year; it takes a skilled professional to stay on top of them.

You don't have to be a professional to incorporate—if you're a self-employed salesman, plumber, real estate agent, antique dealer, hairdresser, this book can save you money. If you can show a net profit, this book can save you money. All you have to do is form a corporation, and this book will show you how it can be done, step by step.

While we'll discuss corporations completely in Chapter 1, "So You Want to Be a Corporation," for now let's define a corporation simply as a body of persons granted a charter that legally recognizes them as a separate entity with its own rights, privileges, and liabilities. But don't let the "body of persons" wording scare you; most states permit one person to incorporate (see chart, Appendix A).

Depending on the state you live in, your business or profession may require you to incorporate as a *professional corporation* (see Appendix A), but this means only that your professional practice is now able to enjoy all the benefits and privileges of corporations that had earlier been prohibited. There is no difference in the *tax* treatment of professional versus business corporations; the only difference is a legal and supervisory one: if you form a professional corporation, all the shareholders and officers of the corporation must be licensed as professional practitioners in the state of incorporation. Your husband or wife and children cannot own stock in the corporation—even as minority stockholders—unless they, too, are licensed as professionals.

Thus, in terms of the law, a professional corporation is more limited in structure than a general business corporation; if your state permits you to choose, it is better to incorporate as a general business corporation. But whatever you do, if you are earning enough money and want to shelter substantial portions of it from taxes, you should consider incorporation.

Now sit back, read carefully, and you, too, can *Inc. Yourself* and *Profit by Setting Up Your Own Corporation.*

1

So You Want to Be a Corporation

Now that your appetite has been sufficiently whetted by visions of tax-free sugarplums, let's get down to basics.

Until now, most self-employed people have been operating as sole (or individual) proprietorships, a form of business organization in which the individual provides the capital, starts and runs the business, and keeps all the net profits and is taxed on them. As a sole proprietorship, the individual assumes total liability.

One step up from the sole proprietorship in complexity is the partnership, in which two or more people act as joint proprietors: they provide joint funding, joint management, and joint financial responsibility. Unfortunately, like the sole proprietorship, the partners are personally liable to an unlimited degree for all the other partners.

A corporation is the most sophisticated—and protective—form of business organization. It is a "legal person," completely separate from the individuals who own and control it. A corporation has the power to do anything any person may do: carry on business, own property, lend and borrow money, sue and be sued. Most important, it offers its shareholders limited liability: its stockholders can lose no more than their original investment; they are not liable for the debts of the corporation.

In terms of limited exposure to liability alone, it pays to incorporate to protect your assets; if you incorporate, no one can attach your house, car, or Ming vases if your business fails or if you lose a lawsuit. While this point is particularly important in such obvious professions as medicine, dentistry, law, architecture, and the construction industry, there are lesser-known areas in which limited liability plays an important role.

One of my friends incorporated himself to produce illustrated science fiction and children's books. For him, too, the primary benefit of incorporation has been limited liability: "I publish authors whose work some people might find offensive, and they might sue me, as the publisher. Rather than reject authors whose work I respected, but who might be dangerous, it seemed safer to incorporate. If I were sued, I wouldn't be personally liable."

Although limited liability may be the most attractive feature of incorporating, there are many others. For many people, there is greater ease in doing business. Some stores favor corporate accounts and offer discounts. Yes, even Tiffany's.

Incorporating can make job possibilities more attractive to new or future employees. There's a feeling of working for a profitable enterprise associated with incorporation, you can offer them greater benefits out of pretax dollars, and, of course, you can always offer them a promotion in title instead of a raise.

Then, too, there are medical, life, and disability insurance benefits. Although the Tax Equity and Fiscal Responsibility Act has finally let Keogh Plan contributions achieve parity with corporate pension contributions, your benefits will be still greater if you incorporate. Incorporation offers you free life and disability insurance. There is even one kind of insurance you can't get as a self-employed person but can get as the employee of your corporation, even if you are the *only* employee—workers' compensation.

Medical benefits alone can make it worth your while to incorporate. If you pay your medical bills as a sole proprietor, their totals are reduced by 7.5 percent of your adjusted gross income. For most people, these deductions can wipe out over $5,000 in medical bills every year.* But your corporation can write off *all* your family's medical bills—they're considered a business expense.

---

*Recently, sole proprietors have been permitted to deduct 25 percent of their health insurance costs in calculating their Adjusted Gross Income, which works out to less than $100 in actual tax dollars for most taxpayers.

Is your business so profitable that you've been investing in stocks? Good. Whereas before, as a sole proprietor, you had to pay income tax on all your dividends, now, if your corporation invests in those stocks, 70 percent of those dividends are completely excluded from income tax, and the remaining 30 percent are taxed at only 15 percent (if your corporate net taxable income was $50,000 or less) and at only 25 percent (if your corporate net taxable income was between $50,000 and $75,000). The maximum rate is 34 percent for corporate net income over $75,000.

That's the good news. There are a few drawbacks, but they're mostly minor ones. There will be more paperwork, and you will have to set yourself a salary and live within it. There will be a greater number of taxes to pay, but your total tax bill will be much lower than it was as a sole proprietorship—especially starting in 1990, when sole proprietors will lose their 2 percent Social Security tax credit and have to pay the same 15.3 percent Social Security tax that incorporated individuals will pay.

It's pretty clear that the advantages far outweigh the disadvantages, and that's why more and more people are following their lawyers' and accountants' advice and incorporating!

THE MYTH OF DOUBLE TAXATION

A little knowledge is a dangerous thing. Here's proof: if you tell friends and colleagues that you're thinking of incorporating, sooner or later one of them will say to you, "But you don't want to do that—you'll be subject to double taxation."

True—and false. You *will* have to pay two taxes—but you won't be taxed twice on the same money. What's more important, *your total taxes will be less*—often by 30 to 50 percent, as compared with an individual proprietorship.

Let's look at some examples. In the first set of figures, our entrepreneur hasn't incorporated. Using 1988 tax rates, he would have to pay $7,494 if he was single and $4,841 if he was married, assuming that he had no children and was filing a joint return with no other income:

	Single	Married
Net income	$40,000	$40,000
Less exemption(s)	1,950	3,900
	$38,050	$36,100
Less standard deduction	3,000	5,000
Net taxable income	$35,050	$31,100
Income tax	$7,494	$4,841

However, if our entrepreneur incorporates, pays himself $20,000 a year, and retains $20,000 in the corporation, the numbers change dramatically:

	Single	Married
Retained corporate earnings	$20,000	$20,000
Taxed at corporate rate	×15%	×15%
Corporate tax	$ 3,000	$ 3,000
Salary	$20,000	$20,000
Less exemption(s)	1,950	3,900
	$18,050	$16,100
Less standard deduction	3,000	5,000
Net taxable income	$15,050	$11,100
Income tax	$ 2,258	$ 1,665
Corporate tax	3,000	3,000
Total taxes	$ 5,258	$ 4,665
Income tax on $40,000	$ 7,494	$ 4,841
Amount saved	$ 2,236*	$ 176*
Percentage saved	30%*	4%*

*The amounts and percentages saved are really much higher than those shown because the $17,000 after-tax corporate income could be invested to produce $1,500 in dividends, of which $1,050 would be tax-free and $450 would be taxed at only 15 percent. Thus, the total tax on $1,500 of dividends would be only $67.50. In comparison, single and married taxpayers whose net income was $40,000 and who received $1,500 in dividends would be taxed $420 on the dividends.

The percentage saved by the single entrepreneur has actually *risen* from 28 percent in the 1986 edition to 30 percent now.

The more money you earn, the more you can save by incorporating. Splitting net income of $50,000 into $25,000 salary and $25,000 retained corporate earnings results in much greater savings, especially for married entrepreneurs, where the percentage of taxes saved zooms from 4 percent to 19 percent:

1988 Corporate Tax Rates		1988 Personal Income-Tax Rates*		
			Single	Married
$0–$50,000	15%	$50,000	33%	28%
$50,000–$75,000	25%			
$75,000+	34%	$75,000	33%	33%

*Net income, after deductions and exemptions.

The table below shows how favorable corporate tax rates are compared to personal income-tax rates:

	Single	Married
Personal income tax on $25,000	$ 3,294	$2,415
Corporate income tax on $25,000	3,750	3,750
	$ 7,044	$6,165
Personal income tax on $50,000	$10,294	$7,641
Amount saved	$ 3,250	$1,476
Percent saved	32%	19%

Thus, for the first $50,000 in income each year, the personal income-tax rates are approximately *double* the corporate tax rates. At that point the gap narrows, but, for most one-person corporations, corporate tax rates are still always lower than or equal to personal tax rates.

But the most important point, of course, is that by incorporating, you can divide your income into *two portions,* as shown earlier, *each of which is taxed at a lower rate.*

ARE YOU EVER TOO YOUNG TO INCORPORATE?

Although the voting age has been lowered to eighteen, in many states you still must be twenty-one to incorporate. From a practical point of view, most experts recommend incorporating as soon as possible. Incorporation has many intangible benefits for young people. The young publisher I mentioned earlier says, "I find it easier to deal as a corporation. I have less trouble in getting good people to work for me; they feel that a corporation is more responsible financially. It seems to increase my financial stature, even in my personal life. I had fewer credit-investigation problems when I wanted to rent an expensive apartment."

ARE YOU EVER TOO OLD?

Of course, the older you are, the fewer years you have in which to accumulate tax-sheltered retirement funds. Still, according to Dean Ridlon of the State Street Bank and Trust Company of Boston, "people in their fifties can still incorporate profitably; it all depends on how much money they're earning every year. A successful professional can certainly make use of incorporation in order to provide substantial retirement funds even if retirement is ten, five, or even only three years away."

ARE YOU EVER TOO RICH TO INCORPORATE?

Yes, Virginia, there is such a thing as making too much money to incorporate. Your corporation can accumulate $150,000/$250,000* —no questions asked. Above that figure, you must prove that your corporation needs the money for business purposes. Otherwise, the IRS will take the position that your company has liquid assets that are "greatly in excess of its reasonable business needs" (IRS regulations quoted) and will impose additional punitive taxes on the corporation.

The corporation then comes to the crossroads, where it must either declare a dividend, on which the stockholders would be taxed; or justify the accumulation by showing "specific, definite, and feasible plans" (IRS regulations quoted) for the use of that accumulation.

---

*The IRS limits corporations whose principal function is "services in the field of law, health, engineering, architecture, accounting, actuarial science, performing arts, or consulting" to $150,000. The limit for all other corporations was raised to $250,000 in 1981.

(Office or inventory expansion would be considered such a reasonable use.) If the accumulation cannot be justified, the IRS sets a penalty tax on the "accumulated taxable income": the retained earnings in excess of $150,000. The tax is 27.5 percent of the first $100,000 of this accumulated taxable income and 38.5 percent of everything in excess of $100,000. This corporate tax is an *additional* tax on top of the normal corporate income tax, so the *total* tax can go as high as 75 percent.

Thus, if your corporation's retained earnings are approaching the $150,000/$250,000 limit, it should pay a dividend to its stockholders in order to avoid this tax.

Only a corporation that has been grossing about $200,000 or $250,000 a year, however, or a corporation that has been in existence a number of years (long enough to have accumulated a substantial surplus) and is considered "mature" is faced with these problems. For most people who are thinking of incorporating, the accumulated earnings tax on surplus is premature and should not be a factor in their decisions.

There's another point, too. Until 1976, the amount a corporation could set aside as surplus without penalty was only $100,000; the Tax Reduction Act of 1975 increased that allowance to $150,000, and the Economic Recovery Tax Act raised that limit for many corporations to $250,000. With inflationary pressures influencing legislation, it is likely that in another five or ten years that allowance will be increased again, just because money today isn't worth what it used to be. If your corporation's net after taxes is $15,000, it would take ten years to reach the IRS limit, and many tax changes are likely between now and then.

ARE YOU EVER TOO POOR?

Yes, again. It doesn't pay for someone who is earning $10,000 or $12,000 a year to incorporate. The real benefits start at around $30,000 a year. At $30,000 net taxable income, a single person is in the 28-percent bracket. A married person is in the 25 percent bracket. However, if either draws a salary of $20,000 instead and retains $10,000 in the corporation, he or she is taxed at approximately 15 percent on the $20,000, and the corporation is taxed at 15 percent on the $10,000.

BUT YOU CAN BE TOO UNDISCIPLINED

For some people, the joys of corporate tax savings just don't outweigh the extra paperwork and planning that are involved. In contrast to the "good old days" of sole proprietorship, when you could write yourself a check or raid petty cash whenever you ran short, now you must clearly differentiate between the corporation and yourself and act in accordance with the fact that you are now an employee of the corporation—even if at the same time you are its president and only employee. The corporation is a *separate legal entity,* and as such, there are certain formalities and restrictions. One of the tests the IRS uses to disqualify a corporation is "the corporate pocketbook"—the mixing together of personal and corporate funds: are you recognizing that you and the corporation are two separate, distinct legal entities, and does your bookkeeping reflect that fact, or are you still commingling corporate and personal income and expenditures? Of course, I know one man who does this and even pays the milkman with a corporate check—he leaves the mess to his accountant, who straightens it out every year. But this procedure is—to say the least—highly inadvisable.

In order to avoid having your corporation disqualified on these grounds, it is necessary that you set yourself a liberal salary—and to live within it, since you can no longer tap the bank account whenever you run short.

MORE TALK ABOUT SALARIES

But deciding on a salary is not as simple as it seems at first glance. If you operate a business as a sole proprietor, you pick up all the income of your business. But if you incorporate and pay yourself a high salary, the IRS may attack your salary as unreasonably high and disallow it. Or the IRS may hold that your salary is reasonable, but that if you don't have a history of paying dividends and your income has been accumulating, part of your salary may be deemed by the IRS to be a dividend and will be taxed to you accordingly.

Part of the question of reasonable versus unreasonable salary depends upon what other people in the same business or profession or a comparable one are earning. However, even this point can be gotten around, to a certain extent. For example, if you are in a creative profession, the IRS really cannot find an equivalent: there's just no way of comparing two artists or two writers—or their income.

But what about too low a salary? If you pay yourself a very low salary, your personal income taxes will be minimal, and your retained corporate earnings, which will be proportionately greater, will also be taxed at minimal corporate rates—15 percent up to $50,000, under the Tax Reform Act of 1986.

This sounds like a wonderful solution, but there are some drawbacks. First, you may not be able to live on a very low salary—and remember, you must avoid the corporate pocketbook at all costs. Second, the more rapidly money accumulates as corporate surplus, the more quickly you may reach the limit of $150,000/$250,000 and be forced to declare a dividend or be liable for the punitive tax on accumulated taxable income over $150,000/$250,000, as explained earlier.

There may also be other considerations involved in how much or how little you pay yourself. If your corporation earns $40,000 a year, the IRS may look askance at your paying yourself $5,000—even if you can live on it—and retaining $35,000 in the corporation at the minimum tax rate of 15 percent. If you drew $15,000 in salary and retained $25,000 in the corporation, there would be less question of the IRS's involvement in the issue of your salary.

Third—and possibly most important—both your Social Security and pension contributions (and eventually payments) are based on your salary; the lower your salary is, the lower these contributions and payments to you will be.

Let's look at that $40,000 to see how this might work with respective salaries of $15,000 and $25,000, based on 1988 rates:

	$15,000 Salary	$25,000 Salary
Net pretax earnings before salary	$40,000	$40,000
Salary	15,000	25,000
	25,000	15,000
Pension contribution (25% of salary)	3,750	6,250
Net corporate earnings	$21,250	$ 8,750
Corporate income tax (15%)	3,188	1,313
Retained earnings—available for investment	$18,062	$ 7,437

Income if invested in common and preferred stocks yielding 10%	$ 1,806	$ 744
Tax-free dividends (70% dividend exclusion)	1,264	521
Salary (single)	$15,000	$25,000
Less exemption ($1,950) and standard deduction ($3,000)	4,950	4,950
Net taxable income	$10,050	$20,050
Personal income tax	$ 1,439	$ 3,365
Corporate tax	3,188	1,313
Total taxes	$ 4,627	$ 4,678
Salary (married)	$15,000	$25,000
Less exemptions ($3,900) and standard deduction ($5,000)	8,900	8,900
Net taxable income	$ 6,100	$16,100
Personal income tax	$ 799	$ 2,299
Corporate tax	3,188	1,313
Total taxes	$ 3,987	$ 3,612

There is no hard-and-fast formula to follow in this area; there are too many individual considerations. Are you single? Are you married? Does your spouse work? How many exemptions do you have? Do you itemize or take the standard deduction? How much money can you keep in your corporation to earn 70 percent tax-free dividends? Discuss these trade-offs with your lawyer and accountant and get their advice. Whatever you decide, recognize that no salary decision must be permanent and inflexible. Your salary can be raised or lowered as long as such provisions are spelled out neatly in the bylaws of your corporation, which will be dealt with at length in Chapter 2, "Getting Ready."

SHOULD YOUR SPOUSE INCORPORATE?

Most certainly, if your spouse is self-employed, and for the same reasons that you should incorporate. Furthermore, if at all possible, your spouse should form his or her own corporation, rather than incorporating with you. Yes, once more it's more paperwork keeping two separate sets of corporate records, but there's a compelling reason to do it this way. Since a corporation can accumulate $150,000/ $250,000 at minimum tax rates whether the corporation has one shareholder or 100, incorporating as two separate corporations permits the two of you to accumulate double that amount, or $300,000/ $500,000.

THE TAXMAN COMETH

If you are a one-person corporation, as I am, the IRS may scrutinize your return very carefully, with an eye toward ruling that your corporation was created to avoid taxes and is therefore illegal. Here are some important arguments you can use to disprove the IRS's claim:

1. Incorporation gives you greater ease in doing business and frequently offers special corporate accounts and discounts.

2. Incorporation increases the attractiveness of your business to new or future employees.

3. Incorporation provides insurance benefits (e.g., workers' compensation) that may not be available to self-employed persons.

4. Incorporation offers greater medical benefits.

5. Incorporation permits limited—rather than unlimited—liability.

But the most important test of whether a corporation is valid depends on how much business activity is being conducted by the corporation. Normally, if the corporation is clearly operating a business and earning income, there would be no reason for the IRS not to accept it as a valid corporation; it would be very difficult for the IRS to attack the corporation as a sham.

THE PERSONAL-HOLDING-CORPORATION TRAP

However, even if your corporation is deemed valid by the IRS, there is still another pitfall to avoid: you do not want to be considered a personal holding corporation. A personal holding corporation is a corporation in which 60 percent or more of corporate income is derived from investments and less than 40 percent comes from actual operation of the business. This situation is to be avoided because personal holding corporations are subject to special heavy taxes and do not enjoy the preferential tax treatment of general business corporations and professional corporations.

In the past, some people who had a great deal of money incorporated and took their investments into the corporation, since, by incorporating, 85 percent of their preferred and common stock dividend income would not be taxed.* These people weren't really conducting a business, they were just managing their investments and collecting dividends. It was a tax loophole.

The personal-holding-corporation regulations, which were designed by the IRS to close this tax loophole and to prevent further tax inequities, provide that if a corporation is held to be a personal holding corporation—and obviously this can vary from year to year depending on annual earned income versus annual dividend income—the personal-holding-company income must be distributed to its shareholders. If it is a one-man corporation, without other shareholders, then he will be taxed on the dividend income as though he himself owned the stocks and not the corporation. If there are several shareholders, they will be taxed on the income as though they themselves owned the stocks and not the corporation.

But there are ways around even this problem. Let's assume that your corporation has a portfolio of $100,000, which yields 7.5 percent, or $7,500 in dividend income, and that for some reason your corporation earned only $5,000. Because the dividend income represents 60 percent—the crucial figure—of total income, your corporation is regarded as a personal holding corporation for that year.

To avoid this problem, you could sell one of the stocks before the final quarterly dividend is paid to avoid reaching the $7,500 figure. Since many corporations pay dividends in December, all you have to do is make certain that your corporation sells the stock before the record date for payment of the dividend.

Then, depending on your financial situation, you might either invest the proceeds of the sale of the stock in a lower-yielding "growth" stock to reduce your dividend income below the 60 percent figure or buy municipal bonds, whose income is not counted by the IRS in making personal holding company determinations.

Tax-free dividends are but one of the many benefits of incorporating. The next chapters will show you how to set up your corporation to start taking advantage of them.

*The Tax Reform Act of 1986 reduced this dividend exclusion to 80 percent, and the Revenue Act of 1987 reduced it further, to 70 percent. It remains a very valuable benefit of incorporation.

2

Getting
Ready

Both incorporating and dissolving your corporation later, when you are ready to retire, or earlier, are especially easy if you are the only stockholder and officer. This is legal in every state.

Once you decide to incorporate, the first, crucial step is applying to the IRS for an Employer Identification Number: you will not be able to open corporate savings or checking accounts without it.

If you already have an Employer Identification Number (e.g., for your Keogh plan account), it's no good—you'll need to apply for another one in the corporate name—even if you're just adding "Inc." to your own name. In the eyes of the IRS, the corporation is a separate "person" and must have a separate number.

The form to file is SS–4, Application for Employer Identification Number. Think of this number as your corporation's Social Security number. The length of time before your number is issued will depend on where you live and on the closeness to April 15—the IRS's busy season. At any rate, it should not take more than six weeks.

Therefore, if you're planning to start your corporate business on January 1, apply for your Employer Identification Number on the preceding October 15 to give yourself plenty of leeway. As soon as you receive this number, apply *immediately* for Subchapter S status if you decide that a Subchapter S corporation is the right choice for you (see pages 15 and 20–21 and Chapter 5, "How to Profit from Your Subchapter S Corporation") by filing IRS Form 2553, "Election by a

Small Business Corporation." This form must be postmarked no later than the fifteenth day of the third month of your corporation's existing tax year. If your corporation is on a calendar year, your deadline is March 15. The IRS will accept no excuses for even one day's lateness: your corporation will not receive S corporation treatment until the following year.

When you are filing these first forms that are crucial to your corporation's existence, it is a good idea to employ the good old "belt-and-suspenders" strategy of dealing with the IRS. Send all forms by certified mail, return receipt requested, so that you will have proof that you filed them before the deadline. Enclose a copy of the form, a self-addressed stamped envelope, and a note asking that your form be stamped "Received" by the IRS and returned to you. Paranoid? Maybe. But anyone who has ever had problems proving to the IRS that forms were sent on time will agree that being supercautious is better than being sorry.

You don't have to have corporate stationery and business cards, but if you want them, order them now so that you will have them on hand before January 1. You may wish to have cards printed and sent to your clients and customers announcing that on January 1 your business or profession will be conducted under your new corporate name:

> As of January 1, 1989
>
> J. ENTREPRENEUR
>
> Will Be Doing Business As
>
> J. ENTREPRENEUR & CO., INC.
>
> 123 EASY STREET
>
> NEW YORK, NEW YORK 10021

Now you're ready for the big step: applying for your Certificate of Incorporation. This is a procedure that varies from state to state; the different state requirements, forms, and fees are shown in Appendix A. In any case, your first step would be writing to the secretary

Leaving. 9/30 8:30 Am

Arriv. 10/1 ~ 1 p.m.

<u>overseas</u>.

8 + 0 + 11 + _ _

852 - 5 - 237695

of state or appropriate department or agency for your state, as shown on the chart.

For purposes of illustration, in this chapter I will walk you through the procedure of incorporation, using New York State laws, procedures, and forms. (Many of the states will differ in detail, but New York State is fairly representative.)

In New York State, the Certificate of Incorporation forms can be bought for approximately 75 cents each at most commercial stationers. Ask for Form A 234—Certificate of Incorporation, Business Corporation Law § (Section) 402, and get several blanks. You'll be sending one copy to Albany, you'll want a duplicate for your files, and you may want one or two forms to practice on.

Following is a sample Certificate of Incorporation. Of course, the purpose of your corporation may be different from the one shown; for the wording you need, consult §§ (Sections) 202 and 402 of the Business Corporation Law. For most small corporations, the broad language already on the form revised in late 1987 and shown here is all that is necessary.*

In New York State, this form is sent to New York State Division of Corporations, 162 Washington Avenue, Albany, New York 12231, along with a money order or bank cashier's check for $110. Unless you are a lawyer, New York State will not accept your personal check.

CHOOSING A FISCAL YEAR

You will note that the IRS Request for Employer Identification Number and the New York State Certificate of Incorporation both ask for your fiscal year.

In the first five editions of *Inc. Yourself,* the recommendations made were very different from the suggestions many tax experts are making now. Back then, the KISS (Keep It Simple, Sweetheart) strategy, which recommended electing a calendar year in order to file fewer tax forms during the first year of incorporation, outweighed the benefits of choosing a different fiscal year in order to implement more sophisticated tax planning.

*For the purpose of this book, I have transferred the material on my original Certificate of Incorporation to this new form.

Certificate of Incorporation

of

JUDITH H. McQUOWN & CO., INC.

under Section 402 of the Business Corporation Law

Filed By: Judith H. McQuown & Co., Inc.

Office and Post Office Address

134 Franklin Avenue
Staten Island, NY 10301

16

A 234—Certificate of Incorporation
Business Corporation Law §402 9-87

© 1975 BY JULIUS BLUMBERG, INC.
PUBLISHER, NYC 10013

Certificate of Incorporation of

JUDITH H. McQUOWN & CO., INC.

under Section 402 of the Business Corporation Law

IT IS HEREBY CERTIFIED THAT:

(1) The name of the proposed corporaton is JUDITH H. McQUOWN & CO., INC.

(2) The purpose or purposes for which this corporation is formed, are as follows, to wit:
To engage in any lawful act or activity for which corporations may be organized under the Business Corporation Law. The corporation is not formed to engage in any act or activity requiring the consent or approval of any state official, department, board, agency or other body.*

The corporation, in furtherance of its corporate purposes above set forth, shall have all of the powers enumerated in Section 202 of the Business Corporation Law, subject to any limitations provided in the Business Corporation Law or any other statute of the State of New York.

*If specific consent or approval is required delete this paragraph, insert specific purposes and obtain consent or approval prior to filing.

17

(3) The office of the corporation is to be located in the County of Richmond State of New York.

(4) The aggregate number of shares which the corporation shall have the authority to issue is

One Hundred (100) no par

(5) The Secretary of State is designated as agent of the corporation upon whom process against it may be served. The post office address to which the Secretary of State shall mail a copy of any process against the corporation served upon him is

134 Franklin Avenue, Staten Island, New York   10301

(6) A director of the corporation shall not be liable to the corporation or its shareholders for damages for any breach of duty in such capacity except for

    (i) liability if a judgment or other final adjudication adverse to a director establishes that his or her acts or omissions were in bad faith or involved intentional misconduct or a knowing violation of law or that the director personally gained in fact a financial profit or other advantage to which he or she was not legally entitled or that the director's acts violated BCL § 719, or

    (ii) liability for any act or omission prior to the adoption of this provision.

The undersigned incorporator, or each of them if there are more than one, is of the age of eighteen years or over.

IN WITNESS WHEREOF, this certificate has been subscribed on December 20,   19 76   by the undersigned who affirm(s) that the statements made herein are true under the penalties of perjury.

Judith H. McQuown
   Type name of incorporator   Signature

134 Franklin Avenue, Staten Island, NY   10301
            Address

   Type name of incorporator   Signature

            Address

   Type name of incorporator   Signature

            Address

Now, though, it's quite clear that the highly profitable deferral strategies available through choosing a fiscal year that differs from the calendar year make it well worth the few hours of extra paperwork in your corporation's first year of life.

Choosing a fiscal year that ends on January 31 will give you the maximum tax-deferral advantage. If your corporation pays your salary annually or semiannually, it can pay you a good part—or all—of your salary in January 1989. The corporation takes its salary deduction for fiscal 1988, which ends on January 31, 1989. But since you, as an individual, are on a calendar year, you will not owe income tax on the salary you received in January 1989 until April 1990. That's a fifteen-month deferral for some people. If you are paying estimated taxes, the actual deferral time may be shorter, but you will still have fifteen months to do your tax planning.

Unfortunately, the Tax Reform Act of 1986 has made it very difficult for certain personal service corporations—defined as those whose principal function is "services in the fields of law, health, engineering, architecture, accounting, actuarial science, performing arts, or consulting"—to elect a fiscal year rather than a calendar year. Now personal service corporations, like Subchapter S corporations, partnerships, and sole proprietorships, must use a calendar year.

Unless your corporation receives special permission, granted by the District Director of the Internal Revenue Service, to use a fiscal year. Here's how to try for it:

You need a clear, documented business reason. If your corporation makes gingerbread houses and most of its income is received in January for sales made in December, you have an excellent business reason for choosing a January fiscal year so that your corporation's income and expenses will fall in the same year.

Even if your services aren't as seasonal as those of a maker of gingerbread houses, you may still have a good chance of convincing the Internal Revenue Service if you can show that a good chunk of your income is received in January. Here's an argument that may work:

"My corporation gets paid in January for work it has done in the preceding year. I have to wait until my clients receive their Christmas bonuses and pay their bills before I know the corporation's income for the year, how many full or partial payments are coming in, and so on. In fact, nearly half of my corporation's income is received in January.

Accordingly, it makes both economic and tax sense not to separate the time period in which the income was received from the time period in which the work was done."

Obviously, this line of reasoning is perfectly logical. You may find that you'll need a more sophisticated argument—consult your accountant or tax lawyer—and up-to-date books whose receivables prove your point if the IRS ever comes knocking at your door; but this argument is the core, and it may very well work for you.

To apply for a fiscal year, file IRS Form 1128 in triplicate (shown on pages 22–24) and cross your fingers. You should receive an answer in six to eight weeks.

The Revenue Act of 1987 gives these personal service corporations another alternative, which may be a better choice for some owners. Under certain circumstances, it may be advantageous—and permissible—to elect a fiscal year that gives you up to a three-month deferral—i.e., a September 30 fiscal year. Consult your tax adviser for details and specific advice. Ask about the "enhanced estimated tax payments" system.

PAR-VALUE VERSUS NO-PAR-VALUE STOCK

Most states' Certificate of Incorporation forms ask whether the corporation plans to issue par-value stock or no-par-value stock, as in the preceding illustration. Par value (sometimes called face value) means the value or price at which the corporation's stock is issued; if a share of stock has a par value of $10, there must be $10 in the treasury to back it when the stock is initially sold or transferred. An entering stockholder would have to pay $1,000 for 100 shares, and the $1,000 would go into the corporate treasury to back the shares of stock ($10 per share).

No-par-value stock has no money behind the shares; no stockholder investment is necessary. Usually, in an ongoing sole proprietorship, the assets and liabilities of the proprietorship are transferred to the corporation in exchange for the corporation's stock.

Generally, if you are offered the option, issue no-par-value stock, rather than par-value stock. No-par-value stock is easier to set up, cheaper, and requires less paperwork. Some states assess taxes based on the par value of the issued and outstanding stock; if you have 100 shares of $100 par-value stock issued and outstanding, your total par

Form **1128** (Rev. June 1987) Department of the Treasury Internal Revenue Service	**Application for Change in Accounting Period** ▶ For Paperwork Reduction Act Notice, see page 1 of separate instructions.		OMB No. 1545-0134 Expires 6-30-89

Name of applicant (if joint return is filed, also show your spouse's name) WONDERFUL CORPORATION	Identifying number (See specific instructions) 13-0000000	Check one:
Address (Number and street) 123 EASY STREET	Service Center where return will be filed HOLTSVILLE, NY	☐ Individual ☐ Partnership ☐ Estate
City or town, state, and ZIP code NEW YORK, NY 10001	Applicant's telephone number (212) 555-1212	☐ Trust ☑ Corporation
Name of person to contact (see specific instructions) I. M. WONDERFUL	Telephone number of contact person (212) 555-1212	☐ S Corporation ☐ Personal Service Corporation

DO NOT FILE FORM 1128 if you meet any of the exceptions under General Instruction B.

DO NOT CHANGE YOUR TAX YEAR UNTIL THE COMMISSIONER HAS APPROVED YOUR REQUEST.

Check one (continued):
☐ IC-DISC
☐ Cooperative (Sec. 1381(a))
☐ Tax-Exempt Organization
☐ Controlled Foreign Corp.
☐ FSC
☐ Foreign Corp.

SECTION A.—All Filers

1a Present tax year ends 12/31/88	1b Permission is requested to change to a tax year ending
1c Permission is requested to adopt tax year ending 1/31/89	2 The period change will require a return for a short period Beginning 1/1 , 1989 Ending 1/31 , 1989

3 Nature of business or principal source of income
DESIGN STUDIO

		Yes	No
4 What is your overall method of accounting? ☑ Cash receipts and disbursements ☐ Accrual ☐ Other (explain) ▶			
5 Are you an individual requesting a change from a fiscal year to a calendar year under Rev. Proc. 66-50, 1966-2 C.B. 1260? (If "Yes," file Form 1128 with the applicable Service Center. See General Instruction C.)			✓
6 In the last 6 years have you changed or requested permission to change your accounting period, your overall method of accounting or the accounting treatment of any item?			✓
If "Yes" and there was a ruling letter issued granting permission to make the change, attach a copy. If a copy of the ruling letter is not available, explain and give the date permission was granted. If a ruling letter was not required, e.g., corporations using Rev. Proc. 84-34, 1984-1 C.B. 508 or Regulations section 1.442-1(c), explain the facts and give the date the change was implemented. If a change in accounting period was granted within the last 6 years, explain in detail the unusual circumstances requiring this change.			
7 Do you have pending any accounting method, accounting period, ruling, or technical advice request in the National Office? If "Yes," attach a statement explaining the type of request (method, period, etc.) and the specific issues involved in each request.			✓
8 Enter the taxable income* or (loss) for the three tax years immediately before the short period and for the short period. If necessary, estimate the amount for the short period. NONE — NEW CORPORATION			
Third preceding year Second preceding year First preceding year Short period $_____ $_____ $_____ $_____			
*Individuals enter adjusted gross income. Partnerships and S corporations enter ordinary income. Section 501(c) organizations enter unrelated business taxable income.			
9 Are you a member of a partnership, a beneficiary of a trust or estate, a shareholder of an S corporation, or a shareholder of an Interest Charge Domestic International Sales Corporation (IC-DISC) or a shareholder in a FSC? If "Yes," attach a statement showing the name, address, identifying number, tax year, percentage of interest in capital and profits, or percentage of interest of each IC-DISC and the amount of income received from each partnership, trust, estate, S corporation, IC-DISC, or FSC for the first preceding year and the short period.			✓
10 Are you an unincorporated syndicate, group, pool, or joint venture that has elected, under the provisions of regulations section 1.761-2(b), not to be treated as a partnership? If yes, provide a copy of the statement described in regulations section 1.761-2(b). If no formal election was made, describe in detail why you are not considered a partnership for Federal income tax purposes.			✓

Form **1128** (Rev. 6-87)

Form 1128 (Rev 6-87)

SECTION A.—All Filers (continued)	Yes	No
11 Are you a U.S. shareholder in a controlled foreign corporation (CFC)?		✓

If "Yes," attach a statement for each CFC stating the name, address, identifying number, tax year, your percentage of total combined voting power, and the amount of income included in your gross income under section 951 for the three tax years immediately before the short period and for the short period.

12 State the reasons for requesting the change. (Attach a separate sheet if you need more space.) ....
.... BULK OF RECEIPTS FOR PRIOR YEAR'S WORK WILL COME ....
.... IN THE FOLLOWING JANUARY ....
....

SECTION B.—Estates or Trusts

1 **Attach a statement showing the following information:**

   a Name, identifying number, address, and tax year of each beneficiary and each person who is an owner or treated as an owner of any portion of the trust.

   b Based on the taxable income of the estate or trust entered in Section A, item 8, show the distribution deduction and the taxable amounts distributable to each beneficiary for the 2 tax years immediately before the short period and for the short period.

   c If the trust is a member of a common trust fund, show name and tax year of that fund.

2 Are you filing for a simple trust as defined in section 651? . . . .

3 Are you filing for a complex trust as defined in section 661? . . . .

4 Are you requesting a change for a trust under Rev. Proc. 68-41, 1968-2 C.B. 943? (If "Yes," file Form 1128 with the applicable Service Center. See General Instruction C.) . . . .

5 Are you filing for a grantor trust as described in regulations section 1.671-1? . . . .

SECTION C.—Partnerships

1 Date business began. (See specific instructions for Section C.) ▶

2 Is any partner applying for a corresponding change in accounting period?

3 Attach a statement showing each partner's name, type of partner (e.g., individual, partnership, estate, trust, corporation, S corporation, IC-DISC, etc.), address, identifying number, tax year, the percentage of interest in capital and profits, and how the interest was acquired.

4 Is any partner of this partnership a member of a personal service corporation as defined in section 269A?
If "Yes," attach a separate sheet providing the name, address, identifying number, tax year, percentage of interest in capital and profits, and the amount of income received from each personal service corporation for the first preceding year and the short period.

SECTION D.—All Corporations

		Yes	No
1 Date of incorporation ▶ 1 2 88			
2 Is the change being requested by a subsidiary who became a member of an affiliated group to join with the parent corporation in the filing of a consolidated return for the short period?			✓
If "Yes," DO NOT FILE THIS FORM. SEE "EXCEPTIONS" IN GENERAL INSTRUCTION B.			✓
3 Is the corporation a member of an affiliated group filing a consolidated return?			

If "Yes," attach a statement showing (a) the name, address, identifying number used on the consolidated return, the tax year, and the Internal Revenue Service Center where the taxpayer files the return; and (b) the name, address, and identifying number of each member of the affiliated group. Designate the parent corporation and the taxable income (loss) of each member for the 3 years immediately before the short period and for the short period.

4 Did the corporation pay any dividends to its shareholders during the short period? . . . .

   If "Yes," furnish the following information:

   (a) Taxable dividends . . . . $

   (b) Nontaxable dividends (explain how determined) . . . . . . $

5 Are you requesting a change for a corporation under Rev. Proc. 84-34? (If "Yes," file Form 1128 with the applicable Service Center. See General Instruction C.) . . . . ✓

6 If you are a personal service corporation, attach a statement showing each shareholder's name, address, identification number, tax year, percentage of ownership, and type of entity (e.g., individual, partnership, corporation, etc.)

Form 1128 (Rev 6-87)   Page **3**

SECTION E.—S Corporations

		Yes	No
1	Date of election ▶		
2	Attach a statement showing each shareholder's name, address, identifying number, tax year, percentage of ownership, and type of entity (e.g., individual, estate, trust, or qualified Subchapter S Trust as defined in section 1361(d)(3)).		
3	Is the corporation a newly electing S corporation required to file Form 2553, Election by a Small Business Corporation, to adopt, retain or change its accounting period? If "Yes," do not file this form. See "Exceptions" in General Instruction B.		

SECTION F.—Tax-Exempt Organizations

1	Form of organization: ☐ Corporation ☐ Trust ☐ Other (specify) ▶		
2	Date of organization ▶		
3	Code section under which you are recognized as exempt ▶		
4	Are you required to file an annual return on either Form 990, 990-C, 990-PF, 990-T, 1120-H, or 1120-POL?		
5	Date exemption was granted ▶ .... Attach a copy of the ruling letter granting exemption. If a copy of the letter is not available, attach explanation.		
6	If a private foundation, is the foundation terminating its status under section 507?		
7	Are you requesting a change for a tax-exempt organization under Rev. Proc. 85-58, 1985-2 C.B. 740, or 76-10, 1976-1 C.B. 548? (If "Yes," see General Instruction C.)		

SECTION G.—Interest Charge Domestic International Sales Corporations or Foreign Sales Corporations

1	Date of election ▶		
2	Attach a statement stating the name, address, identifying number, tax year, and the percentage of ownership and percentage of voting power of each shareholder.		

SECTION H.—Controlled Foreign Corporation

1	Enter the tax year that was used for tax purposes ▶		
2	Attach a statement for each U.S. shareholder (as defined in section 951(b)) stating the name, address, identifying number, tax year, percentage of total combined voting power, and the amount of income included in the gross income under section 951 for the three tax years immediately before the short period and for the short period.		

Signature—ALL FILERS (See specific instructions)

Under penalties of perjury, I declare that I have examined this application, including accompanying schedules and statements, and to the best of my knowledge and belief it is true, correct, and complete. Declaration of preparer (other than applicant) is based on all information of which preparer has any knowledge.

WONDERFUL CORPORATION
_____
Applicant's name   Date

_____
Signature   Title

I. M. WONDERFUL
_____   4/1/88
Signing official's name (Please print or type)   Date

_____   PRESIDENT
Signature of officer of the parent corporation, if applicable   Title

_____
Signature of individual or firm preparing the application other than applicant   Date

_____
Firm or preparer's name

[The next page is 2341.]

[¶1627]

value is $10,000; if those 100 shares have no par value, your total par value is $0.

In most states, corporations that deal in services can choose either par-value or no-par-value stock; it is just those businesses that use a great deal of capital (e.g., manufacturing) which may not be given the choice and would have to issue par-value stock so that the corporation would start with substantial cash assets.

YOUR CORPORATE RECORDS

If you incorporate in New York State, shortly after you submit your Certificate of Incorporation and cashier's check or money order for $110 to the Division of Corporations, you will receive a filing receipt. Now you are able to proceed to the next step: ordering a set of corporate records and a corporation seal at a commercial stationer; both of these are required by law.* Depending on where you live, it may take one to three weeks for you to receive your order. You must present your filing receipt to the stationer, or your order will not be accepted.

The simplest and cheapest corporate record set is a looseleaf binder (approximately $50, including corporation seal) that contains stock certificates, a stock transfer ledger in which the shareholders' names and addresses are recorded, pages to which you attach the filing receipt and a copy of the Certificate of Incorporation, and sample minutes of meetings and bylaws that are set up so that you can just fill in the blanks. (A sample set of corporate minutes and bylaws is shown in Appendix B.) Even if you are the sole stockholder, officer, and employee of your corporation, alas, it is necessary to go through this paperwork. Or, if you put a higher value on your time than on your money, you can have your lawyer set up your corporation.

YOUR CORPORATE BANK ACCOUNTS

After you receive your new Employer Identification Number and your corporate seal, you will be able to open your new corporate bank accounts; I find it best to keep both a savings account and a checking

---

*While some states no longer require a corporate seal, virtually all banks and brokerage houses still require your corporate seal on documents.

account. Both types of accounts require the impression of your corporate seal.

Following is a typical commercial bank checking-account corporate resolution, which you would sign and affix the corporate seal to; since a savings bank corporate resolution is much less detailed, a sample is not given.

TRANSFERRING ASSETS TO YOUR NEW CORPORATION

On the date on which you begin corporate life, you can either cut off your sole proprietorship and start afresh or transfer the proprietorship's assets and liabilities to the new corporation. Note that these are assets and liabilities, such as office equipment and accounts receivable and payable, not earnings and profits from the proprietorship. In general, a corporation's assumption of the proprietorship's liabilities is beneficial; a dentist who had ordered silver would rather have the corporation pay the bill than pay it out of his own pocket.

To the extent that partners in a partnership decide to incorporate, there are theoretically three ways in which the incorporation may take place. Therefore it seems advisable, where substantial sums are involved, that the partners either seek professional advice or use the simplest method. Under this method, the partnership transfers all its assets to the newly formed corporation in exchange for all the outstanding stock of the corporation. The partnership would then terminate, distributing all the stock to its partners in proportion to their partnership interests.

The only danger—in terms of federal tax—is transferring more liabilities than assets, which can lead to unnecessary taxes. This situation can be avoided fairly easily; you can always throw in a personal asset to equalize the balance, even if it's only another chair for your office or a few more reams of paper.

The asset/liability balance is probably a question of magnitude. If the liabilities exceed the assets by $50, it is unlikely that the IRS would bother with your case; if they exceed the assets by $5,000, that's another story. Just to be on the safe side, though, get your accountant's advice; theoretically, even a difference of $50 or $100 could get you in trouble with the IRS.

I, the undersigned, hereby certify to _____ Bank, New York, N. Y., that at a meeting of the Board of Directors of _____

_____

a Corporation organized and existing under the laws of _____

duly called and duly held on the_____day of_____, 19____, the following resolutions were duly adopted, and that the said resolutions have been entered upon the regular minute book of the said Corporation, are in accordance with the By-Laws and are now in full force and effect.

RESOLVED: 1. That the officers of this Corporation, or any one or more of them, are hereby authorized to open a bank account or accounts from time to time with the _____ Bank (hereinafter referred to as the "Bank"), for and in the name of this Corporation with such title or titles as he or they may designate.

2. That the_____

_____of this Corporation,
<small>(Indicate by Title persons authorized to sign, viz.: President, Vice-President, Treasurer, etc.)</small>

signing _____

<small>(Indicate how checks etc. are to be signed, viz.: singly, jointly, any two, etc.)</small>

and their successors in office, and any other person hereafter authorized to sign on behalf of this Corporation, are hereby authorized to sign checks, drafts, notes, acceptances, and other instruments, and orders for the payment or withdrawal of moneys, credits, items and property at any time held by the Bank for account of this Corporation, and the Bank is hereby authorized to honor any or all thereof and other instruments and orders authorized to be paid by the Bank, including such as may bring about an overdraft and such as may be payable to or for the benefit of any signer thereof or other officer or employee individually without inquiry as to the circumstances of the issue or the disposition of the proceeds thereof and without limit as to amount.

3. That the bank is hereby authorized to accept for deposit for the account of this Corporation for credit, or for collection, or otherwise, any or all checks, drafts, notes and other instruments of every kind indorsed by any person or by hand stamp impression in the name of this Corporation or without indorsement.

4. That the_____

_____of this Corporation,
<small>(Indicate by Title persons authorized to effect Loans, Advances, etc., viz.: President, Vice-President, Treasurer, etc.)</small>

signing _____

<small>(Indicate how Notes etc. are to be signed, viz.: singly, jointly, any two, etc.)</small>

and their successors in office are hereby authorized to effect loans and advances at any time for this Corporation from the Bank, and for such loans and advances to make, execute and deliver promissory notes and other written obligations or evidences of indebtedness of this Corporation, applications for letters of credit, and any agreements or undertakings, general or specific, giving liens on, and rights and powers with respect to, any property of this Corporation, and other agreements and undertakings, and as security for the payment of loans, advances, indebtedness and liabilities of this Corporation to pledge, hypothecate, mortgage, assign, transfer, indorse and deliver property of any description, real or personal, and any interest in and evidences of any thereof at any time held by this Corporation, and to execute instruments of transfer, powers of attorney and other instruments which may be necessary or desirable in connection therewith; and also to sell to, or discount with, the Bank commercial paper, bills receivable, accounts receivable and other instruments and evidences of debt at any time held by this Corporation, and to that end to indorse, assign, transfer and deliver the same, and also to give any orders or consents for the delivery, sale, exchange or other disposition of any property or interest therein or evidences thereof belonging to this Corporation and at any time in the hands of the Bank, whether as collateral or otherwise.

5. That all loans, discounts and advances heretofore obtained on behalf of this Corporation and all notes and other obligations or evidences thereof of this Corporation held by the Bank are hereby approved, ratified, and confirmed.

6. That the officers of this Corporation or any one or more of them are hereby authorized to act for this Corporation in all other matters and transactions relating to any of its business with the Bank.

7. That each of the foregoing resolutions and the authority thereby conferred shall remain in full force and effect until written notice of revocation or modification shall be received by the Bank; that the Secretary or any Assistant Secretary or any other officer of this Corporation is hereby authorized and directed to certify, under the seal of this Corporation or not, but with like effect in the latter case, to the Bank the foregoing resolutions, the names of the officers and other representatives of this Corporation, any changes from time to time in the said officers and representatives and specimens of their respective signatures; and that the Bank may conclusively assume that persons at any time certified to it to be officers or other representatives of this Corporation continue as such until receipt by the Bank of written notice to the contrary.

In Witness Whereof. I have hereunto set my hand as Secretary and affixed the seal of the said Corporation this _____day of _____, 19____

*ATTEST:

_____   _____
                                                                    Secretary

<small>Official Designation</small>

(SEAL)

*NOTE: — In case the Secretary is authorized to sign by the above resolutions, this certificate should be attested by a second officer or director of the Corporation.

SEED MONEY

Whether you transfer your sole proprietorship's assets and liabilities to your new corporation or close down everything and start from scratch, there will probably be a period of a month or two in which the corporation will need some kind of seed money until funds start coming into the corporation. This would usually be money for new stationery, petty cash, one month's operating capital, and similar expenses.

Of course, the simplest—but also the most expensive—route would be taking out a 30-, 60-, or 90-day bank loan. But it is possible for you to lend the corporation money as long as the amount of money you are lending the corporation is not too great and as long as the corporation repays you within a short period of time. The IRS suggests that if you choose to lend money to the corporation for start-up expenses, you should limit the loan to no more than about $10,000 and the corporation should repay you within three to six months.

Whether you should charge your corporation interest on the loan or make it an interest-free loan depends on several considerations. Your decision will probably involve less than $400 in interest (a maximum of $10,000 $\times$ 16% $\times$ 3 months), so it really isn't crucial. Among the factors you should consider are whether your corporation will be very successful in its first year, your income from other sources, and whether you need interest income to offset interest you are paying on loans or on your margin account at a brokerage house.

The IRS points out some possible pitfalls in your lending money to the corporation. If the loan is on the corporation's books for an extended period of time and if there is no provision for interest, the IRS could maintain that this money is not really a loan, that instead it is equity capital (money that the corporation must have to stay alive). If the IRS can prove that you need all that money for a fairly long time to keep your business afloat, then, whether or not you call it a loan, the IRS will hold that the money is equity capital.

If the IRS does establish that the loan is really equity capital, then when the loan is repaid, it may be deemed to be a dividend (and therefore taxable to you), rather than a repayment of the loan: you would be distributing part of that equity capital to yourself, and such a distribution is considered a dividend.

However, this is generally a problem that affects only companies which need a great deal of capital; small business and professional corporations can usually stay within the loan-size and repayment-time limitations that satisfy the IRS.

The worksheets that follow show how I handled the problem of seed money for my corporation. In this case, because I had to wait for my Employer Identification Number, I paid some corporate expenses with personal checks and then reimbursed myself when the corporate checking account was activated. I delayed paying myself salary until corporate income could be transferred to the checking account and then paid myself back salary and reimbursed expenses in two large lump-sum checks: one for salary, and one for expenses. This procedure might well work for you and your new corporation.

Shortly after you incorporate, you will have to decide whether you want a Subchapter S corporation and/or whether you want to issue §1244 stock. These are independent choices; you may choose either, both, or neither. *Do not make either decision without consulting a lawyer and/or an accountant.*

SUBCHAPTER S CORPORATIONS

The Revenue Act of 1987 has had a dramatic impact on some entrepreneurs' and professionals' decisions to choose Subchapter S as their corporate form. In a Subchapter S corporation, profits and losses flow through to the individual shareholder(s) and profits are taxed as personal income. In a C (general business) corporation, *you* choose whether corporate profits remain in your corporation or are paid to you.

The key provision of the act—that "certain personal service corporations" (most professional corporations and corporations whose chief source of income is consulting or the performing arts) would be taxed at a flat 34 percent instead of the graduated rates of 15 percent for income under $50,000 and 25 percent for income between $50,000 and $75,000—has made Subchapter S election even more attractive to many people than the 1986 act had made it. By forming a Subchapter S corporation, professionals, consultants, and performers whose net income is $50,000 would be in the 15 percent bracket for part of their income, rather than the mandated 34 percent.

JANUARY 1977

1	Jan 3	Client A		37 50	—	The following Expenses were incurred		
2						at various times and were repaid (or		
3	Jan 7	Client B		485 —		paid) on or after February 15, 1977		
4		Client C		115 80		when employer ID number was issued by IRS		
5								
6	Jan 13	Client D		35 —	Dec 20	New York State —		
7						Corporation Fee		60 —
8	Jan 17	Client B		177 50				
9					Jan 3	Chemical Bank —		
10	Jan 19	Client E		305 60		cash advance to open		
11		Client F		125 —		checking a/c		100 —
12								
13	Jan 25	Client C		90 75	Jan 6	M.T. P/T Sec'y		50 —
14		Client B		75 —		(personal ck #512)		
15								
16	Jan 28	Client B		80 —	Feb 10	Paragon Ans. Svce		52 —
17		Client D		444 —		(personal ck #526)		
18						Eump's - Desk Acc.		14 —
19	Jan 31	Client G		246 —		(personal ck #881)		
20				5899 25		Mrs. Hanover (#822)		26 04
21						business portion		
22						Chemical Bank (#521)		75 54
23		(OF K151:	3000 checking			business portion		
24			500 special savings			Con ED (#528) bus. portion		12 20
25			balance - emp svgs					
26					Feb 15	Print Craft (Xeroxing #907)		58 82
27								
28						Misc. Cash Expenses -		
29						Xeroxing, Car fares,		
30						Supplies, etc.		
31						Jan 1 - Feb 15		100 —
32								
33						Jan + Feb Rent @ 100		200 —
34								
35						ck #1003		748 60
36								

FEBRUARY 1977

Date		Receipts	Date		Disbursements	Amount	
Feb 1	Client B	150 —	Feb 18		Me - Back Salary (#1001)	1429 40	1
					IRS - Back Withholding (#1002)	525 35	2
Feb 7	Client B	162 50			Me - Reimbursement (#1003)	74 60	3
					NY Telephone — Jan (#1004)	75 90	4
Feb 10	Client A	621 —			QED Transcription (#1005)	176 40	5
							6
Feb 15	Client B	595 —	Feb 25		Me - Salary (#1007)	204 20	7
							8
Feb 25	Client B	145 —	Feb 26		Mrs Hanover (#1008)	14 04	9
		1673 50			(Editor's Xmas Present)		10
							11
			Feb 28		Sec'y of State—MD (#___)	2 —	12
					Sec'y of State - CT (#___)	2 —	13
						3177 89	14
							15
							16

As a result of the 1986 and 1987 acts, Subchapter S corporations have become so important that I have devoted an entire chapter to them. In fact, if you think that your corporation might be one of those "certain personal service corporations," finish this overview section and then skip immediately to Chapter 5, "How to Profit from Your Subchapter S Corporation." Deciding whether you should choose an S corporation or a C corporation can be the most important business and tax decision that you make for your new corporation. Obviously, you'll want to consult your tax lawyer and/or accountant before choosing between an S corporation and a C corporation.

§1244 STOCK

If the officers of a corporation decide to issue §1244 stock—a decision that must be made and recorded before the stock is issued—any shareholder who subsequently sells or exchanges that stock at a loss can take the loss as an ordinary loss—as opposed to the less favorable capital loss—on his or her personal income tax return. The rules governing this tax shelter are too technical to describe in detail in a general book like this one; if you feel that issuing §1244 stock might benefit your stockholders and your corporation (usually only if you think that at some point outsiders may buy your stock), you should consult your lawyer and/or your accountant.

Appendix B consists of a sample set of minutes and bylaws for a corporation registered in New York State. They include minutes of the organizational meeting, the bylaws, minutes of a board of directors' meeting, minutes of a shareholders' meeting, and minutes of a special meeting of the board of directors to elect a January fiscal year. Minutes of a special meeting of the board of directors to approve a medical care reimbursement plan and the plan itself are found in Chapter 9, "Medical Benefits."

3

And Now the
Paperwork

Once you've come this far, the rest is easy. Changing from sole proprietor to corporate status doesn't require vastly more complicated bookkeeping; I find that my routine bookkeeping takes me only ten or fifteen minutes a day, or perhaps an hour or so on Saturday morning.

Your corporate bookkeeping can be very simple; any bookkeeping method that you can walk the IRS through is acceptable. For many people, single-entry bookkeeping is much simpler than double-entry. Your ledger can show what funds came in, what was paid out, what money was left, and how it was allocated.

There are now some excellent computer programs to help you with your bookkeeping and corporate records. For around $50, you can find a very adequate program; for around $200, you'll get some extremely sophisticated programs.

No matter how accurate your records are, the IRS may be somewhat reluctant to accept records written on index cards or stray pieces of paper. From the standpoint of creating a good corporate impression, it may be wise to invest in a ledger and to learn to use it. It increases your credibility and, as always, neatness counts.

The worksheets that follow compare several months' books of an individual proprietorship and a corporation. As you can see, the individual proprietorship is taxed far more than the corporation, and much less of its profits can be sheltered from taxes in a pension plan.

Getting down to specifics, always remember that you and your

J. ENTREPRENEUR

October 1977

Oct 3	CLIENT A		300	—	Oct 3	RENT		200	—	1
	CLIENT B		475	—						2
					Oct 14	PHONE		100	—	3
Oct 7	CLIENT C		250	—		ELECTRIC		20	—	4
	CLIENT A		125	—						5
					Oct 31	ENTERTAINMENT		100	—	6
Oct 12	CLIENT B		850	—		(RECEIPTS IN FILE)				7
						MISC. EXPENSES		100	—	8
Oct 21	CLIENT B		500	—		(RECEIPTS IN FILE)				9
								520	—	10
Oct 31	CLIENT A		150	—						11
	CLIENT D		350	—		RETIREMENT PLAN		372	—	12
			3000	—						13
						FEDERAL INCOME				14
						TAX (40%)		893 20		15
										16
						SOCIAL SECURITY		108 62		17
								1843 82		18

34

J. ENTREPRENEUR & Co., INC.

OCTOBER 1977

Date	Description	Amount		Date	Description	Amount	Line
Oct 3	CLIENT A	300 —		Oct 3	RENT	200 —	1
	CLIENT B	475 —					2
				Oct 7	SALARY		3
Oct 7	CLIENT C	250 —			($300 GROSS, $224.95 NET)	224 95	4
	CLIENT A	125 —					5
				Oct 14	SALARY	224 95	6
Oct 12	CLIENT B	850 —			PHONE	100 —	7
					ELECTRIC	20 —	8
Oct 21	CLIENT B	500 —					9
				Oct 21	SALARY	224 95	10
Oct 31	CLIENT A	150 —					11
	CLIENT D	350 —		Oct 28	SALARY	224 95	12
		3000 —					13
				Oct 31	ENTERTAINMENT	100 —	14
					(RECEIPTS IN FILE)		15
					MISC. EXPENSES	100 —	16
					(RECEIPTS IN FILE)		17
						1419 80	18
							19
					FEDERAL INCOME +	300 20	20
					S.S. TAXES		21
							22
					RETIREMENT PLAN	300 —	23
						2020 —	24
							25
							26
							27
							28
							29
							30
							31
							32
							33
							34
							35
							36

J. ENTREPRENGUR

November 1977

Nov 1	CLIENT D		575 —	Nov 4	RENT		200 —	1
								2
Nov 4	CLIENT C		825 —	Nov 18	PHONE		100 —	3
					ELECTRIC		20 —	4
Nov 10	CLIENT A		500 —					5
	CLIENT B		600 —	Nov 30	ENTERTAINMENT		100 —	6
					(RECEIPTS IN FILE)			7
Nov 25	CLIENT C		500 —		MISC. EXPENSES		100 —	8
					(RECEIPTS IN FILE)			9
Nov 30	CLIENT A		500 —				520 —	10
			3000 —					11
					RETIREMENT PLAN		372 —	12
								13
					FEDERAL INCOME		843 20	14
					TAX (40%)			15
								16
					SOCIAL SECURITY		108 62	17
							1843 82	18
								19
								20
								21
								22
								23
								24
								25
								26
								27
								28
								29
								30
								31
								32
								33
								34
								35
								36

J. ENTREPRENEUR + Co., INC.
NOVEMBER 1977

Date	Description	Amount		Date	Description	Amount	
Nov 1	Client D	575 —		Nov 4	Salary	224 95	1
					Rent	200 —	2
							3
Nov 4	Client C	825 —		Nov 11	Salary	224 95	4
							5
Nov 10	Client A	500 —		Nov 18	Salary	224 95	6
	Client B	600 —			Phone	100 —	7
					Electric	20 —	8
Nov 25	Client C	500 —					9
				Nov 25	Salary	224 95	10
Nov 30	Client A	500 —					11
		3000 —		Nov 30	Entertainment	100 —	12
					(Receipts in file)		13
					Misc. Expenses	100 —	14
					(Receipts in file)		15
						1419 80	16
							17
					Federal Income +		18
					SS Taxes	300 20	19
							20
					Retirement Plan	300 —	21
						2020 —	22

J. ENTREPRENEUR

December 1977

Dec 2	CLIENT E	1000 —	Dec 2	RENT	200 —	1
						2
Dec 8	CLIENT A	675 —	Dec 15	EMERGENCY	250 —	3
	CLIENT C	800 —		DENTAL WORK		4
				(TAX-DOLLAR		5
Dec 15	DIVIDENDS	500 —		VALUE OF $1,000 —)		6
						7
Dec 21	CLIENT B	750 —	Dec 16	PHONE	100 —	8
				ELECTRIC	20 —	9
Dec 23	CLIENT A	225 —				10
			Dec 30	ENTERTAINMENT	100 —	11
Dec 30	CLIENT B	550 —		(RECEIPTS IN FILE)		12
		500 —		MISC. EXPENSES	100 —	13
				(RECEIPTS IN FILE)		14
					770 —	15
						16
				RETIREMENT PLAN	522 —	17
						18
	SUMMARY			FEDERAL INCOME		19
	GROSS INCOME	10500 —		TAX (40% OF		20
				$2,188 + 40%		21
	EXPENSE 1,810 —			OF $475 DIVIDENDS:		22
	RETIREMENT 1,266 —			$500 - $25 EXEMPTION)	1065 20	23
	FEDERAL					24
	INCOME + S.S.			SOCIAL SECURITY	1086 3	25
	TAXES 3,077.47				2465 83	26
		6153 47				27
	NET FOR QUARTER	4374 53				28
						29
	TOTAL TAXES FOR QUARTER	3,077.47				30
						31
						32
						33
						34
						35
						36

J. Entrepreneur + Co., Inc.

December 1977

Dec 2	Client E	1000 —	Dec 2	Salary	224 95
				Rent	200 —
Dec 8	Client A	675 —			
	Client C	800 —	Dec 9	Salary	224 95
Dec 15	Dividends	500 —	Dec 15	Emergency	
				Dental Work	
Dec 21	Client B	750 —		(Totally Deductible)	1000 —
Dec 23	Client A	225 —	Dec 16	Salary	224 95
				Phone	100 —
Dec 30	Client B	550 —		Electric	20 —
		4500 —			
			Dec 23	Salary	224 95
	Summary		Dec 30	Salary	224 95
	Gross Income	10500 —		Entertainment	100 —
				(Receipts in File)	
	Expenses* 2560 —			Misc. Expenses	100 —
	Retirement 975 —			(Receipts in File)	
	Federal Income & 975.65				2644 75
	SS Taxes - Employee				
	Federal Income &			Federal Income &	
	SS Taxes - Corp. 911 —			SS Taxes	375 25
		5421.65			
	Net for Quarter	5078.35		Retirement Plan	375 —
					3395 —
	Total Taxes for Quarter	1886.65			
				Tax on 15 % of	
				Dividends	15 —
					3410 —
				Quarterly Fed. Tax	110 60
				Corp. Tax @ 20%	
	*$5,845.35 - $2,924.35 Taken			of Net Income	786 —
	as Salary				4306 60

39

corporation are two separate, distinct legal entities. The corporation is now your employer and should pay your salary regularly, just as any other employer would. It will also withhold taxes from your salary and send them to the appropriate government agencies.

Your corporation will send out all the bills, and all income must now go into corporate bank accounts. I prefer using both a money-market account and a NOW checking account: all income goes directly into a corporate money-market account that earns interest; when money is needed to pay salary and bills, it is transferred from the money-market account to the NOW account.

Paying bills is a little more complicated now than it used to be. As an individual proprietor, your personal check paid for all expenses—personal and business; it was only at the end of the year that you had to figure out what part of a check to a credit-card company covered business expenses and what part represented personal items. Now you will have to make these calculations in advance and pay many bills with two checks: corporate and personal. There is a bonus, though: when you come to the end of the year, your business and personal expenses will already have been segregated, and tax preparation of these items will take no time at all.

You may find it simpler to use one credit card for business only; many people use their American Express or Diner's Club cards for corporate expenditures and their MasterCard or VISA for personal ones.

Paying office bills isn't difficult, but it deserves a chapter all its own; mortgages, rent, phone, and utilities are covered in the next chapter, "Your Office: Home or Away?"

4

Your Office:
Home or Away?

If you have been renting an office as an individual proprietor, corporate status doesn't mean much of a change: from the date of incorporation, you'll be paying your rent and office expenses with company checks instead of personal checks, as you were doing when you were an individual proprietor.

If your office is at home—one or more rooms of an apartment or a house that you rent—you would now use a corporate check to pay for the rent on that portion of the apartment or the house that you use as an office. If your rent was $800 a month for a four-room apartment and you used one room of the apartment exclusively as an office, you would now pay the rent with two checks: a corporate check for $200 for the office portion of your apartment, and a personal check for the personal living portion of your apartment. Using these proportions, you would send the electric utility company a corporate check for 25 percent of your electric bill and a personal check for 75 percent of it. Or you might be able to make a convincing case for a larger share to be allocated to your office—a word processor and lights in constant use, perhaps—and write off 33 or 40 percent as a corporate office expense and 67 or 60 percent for personal use.

In some cases, where your landlord would look askance at your running a business from your second bedroom, it will be more prudent to pay your rent with one single personal check and have your corporation reimburse you monthly with its share of the rent. In this example, you would pay the entire rent of $800 and your corporation would reimburse you $200. Your net rent would still be $600.

Your telephone bill is a bit more complicated. If you have a separate business phone, the bill gets paid with a corporate check, of course, and your private phone bill gets paid with a personal check. If your home office has only one phone, you will have to prorate business and personal use and pay the appropriate shares with corporate and personal checks. Be especially careful to allocate long-distance calls properly; you should be able to document business long-distance calls if the IRS audits your tax return.

Still more complicated is the situation where your office is part of a house, cooperative apartment, or condominium you own and live in. In this case, in order to preserve the separation between your corporation and you, one accountant suggests that the corporation rent its office space from you, the shareholder, in an arm's-length transaction. You may wish to have a lease and corporate resolutions approving the lease—see pages 43–45 to document the arm's-length nature of the transaction. In this kind of transaction, it is clear that there are two separate entities and that there is no favoritism shown, e.g., if you would not rent anyone else office space at $10 per month, you must not rent space to the corporation at this price.

You can even profit from this transaction: as the stockholder, you could take the position that the fair rental value of the corporate offices is higher than the proportionate share of the mortgage and the real estate tax payments you have to make. For example, if your mortgage and tax payments total $1,000 a month and your corporation uses two rooms of your eight-room house, you could conceivably and reasonably argue that $500 a month (rather than the $250 that would be the proportionate share) is a reasonable rent for a two-room office in your neighborhood. Then, as the home-owner (or cooperative or condominium owner), you would be able to take 100 percent of all the deductions on your individual tax return: interest amortization, real estate taxes, etc. You would have to report the rent your corporation pays you as income, but this way you are withdrawing funds from your corporation that will be deductible by the corporation: sales, rentals, anything but dividends, since dividends would be taxed twice.

MINUTES OF A SPECIAL MEETING OF
SHAREHOLDERS
OF
WONDERFUL CORPORATION

MINUTES of a special meeting of shareholders held at 123 Easy Street, New York City, in the State of New York, on the second day of January, 1989, at nine o'clock in the forenoon.

The meeting was duly called to order by the President and sole stockholder, who stated the object of the meeting.

On motion duly made, amended, and unanimously carried, the following resolution was adopted:

WHEREAS, there has been presented to and considered by this meeting a proposed lease from I. M. Wonderful, as Lessor, to this corporation, as Lessee, covering the premises known as 123 Easy Street; and

WHEREAS, said proposed lease is for a term of two years, commencing January 2, 1989, at the annual rental of $6,000.00 (six thousand dollars);

NOW, THEREFORE, BE IT RESOLVED, that the terms and conditions of the proposed lease presented to and considered by this meeting be and the same hereby are approved.

FURTHER RESOLVED, that the President and Secretary of this corporation be and they hereby are authorized to execute said lease in the name of and on behalf of this corporation and in substantially the form approved at this meeting.

There being no further business, the meeting was adjourned.

Dated the second day of January, 1989.

_____
Secretary

_____
President

In fact, there are some excellent reasons to have your corporation pay you as high a rent as is comfortable for your corporation to pay on an annual or biannual basis and that is consistent with neighborhood office-space rents. First, payment of a high rent removes cash

A 35—Lease, Business Premises.
Loft, Office or Store. 2-85

JULIUS BLUMBERG, INC., LAW BLANK PUBLISHERS

This Lease made the SECOND day of JANUARY 1989, between

I. M. WONDERFUL

hereinafter referred to as LANDLORD, and

WONDERFUL CORPORATION

hereinafter jointly, severally and collectively referred to as TENANT.

Witnesseth, that the Landlord hereby leases to the Tenant, and the Tenant hereby hires and takes

from the Landlord **OFFICE SPACE**

in the building known as **123 EASY STREET, NEW YORK, NY 10001**

to be used and occupied by the Tenant

and for no other purpose, for a term to commence on **JANUARY 2** 19**89**, and to end

on **JANUARY 1** 19**91**, unless sooner terminated as hereinafter provided, at the ANNUAL RENT of

$6,000 (SIX THOUSAND DOLLARS)

all payable in equal monthly instalments in advance on the first day of each and every calendar month during said term,

except the first instalment, which shall be paid upon the execution hereof.

THE TENANT JOINTLY AND SEVERALLY COVENANTS:

FIRST.—That the Tenant will pay the rent as above provided.

REPAIRS

SECOND.—That, throughout said term the Tenant will take good care of the demised premises, fixtures and appurtenances, and all alterations, additions and improvements to either; make all repairs in and about the same necessary to preserve them in good order and condition, which repairs shall be, in quality and class, equal to the original work; promptly pay the expense of such repairs; suffer no waste or injury; give prompt notice to the Landlord of any fire that may occur; execute and comply with all laws, rules, orders, ordinances and regulations at any time issued or in force (except those requiring structural alterations), applicable to the demised premises or to the Tenant's occupation thereof, of the Federal, State and Local Governments, and of each and every department, bureau and official thereof, and of the New York Board of Fire Underwriters; permit at all times during usual business hours, the Landlord and representatives of the Landlord to enter the demised premises for the purpose of inspection, and to exhibit them for purposes of sale or rental; suffer the Landlord to make repairs and improvements to all parts of the building, and to comply with all orders and require s of governmental auth ity applicable to said bu'lding or to any occupa'on thereof; suffer the La' lord to erect, r ain, repair and repl' pipes and 'duits in 'mised premises ar' the floors abo' and b ' forever in' ave harmless th' 'ord f' 'air all liability, p ' damages. es 'gments 'y during sa' 'v 'ture, occ' 'olly or '' 'r ac'' 'ons of t' 'hing 'ts, a 'er''
'd t 'd c La 'an, 'as, '0' u' t 'or is , or is if Lan' 'ented 'ed fr' 'oy rea' 'pply 'yed in s' 'equipme. 'ergency de' 'the Pre' of the Un' 'es or in c' 'governm' 'eemption in 'on with a N. or subivision ti' 'f of any go' 'ment agency o' 'y reason of th' 'conditions of ' 'pply and demand ' 'ch have been or '. affected by war or other emergency.

THE LANDLORD COVENANTS:

QUIET POSSESSION

FIRST.—That if and so long as the Tenant pays the rent and "additional rent" reserved hereby, and performs and observes the covenants and provisions hereof, the Tenant shall quietly enjoy the demised premises, subject, however, to the terms of this lease, and to the mortgages above mentioned, provided however, that this covenant shall be conditioned upon the retention of title to the premises by Landlord.

ELEVATOR

HEAT

SECOND.—Subject to the provisions of Paragraph "Fourteenth" above the Landlord will furnish the following respective services: (a) Elevator service, if the building shall contain an elevator or elevators, on all days except Sundays and holidays, from A.M. to P.M. and on Saturdays from A.M. to P.M.; (b) Heat, during the same hours on the same days in the cold season in each year.

And it is mutually understood and agreed that the covenants and agreements contained in the within lease shall be binding upon the parties hereto and upon their respective successors, heirs, executors and administrators.

In Witness Whereof, the Landlord and Tenant have respectively signed and sealed these presents the day and year first above written.

IN PRESENCE OF:

....[L. S.]
Landlord

....[L. S.]
Tenant

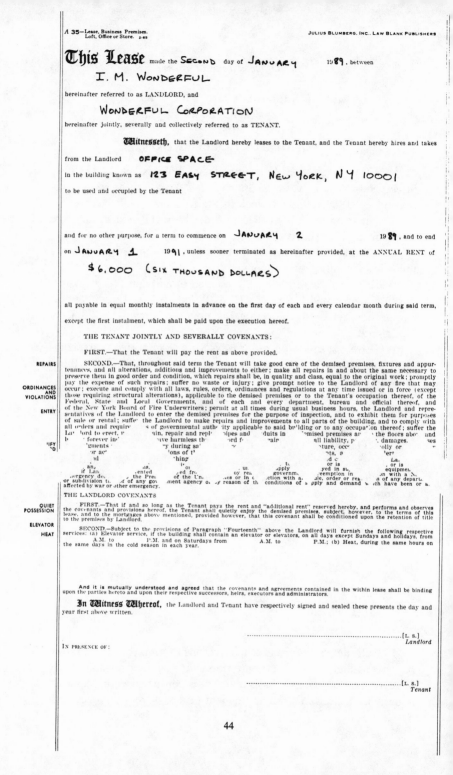

from your corporation. In doing so, it slows down the accumulation of retained earnings and may even lower your corporation's tax bracket. Second, as compared with salary, neither you nor your corporation pays Social Security tax on rent. Third, the rent payments you receive can be offset by depreciation, repairs, cleaning, and other real estate expenses.

As you can see, the corporation is defraying a larger part of your home's expenses than the proportion of the actual physical space it is using, and yet the $500-a-month rent, in this example, is quite reasonable and not likely to be questioned by the IRS.

The key is what the IRS considers reasonable. No matter what comparable office space might cost, the IRS will probably question rent that comes within $100 or so of your house monthly mortgage payment or coop or condominium monthly maintenance charge. Still, *without your being greedy,* these basic guidelines allow a great deal of flexibility. Depending on your office space, its percentage of your total house or apartment space, your monthly rent, maintenance, or mortgage payment, and, to a great extent, your corporation's income, you should be able to charge your corporation rent of anywhere from $400 to $1,000 a month (sometimes more) and still fall within the IRS guidelines of reasonable rent.

Schedule E on the following page shows corporate rental of a portion of a $200,000 apartment. Although the rent is $500 per month—$6,000 per year—in income to the owner, note that only $2,400 of the $6,000 rental is actual taxable income.

Be aware, though, that if you do rent part of your home or apartment to your corporation, when you sell your home or apartment, you'll have to pay tax on the same percentage of any gain as the percentage of the home or apartment you rented to your corporation as well as tax on the recaptured depreciation. Good tax advice can help minimize the bite.

Supplemental Income Schedule

(From rents, royalties, partnerships, estates, trusts, REMICs, etc.)
▶ Attach to Form 1040, Form 1041, or Form 1041S.
▶ See Instructions for Schedule E (Form 1040).

OMB No. 1545-0074

1987

Attachment
Sequence No. **13**

Name(s) as shown on Form 1040	Your social security number
I. M. WONDERFUL	000 : 00 : 0000

Part I Rental and Royalty Income or (Loss)   Caution: Your rental loss may be limited. See Instructions.

1 In the space provided below, show the kind and location of each rental property.	2 For each property listed, did you or a member of your family use for personal purposes any of the properties for more than the greater of 14 days or 10% of the total days rented at fair rental value during the tax year? Yes No	3 For each rental real estate property listed, did you actively participate in the operation of the activity during the tax year? (See Instructions.) Yes No
Property A 123 EASY STREET, NYC – OFFICE SPACE ▶	✓	▶ ✓
Property B .... ▶		▶
Property C .... ▶		▶

Rental and Royalty Income		Properties			Totals (Add columns A, B, and C)	
		A	B	C		
4 Rents received		6,000 00			4	6,000 00
5 Royalties received					5	

Rental and Royalty Expenses						
6 Advertising	6					
7 Auto and travel	7					
8 Cleaning and maintenance	8	600 00				
9 Commissions	9					
10 Insurance	10					
11 Legal and other professional fees	11	500 00				
12 Mortgage interest paid to financial institutions (see Instructions)	12				12	
13 Other interest	13					
14 Repairs	14					
15 Supplies	15					
16 Taxes (Do not include windfall profit tax here. See Part V, line 40.)	16					
17 Utilities	17					
18 Wages and salaries	18					
19 Other (list) ▶ .... DEPRECIATION BASIS: $200,000–5% VALUE OF LAND = $190,000 ÷ 4 (1 RM OF 4-RM APT)= $47,500 ÷ 19 YRS = $2,500/YR. (PLACED IN SERVICE 1984)						
20 Total expenses other than depreciation and depletion. Add lines 6 through 19.	20	1,100 00			20	
21 Depreciation expense (see Instructions), or depletion (see Publication 535).	21	2,500 00			21	
22 Total. Add lines 20 and 21	22	3,600 00				
23 Income or (loss) from rental or royalty properties. Subtract line 22 from line 4 (rents) or 5 (royalties).	23	2,400 00				
24 Deductible rental loss. Caution: Your rental loss on line 23 may be limited. See Instructions to determine if you must file Form 8582, Passive Activity Loss Limitations	24					

25 Profits. Add rental and royalty profits from line 23, and enter the total profits here		25	2,400 00
26 Losses. Add royalty losses from line 23 and rental losses from line 24, and enter the total (losses) here		26 (	)
27 Combine amounts on lines 25 and 26, and enter the net profit or (loss) here		27	2,400 00
28 Net farm rental profit or (loss) from Form 4835. (Also complete Part VI, line 43.)		28	
29 Total rental or royalty income or (loss). Combine amounts on lines 27 and 28, and enter the total here. If Parts II, III, IV, and V on page 2 do not apply to you, enter the amount from line 29 on Form 1040, line 17. Otherwise, include the amount from line 29 in line 42 on page 2 of Schedule E		29	2,400 00

For Paperwork Reduction Act Notice, see Form 1040 Instructions.   Schedule E (Form 1040) 1987

5

How to Profit from Your Subchapter S Corporation

Sooner or later, maybe the new term *S corporation* will catch on. But it's been six years since the Subchapter S Revision Act of 1982 gave these fascinating hybrid corporations their new name, and it hasn't stuck yet. Because you still "elect Subchapter S status" for your corporation, I'll keep to the old name. It's simpler that way.

In a sense, a Subchapter S corporation is a hybrid. It is generally treated like a corporation for legal purposes but like a partnership for income-tax purposes. Think of a Subchapter S corporation as a conduit: its profits and losses are not taxed. Instead, corporate income or losses flow through and are credited or debited to the shareholders in proportion to their shareholdings. Since the shareholders are treated like partners and the corporation like a partnership for tax purposes, shareholders who are owner-employees may benefit from lower individual income-tax rates.

The Tax Reform Act of 1986 suddenly made Subchapter S election very desirable because, for the first time in U.S. tax history, the maximum corporate income-tax rate is now higher than the maximum individual income-tax rate. If you can flow earnings through your corporation and have them taxed at a lower rate, you're better off. You are also getting immediate use of the money. In contrast, if you were to let your corporate profits build up in a C corporation and wanted to liquidate it at some future date, you might be taking a chance. You don't know what the tax rules will be when you liquidate.

There are a few ground rules that are easy to satisfy. A Subchapter S corporation must be a "small business corporation" with no more than thirty-five shareholders—a husband and wife are treated as a single shareholder—all of whom must be U.S. citizens. There must be only one class of stock, and shares cannot be owned by another corporation or a partnership. Some trusts qualify as owners; some don't. You'll need expert legal advice here.

The mechanics of Subchapter S election are simple. You must file Form 2553, shown on pages 49–50, with the District Director of the Internal Revenue Service before the fifteenth day of the third month of your corporation's taxable year, whether calendar or fiscal. (For a calendar-year corporation, the deadline is March 15.) While not mandatory, it's also a good idea to hold a special meeting of your corporation to declare that you have made a Subchapter S election.

PERILOUS PROFESSIONS, OR, NEVER CALL YOURSELF A CONSULTANT

Electing Subchapter S status has become a complex choice. For many people, there are myriad pros and cons. But some people, those in what I call the perilous professions—defined by the IRS as corporations whose principal function is "services in the field of law, health, engineering, architecture, accounting, actuarial science, performing arts, or consulting"—may have an easier choice because the Revenue Act of 1987 raised their corporate taxes to a flat 34 percent. This move has forced most people in these professions and arts into choosing Subchapter S as their corporate form in order to save as much as 19 percent on their income taxes. However, if you use a great deal of expensive equipment in your professional practice, a C corporation may still be a better choice for you. Read this entire chapter, work out the numbers, and get some expert tax advice.

Be aware of the exceptions. Writers, artists, and their agents and representatives do not fall into this group. Neither do people who provide a number of personal or business services. Consultants who

Election by a Small Business Corporation
(Under section 1362 of the Internal Revenue Code)
▶ For Paperwork Reduction Act Notice, see page 1 of instructions.
▶ See separate instructions.

OMB No. 1545-0146

Expires 1-31-89

Note: *This election, to be treated as an "S corporation," can be approved only if all the tests in Instruction B are met.*

Part I Election Information

Name of corporation (see instructions)	Employer identification number (see instructions)	Principal business activity and principal product or service (see instructions)
NEW S COMPANY	13-0000000	EDITORIAL SERVICES

Number and street		Election is to be effective for tax year beginning (month, day, year)
123 ENTREPRENEURIAL ROW		1/1/88

City or town, state and ZIP code		Number of shares issued and outstanding (see instructions)
NEW YORK, NY 10021		100

Is the corporation the outgrowth or continuation of any form of predecessor? . . . . ☐ Yes ☑ No | Date and place of incorporation

If "Yes," state name of predecessor, type of organization, and period of its existence ▶ ------------------------ | 1/1/88 — NEW YORK

A If this election takes effect for the first tax year the corporation exists, enter the earliest of the following: (1) date the corporation first had shareholders, (2) date the corporation first had assets, or (3) date the corporation began doing business. ▶ 1/1/88

B Selected tax year: Annual return will be filed for tax year ending (month and day) ▶ 10/31

See instructions before entering your tax year. If the tax year ends any date other than December 31, you must complete Part II or Part IV on back. You may want to complete Part III to make a back-up request.

C Name of each shareholder, person having a community property interest in the corporation's stock, and each tenant in common, joint tenant, and tenant by the entirety. (A husband and wife (and their estates) are counted as one shareholder in determining the number of shareholders without regard to the manner in which the stock is owned.)	D Shareholders' Consent Statement. We, the undersigned shareholders, consent to the corporation's election to be treated as an "S corporation" under section 1362(a). (Shareholders sign and date below.)*	E Stock owned		F Social security number (employer identification number for estates or trust)	G Tax year ends (month and day)
		Number of shares	Dates acquired		
SAM SMART	Sam Smart	85	1/1/88	000-00-0000	12/31
MARY SMART	Mary Smart	10	1/1/88	000-00-0000	12/31
SAM SMART, JR.	Sam Smart Jr	5	1/1/88	000-00-0000	12/31

*For this election to be valid, the consent of each shareholder, person having a community property interest in the corporation's stock, and each tenant in common, joint tenant, and tenant by the entirety must either appear above or be attached to this form. (See instructions for Column D, if continuation sheet or a separate consent statement is needed.)

Under penalties of perjury, I declare that I have examined this election, including accompanying schedules, and statements, and to the best of my knowledge and belief, it is true, correct, and complete.

Signature and Title of Officer ▶ Sam Smart   President   Date ▶ 1/1/88

See Parts II, III, and IV on back.

Form **2553** (Rev. 2-86)

Part II **Selection of Tax Year Under Revenue Procedure 83-25**

H   Check the applicable box below to indicate whether the corporation is:

☑ Adopting the tax year entered in item B, Part I.

☐ Retaining the tax year entered in item B, Part I.

☐ Changing to the tax year entered in item B, Part I.

I   Check the applicable box below to indicate the representation statement the corporation is making as required under section 7.01 (item 4) of Revenue Procedure 83-25, 1983-1 C.B. 689.

☐ Under penalties of perjury, I represent that shareholders holding more than half of the shares of the stock (as of the first day of the tax year to which the request relates) of the corporation have the same tax year or are concurrently changing to the tax year that the corporation adopts, retains, or changes to per item B, Part I.

☐ Under penalties of perjury, I represent that shareholders holding more than half of the shares of the stock (as of the first day of the tax year to which the request relates) of the corporation have a tax year or are concurrently changing to a tax year that, although different from the tax year the corporation is adopting, retaining, or changing to per item B, Part I, results in a deferment of income to each of these shareholders of three months or less.

☐ Under penalties of perjury, I represent that the corporation is adopting, retaining, or changing to a tax year that coincides with its natural business year as verified by its satisfaction of the requirements of section 4.042(a), (b), (c), and (d) of Revenue Procedure 83-25.

J   Check here ☐ if the tax year entered in item B, Part I, is requested under the provisions of section 8 of Revenue Procedure 83-25. Attach to Form 2553 a statement and other necessary information pursuant to the ruling request requirements of Revenue Procedure 85-1. The statement must include the business purpose for the desired tax year. See instructions.

Part III **Back-Up Request by Certain Corporations Initially Selecting a Fiscal Year (See Instructions.)**

Check here ☑ if the corporation agrees to adopt or to change to a tax year ending December 31 if necessary for IRS to accept this election for S corporation status (temporary regulations section 18.1378-1(b)(2)(ii)(A)). This back-up request does not apply if the fiscal tax year request is approved by IRS or if the election to be an S corporation is not accepted.

Part IV **Request by Corporation for Tax Year Determination by IRS (See Instructions.)**

Check here ☐ if the corporation requests the IRS to determine the permitted tax year for the corporation based on information submitted in Part I (and attached schedules). This request is made under provisions of temporary regulations section 18.1378-1(d).

are clever enough to find another job description for their services may also be able to escape this new corporate trap.

ADVANTAGES OF SUBCHAPTER S

There are four major reasons to elect Subchapter S status for your new corporation:

1. *Lower taxes if you are a member of the perilous professions.* Let's take someone whose corporate income for 1988 is $40,000. The flat rate of 34 percent means that the corporation's federal income tax for the year is $13,600. But if the corporation's owner elects Subchapter S status, the $40,000 corporate income flows through to the owner and is taxed at his or her individual rate. Assuming that there is no other income and that the standard deduction is used, the tax is $7,494 for single taxpayers and $4,841 for married taxpayers—a substantial savings.

However, if you are not a member of the perilous professions, *you can achieve even greater tax savings by using the income-splitting feature of a C corporation,* paying yourself a $20,000 salary and retaining $20,000 in your corporation. (For simplicity's sake, I won't even deduct a permissible $5,000 pension contribution from the corporate profits in making these calculations.) Your corporate income tax is $3,000. Your personal income tax, assuming that you have no other income and that you take the standard deduction, is $2,258 if you are single and $1,665 if you are married—or total taxes of $5,258 and $4,665, respectively. These totals are far lower than the taxes under Subchapter S election—especially for single taxpayers.

2. Because corporate profits flow through to the shareholders, *the IRS can never claim that owner-shareholders are receiving excessive compensation and that some of the compensation is really a dividend* and must be treated as such. Thus *the specter of double taxation cannot rear its frightful head.*

3. Because corporate profits are taxed every year whether or not they are distributed, *there is no buildup of corporate assets,* as there frequently is in a C corporation. *This simplifies matters when you are ready to liquidate your corporation* at some future date. It also removes a great deal of uncertainty because *no one knows how favorably corporate liquidations will be taxed several years down the road.*

4. *Perhaps the greatest advantage is that any losses that are not passive* that your corporation incurs can flow through to you, as an individual taxpayer, to the extent of the basis of the stock in the corporation* (see pages 71–73) *to offset income from other sources immediately, rather than being carried forward from year to year on your C corporation return until they are finally offset by corporate profits.*

There's another significant but subtle advantage, too: corporate tax-loss dollars are worth more when they are used to offset personal-income dollars. For example, $1,000 of corporate-loss carryforward offsets the first $1,000 of corporate income. At current corporate-tax rates, since the first $1,000 of corporate income is taxed at 15 percent, the corporate-loss carryforward is worth only $150.

However, suppose that the $1,000 corporate-loss carryforward flows through to you as a single individual and is used to reduce your investment income and stock-trading profits from $85,000 to $84,000. Since your income places you in the 33 percent federal bracket, that $1,000 corporate-loss carryforward is worth $330 in actual tax dollars and probably even more when state and local income taxes are calculated.

To see the advantages of Subchapter S election in action, look at the sample tax returns on pages 53–70. In each, a successful investor has profits of $30,000 but losses of $20,000 in his new design company. In the first example, he has a Subchapter S corporation; in the second, he doesn't. Our Sub S corporate head is entitled to have his corporation's loss flow through to his own personal tax return to offset his trading profits. As a result, he paid only $764 in federal income taxes. (In 1988 he would have paid only $758.)

The second corporate head can use his corporation's loss only to offset past or future corporate profits. He derives no real immediate benefit and would have paid $4,905 in personal federal income tax in 1987—$4,141 more than our first executive. (In 1988 he would have paid $4,694—$3,936 more than our first executive.) In fact, as you can see, one of the major advantages of a Subchapter S corporation is its ability to pass on its losses to an individual shareholder who has great income from other sources—interest, dividends, rents, stock-market profits, and the like.

---

*Real estate investing has its own rules. You'll need professional help here.

JOSEPHY, STRAUSS & SCHEINTHAL
PUBLIC ACCOUNTANTS AND AUDITORS

are pleased to announce the relocation of their office to

394 Old Country Road
Garden City, New York 11530

Phone Number (516) 741-9770
Fax Number (516) 741-9775

Form **1120S**	**U.S. Income Tax Return for an S Corporation**	OMB No. 1545-0130
Department of the Treasury Internal Revenue Service	For the calendar year 1987 or tax year beginning _____, 1987, ending _____, 19 ___ ▶ **For Paperwork Reduction Act Notice, see page 1 of the instructions.**	**1987**

A Date of election as an S corporation 1/1/87	Use IRS label. Other-wise, please print or type.	Name **NEW CONSULTING, INC.**	C Employer identification number **00-0000000**
B Business code no. (see Specific Instructions) **8999**		Number and street (P.O. Box number if mail is not delivered to street address) **123 EASY STREET**	D Date incorporated **1/1/87**
		City or town, state, and ZIP code **NEW YORK, NY 10021**	E Total assets (see Specific Instructions) Dollars / Cents

F Check applicable boxes: (1) ☑ Initial return (2) ☐ Final return (3) ☐ Change in address (4) ☐ Amended return $

G Check this box if this is an S corporation subject to the consolidated audit procedures of sections 6241 through 6245 (see instructions) . . . . ▶ ☐

H Was this corporation in operation at the end of 1987 (see instructions)? . . . . Yes ☑ No ☐

I How many months in 1987 was this corporation in operation (see instructions)? . . . . ▶ 12

Caution: Include **only** trade or business income and expenses on lines 1a through 21. See the instructions for more information.

	Income		
1a	Gross receipts or sales _____ b Less returns and allowances _____ Balance ▶	1c	
2	Cost of goods sold and/or operations (Schedule A, line 7)	2	
3	Gross profit (subtract line 2 from line 1c)	3	
4	Net gain (or loss) from Form 4797, line 18 (see instructions)	4	
5	Other income (see instructions—attach schedule)	5	
6	TOTAL income (loss)—Combine lines 3, 4 and 5 and enter here . ▶	6	(20,000)

	Deductions (See instructions for limitations.)		
7	Compensation of officers	7	
8a	Salaries and wages _____ b Less jobs credit _____ Balance ▶	8c	
9	Repairs	9	
10	Bad debts (see instructions)	10	
11	Rents	11	
12	Taxes	12	
13	Deductible interest expense not claimed or reported elsewhere on return (see instructions) . .	13	
14a	Depreciation from Form 4562 (attach Form 4562).	14a	
b	Depreciation reported on Schedule A and elsewhere on return . .	14b	
c	Subtract line 14b from line 14a	14c	
15	Depletion (**Do not deduct oil and gas depletion.** See instructions.)	15	
16	Advertising	16	
17	Pension, profit-sharing, etc. plans	17	
18	Employee benefit programs	18	
19	Other deductions (attach schedule)	19	
20	TOTAL deductions—Add lines 7 through 19 and enter here . ▶	20	
21	Ordinary income (loss) from trade or business activity(ies)—Subtract line 20 from line 6 . .	21	(20,000)

	Tax and Payments		
22	Tax:		
a	Excess net passive income tax (attach schedule) . .	22a	
b	Tax from Schedule D (Form 1120S)	22b	
c	Add lines 22a and 22b	22c	0
23	Payments:		
a	Tax deposited with Form 7004	23a	
b	Credit for Federal tax on gasoline and special fuels (attach Form 4136)	23b	
c	Add lines 23a and 23b	23c	0
24	**TAX DUE** (subtract line 23c from line 22c). See instructions for Paying the Tax . . . ▶	24	0
25	**OVERPAYMENT** (subtract line 22c from line 23c) . . . . ▶	25	0

Please Sign Here

Under penalties of perjury, I declare that I have examined this return, including accompanying schedules and statements, and to the best of my knowledge and belief, it is true, correct, and complete. Declaration of preparer (other than taxpayer) is based on all information of which preparer has any knowledge.

▶ Signature of officer _____ Date 3/15/88 ▶ Title PRESIDENT

Paid Preparer's Use Only	Preparer's signature ▶	Date	Check if self-employed ▶ ☐	Preparer's social security number
	Firm's name (or yours if self-employed) and address ▶		E.I. No. ▶	
			ZIP code ▶	

Form **1120S** (1987)

Schedule A Cost of Goods Sold and/or Operations (See instructions for Schedule A.)

1 Inventory at beginning of year	**1**	
2 Purchases	**2**	
3 Cost of labor	**3**	
4a Additional section 263A costs (attach schedule)	**4a**	
b Other costs (attach schedule)	**4b**	
5 Total—Add lines 1 through 4b	**5**	
6 Inventory at end of year	**6**	
7 Cost of goods sold and/or operations—Subtract line 6 from line 5. Enter here and on line 2, page 1.	**7**	N/A

8a Check all methods used for valuing closing inventory:
  (i) ☐ Cost
  (ii) ☐ Lower of cost or market as described in Regulations section 1.471-4 (see instructions)
  (iii) ☐ Writedown of "subnormal" goods as described in Regulations section 1.471-2(c) (see instructions)
  (iv) ☐ Other (Specify method used and attach explanation) ▶

b Check this box if the LIFO inventory method was adopted this tax year for any goods (if checked, attach Form 970) . . . ☐
c If the LIFO inventory method was used for this tax year, enter percentage (or amounts) of closing inventory computed under LIFO **8c**

d Do the rules of section 263A (with respect to property produced or acquired for resale) apply to the corporation? . . . ☐ Yes ☐ No
e Was there any change (other than for section 263A purposes) in determining quantities, cost, or valuations between opening and closing inventory? (If "Yes," attach explanation.) . . . ☐ Yes ☐ No

Additional Information Required

	Yes	No
J Did you at the end of the tax year own, directly or indirectly, 50% or more of the voting stock of a domestic corporation? (For rules of attribution, see section 267(c).) If "Yes," attach a schedule showing: (1) Name, address, and employer identification number; (3) Highest amount owed by you to such corporation during the year; and (2) Percentage owned; (4) Highest amount owed to you by such corporation during the year. (Note: For purposes of J(3) and J(4), "highest amount owed" includes loans and accounts receivable/payable.)		✓
K Refer to the listing of business activity codes at the end of the Instructions for Form 1120S and state your principal: Business activity ▶ .... : Product or service ▶ EDITORIAL SERVICES		
L Were you a member of a controlled group subject to the provisions of section 1561?		✓
M Did you claim a deduction for expenses connected with:		
(1) Entertainment facilities (boat, resort, ranch, etc.)?		✓
(2) Living accommodations (except for employees on business)?		✓
(3) Employees attending conventions or meetings outside the North American area? (See section 274(h).)		✓
(4) Employees' families at conventions or meetings?		✓
If "Yes," were any of these conventions or meetings outside the North American area? (See section 274(h).)		✓
(5) Employee or family vacations not reported on Form W-2?		✓
N At any time during the tax year, did you have an interest in or a signature or other authority over a financial account in a foreign country (such as a bank account, securities account, or other financial account)? (See instructions for exceptions and filing requirements for form TD F 90-22.1.) If "Yes," enter the name of the foreign country ▶		✓
O Were you the grantor of, or transferor to, a foreign trust which existed during the current tax year, whether or not you have any beneficial interest in it? If "Yes," you may have to file Forms 3520, 3520-A, or 926		✓
P During this tax year did you maintain any part of your accounting/tax records on a computerized system?	✓	
Q Check method of accounting: (1) ☐ Cash (2) ☐ Accrual (3) ☐ Other (specify) ▶		
R Check this box if the S corporation has filed or is required to file **Form 8264,** Application for Registration of a Tax Shelter. . . . ▶ ☐		
S Check this box if the corporation issued publicly offered debt instruments with original issue discount . . . ▶ ☐ If so, the corporation may have to file Form 8281, Information Return for Publicly Offered Original Issue Discount Instruments.		
T If section 1374 (new built-in gains tax) applies to the corporation, enter the corporation's net unrealized built-in gain as defined in section 1374(d)(1) (see instructions) ▶		

Designation of Tax Matters Person

The following shareholder is hereby designated as the tax matters person (TMP) for the tax year for which this tax return is filed:

Name of designated TMP ▶   Identifying number of TMP ▶

Address of designated TMP ▶

Schedule K	Shareholders' Shares of Income, Credits, Deductions, etc. (See Instructions.)		
	(a) Distributive share items		(b) Total amount

Income (Losses) and Deductions

1	Ordinary income (loss) from trade or business activity(ies) (page 1, line 21)	**1**	(20,000)
2a	Gross income from rental real estate activity(ies). **2a**		
b	Minus expenses (attach schedule) **2b**		
c	Balance: net income (loss) from rental real estate activity(ies).	**2c**	
3a	Gross income from other rental activity(ies) **3a**		
b	Minus expenses (attach schedule) **3b**		
c	Balance: net income (loss) from other rental activity(ies)	**3c**	
4	Portfolio income (loss):		
a	Interest income	**4a**	
b	Dividend income	**4b**	
c	Royalty income	**4c**	
d	Net short-term capital gain (loss) (Schedule D (Form 1120S)).	**4d**	
e	Net long-term capital gain (loss) (Schedule D (Form 1120S))	**4e**	
f	Other portfolio income (loss) (attach schedule)	**4f**	
5	Net gain (loss) under section 1231 (other than due to casualty or theft)	**5**	
6	Other income (loss) (attach schedule)	**6**	
7	Charitable contributions (attach schedule)	**7**	
8	Section 179 expense deduction (attach schedule)	**8**	
9	Expenses related to portfolio income (loss) (attach schedule) (see instructions)	**9**	
10	Other deductions (attach schedule)	**10**	

Credits

11a	Jobs credit (attach Form 5884)	**11a**	
b	Low-income housing credit (attach Form 8586)	**11b**	
c	Qualified rehabilitation expenditures related to rental real estate activity(ies) (attach schedule)	**11c**	
d	Credits related to rental real estate activity(ies) other than on lines 11b and 11c (attach schedule)	**11d**	
e	Credit(s) related to rental activity(ies) other than on lines 11b, 11c, and 11d (attach schedule)	**11e**	
12	Other credits (attach schedule)	**12**	

Tax Preference and Adjustment Items

13a	Accelerated depreciation of real property placed in service before 1987	**13a**	
b	Accelerated depreciation of leased personal property placed in service before 1987	**13b**	
c	Depreciation adjustment on property placed in service after 1986	**13c**	
d	Depletion (other than oil and gas)	**13d**	
e	(1) Gross income from oil, gas, or geothermal properties	**13e(1)**	
	(2) Gross deductions allocable to oil, gas, or geothermal properties	**13e(2)**	
f	Other items (attach schedule)	**13f**	

Investment Interest

14a	Interest expense on investment debts	**14a**	
b	(1) Investment income included on lines 4a through 4f, Schedule K	**14b(1)**	
	(2) Investment expenses included on line 9, Schedule K	**14b(2)**	

Foreign Taxes

15a	Type of income		
b	Name of foreign country or U.S. possession		
c	Total gross income from sources outside the U.S. (attach schedule)	**15c**	
d	Total applicable deductions and losses (attach schedule)	**15d**	
e	Total foreign taxes (check one): ▶ ☐ Paid ☐ Accrued	**15e**	
f	Reduction in taxes available for credit (attach schedule)	**15f**	
g	Other (attach schedule)	**15g**	

Other Items

16	Total property distributions (including cash) other than dividend distributions reported on line 18, Schedule K	**16**	
17	Other items and amounts not included in lines 1 through 16, Schedule K, that are required to be reported separately to shareholders (attach schedule)		
18	Total dividend distributions paid from accumulated earnings and profits contained in other retained earnings (line 26 of Schedule L)	**18**	

Schedule L — Balance Sheets

Assets	Beginning of tax year		End of tax year	
	(a)	(b)	(c)	(d)
1 Cash		5,000		6,000
2 Trade notes and accounts receivable	2,000		5,000	
a Less allowance for bad debts		2,000		5,000
3 Inventories				
4 Federal and state government obligations				
5 Other current assets (attach schedule)				
6 Loans to shareholders				
7 Mortgage and real estate loans				
8 Other investments (attach schedule)		25,000		5,000
9 Buildings and other depreciable assets				
a Less accumulated depreciation				
10 Depletable assets				
a Less accumulated depletion				
11 Land (net of any amortization)				
12 Intangible assets (amortizable only)				
a Less accumulated amortization				
13 Other assets (attach schedule)				
14 Total assets		32,000		16,000
Liabilities and Shareholders' Equity				
15 Accounts payable		3,000		4,000
16 Mortgages, notes, bonds payable in less than 1 year				
17 Other current liabilities (attach schedule)				
18 Loans from shareholders		2,000		5,000
19 Mortgages, notes, bonds payable in 1 year or more				
20 Other liabilities (attach schedule)				
21 Capital stock		1,000		1,000
22 Paid-in or capital surplus				
23 Accumulated adjustments account				
24 Other adjustments account				
25 Shareholders' undistributed taxable income previously taxed				
26 Other retained earnings (see instructions). Check this box if the corporation has subchapter C earnings and profits at the close of the tax year ▶ ☐ (see instructions)				
27 Total retained earnings per books—Combine amounts on lines 23 through 26, columns (a) and (c) (see instructions)		26,000		6,000
28 Less cost of treasury stock	(	)	(	)
29 Total liabilities and shareholders' equity		32,000		16,000

Schedule M — Analysis of Accumulated Adjustments Account, Other Adjustments Account, and Shareholders' Undistributed Taxable Income Previously Taxed

(If Schedule L, column (c), amounts for lines 23, 24, or 25 are not the same as corresponding amounts on line 9 of Schedule M, attach a schedule explaining any differences. See instructions.)

	Accumulated adjustments account	Other adjustments account	Shareholders' undistributed taxable income previously taxed
1 Balance at beginning of year	26,000		
2 Ordinary income from page 1, line 21			
3 Other additions			
4 Total of lines 1, 2, and 3	26,000		
5 Distributions other than dividend distributions	—		
6 Loss from page 1, line 21	20,000		
7 Other reductions	—		
8 Add lines 5, 6, and 7	20,000		
9 Balance at end of tax year—Subtract line 8 from line 4	6,000		

Form 1040 Department of the Treasury—Internal Revenue Service
U.S. Individual Income Tax Return 1987

For the year Jan.–Dec. 31, 1987, or other tax year beginning , 1987, ending , 19 | OMB No. 1545-0074

Label

Use IRS label. Otherwise, please print or type.

Your first name and initial (if joint return, also give spouse's name and initial) | Last name
J. Fox ENTREPRENEUR

Your social security number
000 00 0000

Present home address (number and street or rural route). (If you have a P.O. Box, see page 6 of Instructions.)
123 EASY STREET

Spouse's social security number

City, town or post office, state, and ZIP code
NEW YORK, NY 10021

For Privacy Act and Paperwork Reduction Act Notice, see Instructions.

Presidential Election Campaign ▶ Do you want $1 to go to this fund? . . . . Yes / **No** ✓
If joint return, does your spouse want $1 to go to this fund? . . . Yes / **No**

Note: Checking "Yes" will not change your tax or reduce your refund.

Filing Status

Check only one box.

1 ✓ Single
2 Married filing joint return (even if only one had income)
3 Married filing separate return. Enter spouse's social security no. above and full name here. _____
4 Head of household (with qualifying person). (See page 7 of Instructions.) If the qualifying person is your child but not your dependent, enter child's name here. _____
5 Qualifying widow(er) with dependent child (year spouse died ▶ 19). (See page 7 of Instructions.)

Exemptions

(See Instructions on page 7.)

Caution: If you can be claimed as a dependent on another person's tax return (such as your parents' return), do not check box 6a. But be sure to check the box on line 32b on page 2.

No. of boxes checked on 6a and 6b ▶ **1**

6a ✓ Yourself 6b ☐ Spouse

c Dependents

(1) Name (first, initial, and last name)	(2) Check if under age 5	(3) If age 5 or over, dependent's social security number	(4) Relationship	(5) No. of months lived in your home in 1987

No. of children on 6c who lived with you ▶ **0**

No. of children on 6c who didn't live with you due to divorce or separation ▶ **0**

If more than 7 dependents, see Instructions on page 7.

No. of parents listed on 6c ▶ **0**

No. of other dependents listed on 6c ▶ **0**

d If your child didn't live with you but is claimed as your dependent under a pre-1985 agreement, check here . ▶ ☐

Add numbers entered in boxes above ▶ **1**

e Total number of exemptions claimed (also complete line 35) . . . . . ▶

Income

Please attach Copy B of your Forms W-2, W-2G, and W-2P here.

If you do not have a W-2, see page 6 of Instructions.

7 Wages, salaries, tips, etc. (attach Form(s) W-2) . . . . . | 7 | 0
8 Taxable interest income (also attach Schedule B if over $400) . . . | 8 | 0
9 Tax-exempt interest income (see page 10). DON'T include on line 8 | 9 |
10 Dividend income (also attach Schedule B if over $400) . . . . | 10 | 0
11 Taxable refunds of state and local income taxes, if any, from worksheet on page 11 of Instructions . | 11 | 0
12 Alimony received . . . . | 12 | 0
13 Business income or (loss) (attach Schedule C). . . . . . | 13 | 0
14 Capital gain or (loss) (attach Schedule D) . . . . . . | 14 | 30,000
15 Other gains or (losses) (attach Form 4797) . . . . . . | 15 |
16a Pensions, IRA distributions, annuities, and rollovers. Total received | 16a |
b Taxable amount (see page 11) . . . . | 16b | 0
17 Rents, royalties, partnerships, estates, trusts, etc. (attach Schedule E) 1120S attached | 17 | (20,000)
18 Farm income or (loss) (attach Schedule F) . . . . . . | 18 | 0
19 Unemployment compensation (insurance) (see page 11) . . . | 19 | 0

Please attach check or money order here.

20a Social security benefits (see page 12) | 20a |
b Taxable amount, if any, from the worksheet on page 12 . . . | 20b | 0
21 Other income (list type and amount—see page 12) . . . . | 21 | 0
22 Add the amounts shown in the far right column for lines 7, 8, and 10–21. This is your **total income** ▶ | 22 | 10,000

Adjustments to Income

(See Instructions on page 12.)

23 Reimbursed employee business expenses from Form 2106 . | 23 |
24a Your IRA deduction, from applicable worksheet on page 13 or 14 | 24a |
b Spouse's IRA deduction, from applicable worksheet on page 13 or 14 . | 24b |
25 Self-employed health insurance deduction, from worksheet on page 14 . | 25 |
26 Keogh retirement plan and self-employed SEP deduction. . . | 26 |
27 Penalty on early withdrawal of savings . . . . . . | 27 |
28 Alimony paid (recipient's last name _____ and social security no. _____) . | 28 |
29 Add lines 23 through 28. These are your **total adjustments** . . . . ▶ | 29 | 0

Adjusted Gross Income

30 Subtract line 29 from line 22. This is your **adjusted gross income.** *If this line is less than $15,432 and a child lived with you, see "Earned Income Credit" (line 56) on page 18 of the Instructions. If you want IRS to figure your tax, see page 15 of the Instructions* . . ▶ | 30 | 10,000

Tax Computation	**31**	Amount from line 30 (adjusted gross income)	**31**	10,000
	32a	Check if: ☐ **You** were 65 or over ☐ **Blind;** ☐ **Spouse** was 65 or over ☐ Blind.		
		Add the number of boxes checked and enter the total here . . . . ▶	32a	
	b	If you can be claimed as a dependent on another person's return, check here . . ▶	32b ☐	
	c	If you are married filing a separate return and your spouse itemizes deductions, or you are a dual-status alien, see page 15 and check here . . . . ▶	32c ☐	
	33a	**Itemized deductions.** See page 15 to see if you should itemize. If you don't itemize, enter zero. If you do itemize, attach Schedule A, enter the amount from Schedule A, line 26, **AND** skip line 33b .	**33a**	0
Caution: ◀ If you checked any box on line 32a, b, or c **and you don't** itemize, see page 16 for the amount to enter on line 33b.	**b**	**Standard deduction.** Read **Caution** to left. If it applies, see page 16 for the amount to enter. If **Caution** doesn't apply and your filing status from page 1 is: { Single or Head of household, enter $2,540 / Married filing jointly or Qualifying widow(er), enter $3,760 / Married filing separately, enter $1,880 }	**33b**	2,540
	34	Subtract line 33a or 33b, whichever applies, from line 31. Enter the result here	**34**	7,460
	35	Multiply $1,900 by the total number of exemptions claimed on line 6e or see chart on page 16 .	**35**	1,900
	36	**Taxable income.** Subtract line 35 from line 34. Enter the result (but not less than zero) .	**36**	5,560
		Caution: If under age 14 and you have more than $1,000 of investment income, check here ▶☐ and see page 16 to see if you have to use Form 8615 to figure your tax.		
	37	Enter tax. Check if from ☑ Tax Table, ☐ Tax Rate Schedules, ☐ Schedule D, or ☐ Form 8615	**37**	764
	38	Additional taxes (see page 16). Check if from ☐ Form 4970 or ☐ Form 4972	**38**	0
	39	Add lines 37 and 38. Enter the total . . . . ▶	**39**	764
Credits (See Instructions on page 17.)	**40**	Credit for child and dependent care expenses *(attach Form 2441)*	40	
	41	Credit for the elderly or for the permanently and totally disabled *(attach Schedule R)*	41	
	42	Add lines 40 and 41. Enter the total	**42**	0
	43	Subtract line 42 from line 39. Enter the result (but not less than zero)	**43**	764
	44	Foreign tax credit *(attach Form 1116)*	44	
	45	General business credit. Check if from ☐ Form 3800, ☐ Form 3468, ☐ Form 5884, ☐ Form 6478, ☐ Form 6765, or ☐ Form 8586 . .	45	
	46	Add lines 44 and 45. Enter the total	**46**	0
	47	Subtract line 46 from line 43. Enter the result (but not less than zero) . . . . . . ▶	**47**	764
Other Taxes (Including Advance EIC Payments)	**48**	Self-employment tax *(attach Schedule SE)*	**48**	
	49	Alternative minimum tax *(attach Form 6251)*	**49**	
	50	Tax from recapture of investment credit *(attach Form 4255)*	**50**	
	51	Social security tax on tip income not reported to employer *(attach Form 4137)*	**51**	
	52	Tax on an IRA or a qualified retirement plan *(attach Form 5329)*	**52**	
	53	Add lines 47 through 52. This is your **total tax** . . . . ▶	**53**	764
Payments Attach Forms W-2, W-2G, and W-2P to front.	**54**	Federal income tax withheld (including tax shown on Form(s) 1099)	54	
	55	1987 estimated tax payments and amount applied from 1986 return	55	
	56	Earned income credit (see page 18)	56	
	57	Amount paid with Form 4868 (extension request)	57	
	58	Excess social security tax and RRTA tax withheld (see page 19)	58	
	59	Credit for Federal tax on gasoline and special fuels *(attach Form 4136)*	59	
	60	Regulated investment company credit *(attach Form 2439)* . . .	60	
	61	Add lines 54 through 60. These are your **total payments** . . . . ▶	**61**	0
Refund or Amount You Owe	**62**	If line 61 is larger than line 53, enter amount **OVERPAID** . . . . ▶	**62**	
	63	Amount of line 62 to be **REFUNDED TO YOU** . . . . ▶	**63**	
	64	Amount of line 62 to be applied to your 1988 estimated tax . . ▶	64	
	65	If line 53 is larger than line 61, enter **AMOUNT YOU OWE.** Attach check or money order for full amount payable to "Internal Revenue Service." Write your social security number, daytime phone number, and "1987 Form 1040" on it	**65**	764
		Check ▶ ☐ if Form 2210 (2210F) is attached. See page 20. **Penalty: $**		

Please Sign Here

Under penalties of perjury, I declare that I have examined this return and accompanying schedules and statements, and to the best of my knowledge and belief, they are true, correct, and complete. Declaration of preparer (other than taxpayer) is based on all information of which preparer has any knowledge.

Your signature	Date 4/15/88	Your occupation EXECUTIVE
Spouse's signature (if joint return, BOTH must sign)	Date	Spouse's occupation

Paid Preparer's Use Only

Preparer's signature ▶	Date	Check if self-employed ☐	Preparer's social security no.
Firm's name (or yours if self-employed) and address ▶		E.I. No.	
		ZIP code	

SCHEDULE D
(Form 1040)

Department of the Treasury
Internal Revenue Service

Capital Gains and Losses
and Reconciliation of Forms 1099-B

▶ Attach to Form 1040. ▶ See Instructions for Schedule D (Form 1040).

For Paperwork Reduction Act Notice, see Form 1040 Instructions.

OMB No. 1545-0074

1987

Attachment
Sequence No. 12

Name(s) as shown on Form 1040	Your social security number
J. FOX ENTREPRENEUR	000 00 0000

1 Report here, the total sales of stocks, bonds, etc., reported for 1987 by your broker to you on Form(s) 1099-B or an equivalent substitute statement(s). If this amount differs from the total of lines 2b and 9b, column (d), attach a statement explaining the difference. See the Instructions for line 1 for examples. Do not include real estate transactions reported to you on a Form 1099-B on line 1, 2a, or 9a **1**

Part I Short-term Capital Gains and Losses—Assets Held Six Months or Less

(a) Description of property (Example. 100 shares 7% preferred of "Z" Co.)	(b) Date acquired (Mo., day, yr.)	(c) Date sold (Mo., day, yr.)	(d) Sales price (see Instructions)	(e) Cost or other basis (see Instructions)	(f) LOSS If (e) is more than (d), subtract (d) from (e)	(g) GAIN If (d) is more than (e), subtract (e) from (d)
2a Form 1099-B Transactions (Sales of Stocks, Bonds, etc.): (Do not report real estate transactions here. See the instructions for lines 2a and 9a.)						
2b Total (add column (d)) . . . . . ▶						
2c Other Transactions:						

3 Short-term gain from sale or exchange of a principal residence from Form 2119, lines 8 or 14	**3**			0
4 Short-term gain from installment sales from Form 6252, lines 23 or 31 . . .	**4**			0
5 Net short-term gain or (loss) from partnerships, S corporations, and fiduciaries .	**5**	0		0
6 Short-term capital loss carryover	**6**	0		
7 Add all of the transactions on lines 2a and 2c and lines 3 through 6 in columns (f) and (g) . . .	**7**	(0)		30,000
8 Net short-term gain or (loss), combine columns (f) and (g) of line 7			**8**	30,000

Part II Long-term Capital Gains and Losses—Assets Held More Than Six Months

9a Form 1099-B Transactions (Sales of Stocks, Bonds, etc.): (Do not report real estate transactions here. See the instructions for lines 2a and 9a.)						
9b Total (add column (d)) . . . . ▶						
9c Other Transactions:						

10 Long-term gain from sale or exchange of a principal residence from Form 2119, lines 8, 10, or 14	**10**			
11 Long-term gain from installment sales from Form 6252, lines 23 or 31	**11**			
12 Net long-term gain or (loss) from partnerships, S corporations, and fiduciaries .	**12**			
13 Capital gain distributions	**13**			
14 Enter gain from Form 4797, line 7 or 9	**14**			
15 Long-term capital loss carryover	**15**			
16 Add all of the transactions on lines 9a and 9c and lines 10 through 15 in columns (f) and (g) . .	**16**	( )		
17 Net long-term gain or (loss), combine columns (f) and (g) of line 16			**17**	

Schedule D (Form 1040) 1987

Name(s) as shown on Form 1040 (Do not enter name and social security number if shown on other side.)	Your social security number

Part III   Summary of Parts I and II

18	Combine lines 8 and 17, and enter the net gain or (loss) here. If result is a gain, also enter the gain on Form 1040, line 14	18	30,000
	Note: If lines 17 and 18 are net gains and your taxable income is taxed over the 28% tax rate, see Part IV below. You may be able to reduce your tax if you qualify for the alternative tax computation.		
19	If line 18 is a loss, enter here and as a loss on Form 1040, line 14, the **smaller** of:		
a	The amount on line 18; **or b** $3,000 ($1,500 if married filing a separate return)	19	—

Part IV   Alternative Tax Computation
First complete Form 1040 through line 36.

Use Part IV if both lines 17 and 18 show net gains, **AND**:

You checked filing status box:	AND	Form 1040, line 36 is over:	You checked filing status box:	AND	Form 1040, line 36 is over:
1		$27,000	3		$22,500
2 or 5		45,000	4		38,000

20	Enter amount from Form 1040, line 36	20	
21	Enter the smaller of the gain on line 17 or the gain on line 18	21	
22	Subtract line 21 from 20 and enter the result	22	
23	Enter: **a** $16,800 if you checked filing status box 1; **b** $28,000 if you checked filing status box 2 or 5; **c** $14,000 if you checked filing status box 3; **or d** $23,000 if you checked filing status box 4	23	
24	Enter the **greater** of line 22 or line 23	24	
25	Subtract line 24 from line 20	25	
26	Figure the amount of tax on line 24. Use the Tax Table or Tax Rate Schedules, whichever applies . . .	26	
27	Multiply line 25 by 28% (.28) and enter the result	27	
28	Add lines 26 and 27. Enter the result here and on Form 1040, line 37 and check the box for Schedule D	28	

Part V   Computation of Capital Loss Carryovers From 1987 to 1988
(Complete this part if the loss on line 18 is more than the loss on line 19.)

29	Enter the loss shown on line 8; if none, enter zero and skip lines 30 through 33.	29	
30	Enter gain shown on line 17. If that line is blank or shows a loss, enter zero	30	
31	Subtract line 30 from line 29	31	
32	Enter the smaller of line 19 or 31	32	
33	Subtract line 32 from line 31. This is your **short-term capital loss carryover from 1987 to 1988**	33	
34	Enter loss from line 17; if none, enter zero and skip lines 35 through 38	34	
35	Enter gain shown on line 8. If that line is blank or shows a loss, enter zero	35	
36	Subtract line 35 from line 34	36	
37	Subtract line 32 from line 19. (**Note:** If you skipped lines 30 through 33, enter the amount from line 19.)	37	
38	Subtract line 37 from line 36. This is your **long-term capital loss carryover from 1987 to 1988** . .	38	

Part VI   Complete This Part Only If You Elect Out of the Installment Method and Report a Note or Other Obligation at Less Than Full Face Value

39	Check here if you elect out of the installment method . . . . ▶ ☐	
40	Enter the face amount of the note or other obligation . . . . ▶	
41	Enter the percentage of valuation of the note or other obligation . . . . ▶	

Part VII   Reconciliation of Forms 1099-B for Bartering Transactions
Complete this part if you received one or more Form(s) 1099-B or an equivalent substitute statement(s) reporting bartering income.

			Amount of bartering income from Form 1099-B or equivalent statement reported on form or schedule
42	Form 1040, line 21	42	
43	Schedule C (Form 1040)	43	
44	Schedule D (Form 1040)	44	
45	Schedule E (Form 1040)	45	
46	Schedule F (Form 1040)	46	
47	Other (identify) (if not taxable, indicate reason—attach additional sheets if necessary) ▶	47	
48	Total (add lines 42 through 47)	48	
	Note: The amount on line 48 should be the same as the total bartering income on all Forms 1099-B or equivalent statements received.		

SCHEDULE E
(Form 1040)

Department of the Treasury
Internal Revenue Service

Supplemental Income Schedule

(From rents, royalties, partnerships, estates, trusts, REMICs, etc.)
► Attach to Form 1040, Form 1041, or Form 1041S.
► See Instructions for Schedule E (Form 1040).

OMB No 1545-0074

1987

Attachment
Sequence No 13

Name(s) as shown on Form 1040	Your social security number
J. FOX ENTREPRENEUR	000 : 00 : 0000

Part I Rental and Royalty Income or (Loss) Caution: Your rental loss may be limited. See Instructions.

1 In the space provided below, show the kind and location of each rental property.	2 For each property listed, did you or a member of your family use for personal purposes any of the properties for more than the greater of 14 days or 10% of the total days rented at fair rental value during the tax year?		3 For each rental real estate property listed, did you actively participate in the operation of the activity during the tax year? (See Instructions.)		
		Yes	No		Yes	No

Property A .... ►
Property B .... ►
Property C .... ►

Rental and Royalty Income		Properties			Totals (Add columns A, B, and C)
		A	B	C	
4 Rents received					4
5 Royalties received					5

Rental and Royalty Expenses

		A	B	C	Totals
6 Advertising.	6				
7 Auto and travel	7				
8 Cleaning and maintenance . . .	8				
9 Commissions	9				
10 Insurance	10				
11 Legal and other professional fees	11				
12 Mortgage interest paid to financial institutions (see Instructions). . .	12				12
13 Other interest.	13				
14 Repairs	14				
15 Supplies	15				
16 Taxes (Do **not** include windfall profit tax here. See Part V, line 40.). .	16				
17 Utilities	17				
18 Wages and salaries	18				
19 Other (list) ►					
....					
....					
....					
20 Total expenses other than depreciation and depletion. Add lines 6 through 19.	20				20
21 Depreciation expense (see Instructions), or depletion (see Publication 535). .	21				21
22 Total. Add lines 20 and 21 . . .	22				
23 Income or (loss) from rental or royalty properties. Subtract line 22 from line 4 (rents) or 5 (royalties) .	23				
24 Deductible rental loss. **Caution:** Your rental loss on line 23 may be limited. See Instructions to determine if you must file **Form 8582**, Passive Activity Loss Limitations	24				

25 **Profits.** Add rental and royalty profits from line 23, and enter the total profits here	25	
26 **Losses.** Add royalty losses from line 23 and rental losses from line 24, and enter the total (losses) here .	26 (	)
27 Combine amounts on lines 25 and 26, and enter the net profit or (loss) here	27	
28 Net farm rental profit or (loss) from Form 4835. (Also complete Part VI, line 43.)	28	
29 Total rental or royalty income or (loss). Combine amounts on lines 27 and 28, and enter the total here. If Parts II, III, IV, and V on page 2 do not apply to you, enter the amount from line 29 on Form 1040, line 17. Otherwise, include the amount from line 29 in line 42 on page 2 of Schedule E . . . •	29	0

For Paperwork Reduction Act Notice, see Form 1040 Instructions.

Schedule E (Form 1040) 1987

Name(s) as shown on Form 1040. (Do not enter name and social security number if shown on other side.)   Your social security number

Part II   Income or (Loss) from Partnerships and S Corporations

If you report a loss below and have amounts invested in that activity for which you are **not at risk**, you MUST check "Yes" in column (e) and attach Form 6198. Otherwise, you must check "No." See Instructions.

	(a) Name	(b) Enter P for partnership; S for S Corporation	(c) Check if foreign partnership	(d) Employer identification number	(e) Not at-Risk? Yes	No
A	NEW CONSULTING, INC.	S		00-0000000		✓
B						
C						
D						
E						

	Passive Activities		Nonpassive Activities		
	(f) Passive loss allowed from Form 8582	(g) Passive income from Schedule K-1	(h) Nonpassive loss from Schedule K-1	(i) Section 179 deduction	(j) Nonpassive income from Schedule K-1
A					
B					
C					
D					
E					
30a Totals					
b Totals			(20,000)		

31 Add amounts in columns (g) and (j), line 30a. Enter total income here . . . . **31**   O

32 Add amounts in columns (f), (h), and (i), line 30b. Enter total here **32** (20,000)

33 Total partnership and S corporation income or (loss). Combine amounts on lines 31 and 32. Enter the total here and include in line 42 below **33** (20,000)

Part III   Income or (Loss) from Estates and Trusts

	(a) Name	(b) Employer identification number
A		
B		
C		

	Passive Activities		Nonpassive Activities	
	(c) Passive deduction or loss allowed from Form 8582	(d) Passive income from Schedule K-1	(e) Deduction or loss from Schedule K-1	(f) Other income from Schedule K-1
A				
B				
C				
34a Totals				
b Totals				

35 Add amounts in columns (d) and (f), line 34a. Enter total income here **35**

36 Add amounts in columns (c) and (e), line 34b. Enter total (loss) here . . . . **36** ( )

37 Total estate and trust income or (loss). Combine amounts on lines 35 and 36. Enter the total here and include in line 42 below **37**

Part IV   Income or (Loss) from Real Estate Mortgage Investment Conduits (REMICs)—Residual Holder

(a) Name	(b) Employer identification number	(c) Excess inclusion from Schedules Q, line 2c (see Instructions)	(d) Taxable income (net loss) from Schedules Q, line 1b	(e) Income from Schedules Q, line 3b

38 Combine columns (d) and (e) only. Enter the total here and include in line 42 below **38**

Part V   Windfall Profit Tax Summary

39 Windfall profit tax credit or refund received in 1987 (see Instructions) **39**

40 Windfall profit tax withheld in 1987 (see Instructions) . . . . **40** ( )

41 Combine amounts on lines 39 and 40. Enter the total here and include in line 42 below **41**

Part VI   Summary

42 TOTAL income or (loss). Combine lines 29, 33, 37, 38, and 41. Enter total here and on Form 1040, line 17 . . . . ▶ **42** (20,000)

43 Farmers and fishermen: Enter your share of GROSS FARMING AND FISHING INCOME applicable to Parts I, II, and III (see Instructions) . . . **43**

Form 1120

U.S. Corporation Income Tax Return

OMB No. 1545-0123

Department of the Treasury
Internal Revenue Service

For calendar 1987 or tax year beginning _____, 1987, ending _____, 19 ____
▶ For Paperwork Reduction Act Notice, see page 1 of the instructions.

1987

Check if a—		
A Consolidated return ☐		
B Personal Holding Co. ☐		
C Business Code No. (See the list in the instructions.) **8999**		

Use IRS label. Otherwise please print or type.

Name REARGUARD DESIGNS, INC.

Number and street 999 EASY STREET

City or town, state, and ZIP code NEW YORK, NY 10021

D Employer identification number 00-0000000

E Date incorporated 1/1/87

F Total assets (See Specific Instructions.)

	Dollars	Cents
$		

G Check applicable boxes: (1) ☑ Initial return (2) ☐ Final return (3) ☐ Change in address

Income

		Dollars	Cents
1a	Gross receipts or sales _____ **b** Less returns and allowances _____ Balance ▶	1c	
2	Cost of goods sold and/or operations (Schedule A)	2	
3	Gross profit (line 1c less line 2)	3	
4	Dividends (Schedule C)	4	
5	Interest	5	
6	Gross rents	6	
7	Gross royalties	7	
8	Capital gain net income (attach separate Schedule D)	8	
9	Net gain or (loss) from Form 4797, line 18, Part II (attach Form 4797)	9	
10	Other income (see instructions—attach schedule)	10	
11	TOTAL income—Add lines 3 through 10 and enter here ▶	11	(20,000)

Deductions (See Instructions for limitations on deductions)

			Dollars	Cents
12	Compensation of officers (Schedule E)		12	
13a	Salaries and wages _____ **b** Less jobs credit _____ Balance ▶		13c	
14	Repairs		14	
15	Bad debts (see instructions)		15	
16	Rents		16	
17	Taxes		17	
18	Interest		18	
19	Contributions (see instructions for 10% limitation)		19	
20	Depreciation (attach Form 4562)	20		
21	Less depreciation claimed in Schedule A and elsewhere on return	21a	21b	
22	Depletion		22	
23	Advertising		23	
24	Pension, profit-sharing, etc., plans		24	
25	Employee benefit programs		25	
26	Other deductions (attach schedule)		26	
27	TOTAL deductions—Add lines 12 through 26 and enter here ▶		27	
28	Taxable income before net operating loss deduction and special deductions (line 11 less line 27)		28	(20,000)
29	Less: **a** Net operating loss deduction (see instructions)	29a		
	b Special deductions (Schedule C)	29b	29c	0
30	Taxable income (line 28 less line 29c)		30	(20,000)
31	TOTAL TAX (Schedule J)		31	0

Tax and Payments

				Dollars	Cents
32	Payments: **a** 1986 overpayment credited to 1987				
	b 1987 estimated tax payments				
	c Less 1987 refund applied for on Form 4466 ( )				
	d Tax deposited with Form 7004				
	e Credit from regulated investment companies (attach Form 2439)				
	f Credit for Federal tax on gasoline and special fuels (attach Form 4136)		32		
33	Enter any PENALTY for underpayment of estimated tax—check ▶ ☐ if Form 2220 is attached		33		
34	TAX DUE—If the total of lines 31 and 33 is larger than line 32, enter AMOUNT OWED		34	0	
35	OVERPAYMENT—If line 32 is larger than the total of lines 31 and 33, enter AMOUNT OVERPAID		35		
36	Enter amount of line 35 you want: Credited to 1988 estimated tax ▶ _____ Refunded ▶		36		

Please Sign Here

Under penalties of perjury, I declare that I have examined this return, including accompanying schedules and statements, and to the best of my knowledge and belief, it is true, correct, and complete. Declaration of preparer (other than taxpayer) is based on all information of which preparer has any knowledge.

▶ _____ Signature of officer   Date 3/15/88   Title PRESIDENT

Paid Preparer's Use Only

Preparer's signature ▶		Date	Check if self-employed ☐	Preparer's social security number
Firm's name (or yours, if self-employed) and address ▶			E.I. No. ▶	
			ZIP code ▶	

Schedule A　Cost of Goods Sold and/or Operations (See instructions for line 2, page 1.)

1 Inventory at beginning of year	1	
2 Purchases	2	
3 Cost of labor	3	
4a Additional section 263A costs (see instructions)	4a	
b Other costs (attach schedule)	4b	
5 Total—Add lines 1 through 4b	5	
6 Inventory at end of year	6	
7 Cost of goods sold and/or operations—Line 5 less line 6. Enter here and on line 2, page 1	7	N/A

8a Check all methods used for valuing closing inventory:

  (i) ☐ Cost　(ii) ☐ Lower of cost or market as described in Regulations section 1.471-4 (see instructions)

  (iii) ☐ Writedown of "subnormal" goods as described in Regulations section 1.471-2(c) (see instructions)

  (iv) ☐ Other (Specify method used and attach explanation.) ▶ --------------------------------

  b Check if the LIFO inventory method was adopted this tax year for any goods (if checked, attach Form 970) ☐

  c If the LIFO inventory method was used for this tax year, enter percentage (or amounts) of closing inventory computed under LIFO | 8c |

  d Do the rules of section 263A (with respect to property produced or acquired for resale) apply to the corporation? ☐ Yes ☐ No

  e Was there any change (other than for section 263A purposes) in determining quantities, cost, or valuations between opening and closing inventory? If "Yes," attach explanation ☐ Yes ☐ No

Schedule C　Dividends and Special Deductions (See Schedule C instructions.)

	(a) Dividends received	(b) %	(c) Special deductions: multiply (a) × (b)
1 Domestic corporations subject to section 243(a) deduction (other than debt-financed stock)		see instructions	
2 Debt-financed stock of domestic and foreign corporations (section 246A)		see instructions	
3 Certain preferred stock of public utilities		see instructions	
4 Foreign corporations and certain FSCs subject to section 245 deduction		see instructions	
5 Wholly owned foreign subsidiaries and FSCs subject to 100% deduction (sections 245(b) and (c))		100	
6 Total—Add lines 1 through 5. See instructions for limitation			
7 Affiliated groups subject to the 100% deduction (section 243(a)(3))		100	
8 Other dividends from foreign corporations not included in lines 4 and 5			
9 Income from controlled foreign corporations under subpart F (attach Forms 5471)			
10 Foreign dividend gross-up (section 78)			
11 IC-DISC or former DISC dividends not included in lines 1 and/or 2 (section 246(d))			
12 Other dividends			
13 Deduction for dividends paid on certain preferred stock of public utilities (see instructions)			
14 Total dividends—Add lines 1 through 12. Enter here and on line 4, page 1 ▶			
15 Total deductions—Add lines 6, 7, and 13. Enter here and on line 29b, page 1 ▶			

Schedule E　Compensation of Officers (See instructions for line 12, page 1.)

Complete Schedule E only if total receipts (line 1a, plus lines 4 through 10, of page 1, Form 1120) are $150,000 or more.

(a) Name of officer	(b) Social security number	(c) Percent of time devoted to business	Percent of corporation stock owned (d) Common	(e) Preferred	(f) Amount of compensation
		%	%	%	
		%	%	%	
		%	%	%	
		%	%	%	
		%	%	%	
		%	%	%	
		%	%	%	

Total compensation of officers—Enter here and on line 12, page 1.

Schedule J — Tax Computation (See instructions.)

1 Check if you are a member of a controlled group (see sections 1561 and 1563) . . . . ▶ ☐

2 If line 1 is checked, see instructions. If your tax year includes June 30, 1987, complete both a and b below. Otherwise, complete only b.

a (i) $ _____ (ii) $ _____ (iii) $ _____ (iv) $ _____

b (i) $ _____ (ii) $ _____

3 Income tax (see instructions to figure the tax; enter this tax or alternative tax from Schedule D, whichever is less). Check if from Schedule D ▶ ☐	**3**	
4a Foreign tax credit (attach Form 1118)	**4a**	
b Possessions tax credit (attach Form 5735)	**b**	
c Orphan drug credit (attach Form 6765)	**c**	
d Credit for fuel produced from a nonconventional source (see instructions)	**d**	
e General business credit. Enter here and check which forms are attached ☐ Form 3800 ☐ Form 3468 ☐ Form 5884 ☐ Form 6478 ☐ Form 6765 ☐ Form 8586	**e**	
5 Total—Add lines 4a through 4e	**5**	
6 Line 3 less line 5	**6**	
7 Personal holding company tax (attach Schedule PH (Form 1120))	**7**	
8 Tax from recomputing prior-year investment credit (attach Form 4255)	**8**	
9a Alternative minimum tax (see instructions—attach Form 4626)	**9a**	
b Environmental tax (see instructions—attach Form 4626)	**9b**	
10 Total—Add lines 6 through 9b. Enter here and on line 31, page 1	**10**	O

Additional Information (See instruction F.)

	Yes	No
H Did the corporation claim a deduction for expenses connected with:		
(1) An entertainment facility (boat, resort, ranch, etc.)? . . .		✓
(2) Living accommodations (except employees on business)? . .		✓
(3) Employees attending conventions or meetings outside the North American area? (See section 274(h).)		✓
(4) Employees' families at conventions or meetings?		✓
If "Yes," were any of these conventions or meetings outside the North American area? (See section 274(h).) . . .		
(5) Employee or family vacations not reported on Form W-2? . .		✓

I (1) Did the corporation at the end of the tax year own, directly or indirectly, 50% or more of the voting stock of a domestic corporation? (For rules of attribution, see section 267(c).) . .

If "Yes," attach a schedule showing: (a) name, address, and identifying number; (b) percentage owned; (c) taxable income or (loss) before NOL and special deductions of such corporation for the tax year ending with or within your tax year; (d) highest amount owed by the corporation to such corporation during the year; and (e) highest amount owed to the corporation by such corporation during the year.

(2) Did any individual, partnership, corporation, estate, or trust at the end of the tax year own, directly or indirectly, 50% or more of the corporation's voting stock? (For rules of attribution, see section 267(c).) If "Yes," complete (a) through (d) . . . ✓

(a) Attach a schedule showing name, address and identifying number. Enter percentage owned ▶ GARDOU J. ENTREPRENEUR-100

(b) Was the owner of such voting stock a person other than a U.S. person? (See instructions.) **Note:** *If "Yes," the corporation may have to file Form 5472.* ✓

If "Yes," enter owner's country ▶ _____

(c) Enter highest amount owed by the corporation to such owner during the year ▶ _____

(d) Enter highest amount owed to the corporation by such owner during the year ▶ _____

Note: *For purposes of I(1) and I(2), "highest amount owed" includes loans and accounts receivable/payable.*

	Yes	No
J Refer to the list in the instructions and state the principal: Business activity ▶ _____ Product or service ▶ GRAPHIC DESIGN _____		
K Was the corporation a U.S. shareholder of any controlled foreign corporation? (See sections 951 and 957.)		✓
If "Yes," attach Form 5471 for each such corporation.		
L At any time during the tax year, did the corporation have an interest in or a signature or other authority over a financial account in a foreign country (such as a bank account, securities account, or other financial account)?		✓
(See instruction F and filing requirements for form TD F 90-22.1.)		
If "Yes," enter name of foreign country ▶ _____		
M Was the corporation the grantor of, or transferor to, a foreign trust which existed during the current tax year, whether or not the corporation has any beneficial interest in it?		✓
If "Yes," the corporation may have to file Forms 3520, 3520-A, or 926.		
N During this tax year, did the corporation pay dividends (other than stock dividends and distributions in exchange for stock) in excess of the corporation's current and accumulated earnings and profits? (See sections 301 and 316.)		✓
If "Yes," file Form 5452. If this is a consolidated return, answer here for parent corporation and on Form 851, Affiliations Schedule, for each subsidiary.		
O During this tax year did the corporation maintain any part of its accounting/tax records on a computerized system? . . .		✓
P Check method of accounting: (1) ☑ Cash (2) ☐ Accrual (3) ☐ Other (specify) ▶ _____		
Q Check this box if the corporation issued publicly offered debt instruments with original issue discount . . . . ☐ If so, the corporation may have to file Form 8281.		
R Enter the amount of tax-exempt interest received or accrued during the tax year ▶ _____		
S If you are a member of a controlled group, enter the amount of taxable income for the entire group ▶ _____		

Schedule L	Balance Sheets	Beginning of tax year		End of tax year	
	Assets	(a)	(b)	(c)	(d)
1	Cash		5,000		6,000
2	Trade notes and accounts receivable	2,000		5,000	
a	Less allowance for bad debts		2,000		5,000
3	Inventories				
4	Federal and state government obligations				
5	Other current assets (attach schedule)				
6	Loans to stockholders				
7	Mortgage and real estate loans				
8	Other investments (attach schedule)		25,000		5,000
9	Buildings and other depreciable assets				
a	Less accumulated depreciation				
10	Depletable assets				
a	Less accumulated depletion				
11	Land (net of any amortization)				
12	Intangible assets (amortizable only)				
a	Less accumulated amortization				
13	Other assets (attach schedule)				
14	Total assets		32,000		16,000
	Liabilities and Stockholders' Equity				
15	Accounts payable		3,000		4,000
16	Mortgages, notes, bonds payable in less than 1 year				
17	Other current liabilities (attach schedule)				
18	Loans from stockholders		2,000		5,000
19	Mortgages, notes, bonds payable in 1 year or more				
20	Other liabilities (attach schedule)				
21	Capital stock: a preferred stock				
	b common stock	1,000	1,000	1,000	1,000
22	Paid-in or capital surplus				
23	Retained earnings—Appropriated (attach schedule)		26,000		6,000
24	Retained earnings—Unappropriated				
25	Less cost of treasury stock		( )		( )
26	Total liabilities and stockholders' equity		32,000		16,000

Schedule M-1 **Reconciliation of Income per Books With Income per Return** You are not required to complete this schedule if the total assets on line 14, column (d), of Schedule L are less than $25,000.

1	Net income per books	(20,000)	7	Income recorded on books this year not included in this return (itemize)	
2	Federal income tax			a Tax-exempt interest $	
3	Excess of capital losses over capital gains				
4	Income subject to tax not recorded on books this year (itemize)		8	Deductions in this tax return not charged against book income this year (itemize)	
5	Expenses recorded on books this year not deducted in this return (itemize)			a Depreciation $	
a	Depreciation $			b Contributions carryover $	
b	Contributions carryover $		9	Total of lines 7 and 8	0
6	Total of lines 1 through 5	(20,000)	10	Income (line 28, page 1)—line 6 less line 9	(20,000)

Schedule M-2 **Analysis of Unappropriated Retained Earnings per Books (line 24, Schedule L)** You are not required to complete this schedule if the total assets on line 14, column (d), of Schedule L are less than $25,000.

1	Balance at beginning of year		5	Distributions: a Cash	
2	Net income per books			b Stock	
3	Other increases (itemize)			c Property	
			6	Other decreases (itemize)	
			7	Total of lines 5 and 6	
4	Total of lines 1, 2, and 3		8	Balance at end of year (line 4 less line 7)	

Form 1040 — Department of the Treasury—Internal Revenue Service
U.S. Individual Income Tax Return 1987

For the year Jan.–Dec. 31, 1987, or other tax year beginning _____ , 1987, ending _____ , 19 ___   OMB No 1545-0074

Label

Use IRS label.
Otherwise,
please print or
type.

Your first name and initial (if joint return, also give spouse's name and initial)   Last name
REARDON   J.   ENTREPRENEUR

Present home address (number and street or rural route). (If you have a P.O. Box, see page 6 of Instructions.)
999 EASY STREET

City, town or post office, state, and ZIP code
NEW YORK, NY 10021

Your social security number   000 00 0000
Spouse's social security number

For Privacy Act and Paperwork Reduction Act Notice, see Instructions.

Presidential Election Campaign ▶
Do you want $1 to go to this fund? — Yes [ ] No [✓]
If joint return, does your spouse want $1 to go to this fund? — Yes [ ] No [ ]

Note: Checking "Yes" will not change your tax or reduce your refund

Filing Status

Check only one box.

1. [✓] Single
2. [ ] Married filing joint return (even if only one had income)
3. [ ] Married filing separate return. Enter spouse's social security no. above and full name here. _____
4. [ ] Head of household (with qualifying person). (See page 7 of Instructions.) If the qualifying person is your child but not your dependent, enter child's name here. _____
5. [ ] Qualifying widow(er) with dependent child (year spouse died ▶ 19 ___). (See page 7 of Instructions.)

Exemptions

(See Instructions on page 7.)

Caution: If you can be claimed as a dependent on another person's tax return (such as your parents' return), do not check box 6a. But be sure to check the box on line 32b on page 2.

| | | | | | No. of boxes checked on 6a and 6b ▶ | 1 |

6a [✓] Yourself   6b [ ] Spouse

c Dependents

(1) Name (first, initial, and last name)	(2) Check if under age 5	(3) If age 5 or over, dependent's social security number	(4) Relationship	(5) No. of months lived in your home in 1987

If more than 7 dependents, see Instructions on page 7.

No. of children on 6c who lived with you ▶ 0
No. of children on 6c who didn't live with you due to divorce or separation ▶ 0
No. of parents listed on 6c ▶ 0
No. of other dependents listed on 6c ▶ 0

d If your child didn't live with you but is claimed as your dependent under a pre-1985 agreement, check here . ▶ [ ]

e Total number of exemptions claimed (also complete line 35) . . . .

Add numbers entered in boxes above ▶ 1

Income

Please attach Copy B of your Forms W-2, W-2G, and W-2P here.

If you do not have a W-2, see page 6 of Instructions.

7	Wages, salaries, tips, etc. (attach Form(s) W-2)	7	
8	Taxable interest income (also attach Schedule B if over $400)	8	
9	Tax-exempt interest income (see page 10). DON'T include on line 8 9 ____		
10	Dividend income (also attach Schedule B if over $400)	10	
11	Taxable refunds of state and local income taxes, if any, from worksheet on page 11 of Instructions.	11	
12	Alimony received	12	
13	Business income or (loss) (attach Schedule C).	13	
14	Capital gain or (loss) (attach Schedule D) . .	14	30,000
15	Other gains or (losses) (attach Form 4797)	15	
16a	Pensions, IRA distributions, annuities, and rollovers. Total received 16a ____		
b	Taxable amount (see page 11)	16b	
17	Rents, royalties, partnerships, estates, trusts, etc. (attach Schedule E)	17	
18	Farm income or (loss) (attach Schedule F)	18	
19	Unemployment compensation (insurance) (see page 11)	19	
20a	Social security benefits (see page 12) . . . 20a ____		
b	Taxable amount, if any, from the worksheet on page 12	20b	
21	Other income (list type and amount—see page 12)	21	
22	Add the amounts shown in the far right column for lines 7, 8, and 10–21. This is your **total income** ▶	22	30,000

Please attach check or money order here.

Adjustments to Income

(See Instructions on page 12.)

23	Reimbursed employee business expenses from Form 2106 . .	23	
24a	Your IRA deduction, from applicable worksheet on page 13 or 14	24a	
b	Spouse's IRA deduction, from applicable worksheet on page 13 or 14	24b	
25	Self-employed health insurance deduction, from worksheet on page 14 .	25	
26	Keogh retirement plan and self-employed SEP deduction. . .	26	
27	Penalty on early withdrawal of savings	27	
28	Alimony paid (recipient's last name _____ and social security no. _____) .	28	
29	Add lines 23 through 28. These are your **total adjustments** . . . . . . ▶	29	0

Adjusted Gross Income

30	Subtract line 29 from line 22. This is your **adjusted gross income**. If this line is less than $15,432 and a child lived with you, see "Earned Income Credit" (line 56) on page 18 of the Instructions. If you want IRS to figure your tax, see page 15 of the Instructions . . . ▶	30	30,000

67

Tax Compu- tation	31	Amount from line 30 (adjusted gross income)	31	30,000
	32a	Check if: ☐ **You** were 65 or over ☐ Blind; ☐ **Spouse** was 65 or over ☐ Blind.		
		Add the number of boxes checked and enter the total here . . . . ▶	32a	
	b	If you can be claimed as a dependent on another person's return, check here . . ▶	32b ☐	
	c	If you are married filing a separate return and your spouse itemizes deductions, or you are a dual-status alien, see page 15 and check here . . . . ▶	32c ☐	
	33a	**Itemized deductions.** See page 15 to see if you should itemize. If you don't itemize, enter zero. If you do itemize, attach Schedule A, enter the amount from Schedule A, line 26, **AND** skip line 33b .	33a	O
Caution: ◀— If you checked any box on line 32a, b, or c **and** you don't itemize, see page 16 for the amount to enter on line 33b.	b	**Standard deduction.** Read Caution to left. If it applies, see page 16 for the amount to enter. If **Caution** doesn't apply and your filing status from page 1 is: { Single or Head of household, enter $2,540 ⎫ Married filing jointly or Qualifying widow(er), enter $3,760 ⎬ . . . . . Married filing separately, enter $1,880 ⎭	33b	2,540
	34	Subtract line 33a or 33b, whichever applies, from line 31. Enter the result here	34	27,460
	35	Multiply $1,900 by the total number of exemptions claimed on line 6e or see chart on page 16 . .	35	1,900
	36	**Taxable income.** Subtract line 35 from line 34. Enter the result (but not less than zero) . .	36	25,560
		Caution: If under age 14 and you have more than $1,000 of investment income, check here ▶☐ and see page 16 to see if you have to use Form 8615 to figure your tax.		
	37	Enter tax. Check if from ☑Tax Table, ☐ Tax Rate Schedules, ☐ Schedule D, or ☐ Form 8615	37	4,905
	38	Additional taxes (see page 16). Check if from ☐ Form 4970 or ☐ Form 4972	38	O
	39	Add lines 37 and 38. Enter the total . . . . ▶	39	4,905
Credits (See Instructions on page 17.)	40	Credit for child and dependent care expenses (attach Form 2441)	40		
	41	Credit for the elderly or for the permanently and totally disabled (attach Schedule R)	41		
	42	Add lines 40 and 41. Enter the total	42	O
	43	Subtract line 42 from line 39. Enter the result (but not less than zero)	43	4,905
	44	Foreign tax credit (attach Form 1116)	44		
	45	General business credit. Check if from ☐ Form 3800, ☐ Form 3468, ☐ Form 5884, ☐ Form 6478, ☐ Form 6765, or ☐ Form 8586	45		
	46	Add lines 44 and 45. Enter the total	46	O
	47	Subtract line 46 from line 43. Enter the result (but not less than zero) . . . ▶	47	4,905
Other Taxes (Including Advance EIC Payments)	48	Self-employment tax (attach Schedule SE)	48	
	49	Alternative minimum tax (attach Form 6251)	49	
	50	Tax from recapture of investment credit (attach Form 4255)	50	
	51	Social security tax on tip income not reported to employer (attach Form 4137) . .	51	
	52	Tax on an IRA or a qualified retirement plan (attach Form 5329)	52	
	53	Add lines 47 through 52. This is your **total tax** . . . . ▶	53	4,905
Payments Attach Forms W-2, W-2G, and W-2P to front.	54	Federal income tax withheld (including tax shown on Form(s) 1099)	54		
	55	1987 estimated tax payments and amount applied from 1986 return	55	4,000	
	56	Earned income credit (see page 18)	56		
	57	Amount paid with Form 4868 (extension request) .	57		
	58	Excess social security tax and RRTA tax withheld (see page 19)	58		
	59	Credit for Federal tax on gasoline and special fuels (attach Form 4136)	59		
	60	Regulated investment company credit (attach Form 2439)	60		
	61	Add lines 54 through 60. These are your **total payments** . . . . ▶	61	4,000
Refund or Amount You Owe	62	If line 61 is larger than line 53, enter amount **OVERPAID** . . . . ▶	62	
	63	Amount of line 62 to be **REFUNDED TO YOU** . . . . ▶	63	
	64	Amount of line 62 to be applied to your 1988 estimated tax . . ▶	64	
	65	If line 53 is larger than line 61, enter **AMOUNT YOU OWE.** Attach check or money order for full amount payable to "Internal Revenue Service." Write your social security number, daytime phone number, and "1987 Form 1040" on it . . . . ▶ Check ▶ ☐ if Form 2210 (2210F) is attached. See page 20. **Penalty: $**	65	905

Please Sign Here

Under penalties of perjury, I declare that I have examined this return and accompanying schedules and statements, and to the best of my knowledge and belief, they are true, correct, and complete. Declaration of preparer (other than taxpayer) is based on all information of which preparer has any knowledge.

Your signature	Date 4/15/88	Your occupation EXECUTIVE
Spouse's signature (if joint return, BOTH must sign)	Date	Spouse's occupation

Paid Preparer's Use Only

Preparer's signature	Date	Check if self-employed ☐	Preparer's social security no.
Firm's name (or yours if self-employed) and address ▶		E.I. No.	
		ZIP code	

GLBF FORM 2853 - CALL (616) 243-8267

SCHEDULE D
(Form 1040)

Capital Gains and Losses and Reconciliation of Forms 1099-B

OMB No. 1545-0074

19 87

► Attach to Form 1040.   ► See Instructions for Schedule D (Form 1040).

For Paperwork Reduction Act Notice, see Form 1040 Instructions.

Department of the Treasury
Internal Revenue Service

Attachment
Sequence No. **12**

Name(s) as shown on Form 1040

REARDON   J. ENTREPRENEUR

Your social security number

000 : 00 : 0000

1 Report here, the total sales of stocks, bonds, etc., reported for 1987 by your broker to you on Form(s) 1099-B or an equivalent substitute statement(s). If this amount differs from the total of lines 2b and 9b, column (d), attach a statement explaining the difference. See the Instructions for line 1 for examples. Do not include real estate transactions reported to you on a Form 1099-B on line 1, 2a, or 9a. **1**

Part I   Short-term Capital Gains and Losses—Assets Held Six Months or Less

(a) Description of property (Example, 100 shares 7% preferred of "Z" Co.)	(b) Date acquired (Mo., day, yr.)	(c) Date sold (Mo., day, yr.)	(d) Sales price (see Instructions)	(e) Cost or other basis (see Instructions)	(f) LOSS If (e) is more than (d), subtract (d) from (e)	(g) GAIN If (d) is more than (e), subtract (e) from (d)
2a Form 1099-B Transactions (Sales of Stocks, Bonds, etc.): (Do not report real estate transactions here. See the instructions for lines 2a and 9a.)						

2b **Total** (add column (d)) . . . . . ►

2c **Other Transactions:**

3 Short-term gain from sale or exchange of a principal residence from Form 2119, lines 8 or 14	**3**		O
4 Short-term gain from installment sales from Form 6252, lines 23 or 31	**4**		O
5 Net short-term gain or (loss) from partnerships, S corporations, and fiduciaries .	**5**	O	O
6 Short-term capital loss carryover	**6**	O	
7 Add all of the transactions on lines 2a and 2c and lines 3 through 6 in columns (f) and (g) . . .	**7** (O)		30,000
8 Net short-term gain or (loss), combine columns (f) and (g) of line 7	**8**		30,000

Part II   Long-term Capital Gains and Losses—Assets Held More Than Six Months

9a Form 1099-B Transactions (Sales of Stocks, Bonds, etc.): (Do not report real estate transactions here. See the instructions for lines 2a and 9a.)

9b **Total** (add column (d)) . . . . ►

9c **Other Transactions:**

10 Long-term gain from sale or exchange of a principal residence from Form 2119, lines 8, 10, or 14	**10**		
11 Long-term gain from installment sales from Form 6252, lines 23 or 31	**11**		
12 Net long-term gain or (loss) from partnerships, S corporations, and fiduciaries .	**12**		
13 Capital gain distributions	**13**		
14 Enter gain from Form 4797, line 7 or 9	**14**		
15 Long-term capital loss carryover	**15**		
16 Add all of the transactions on lines 9a and 9c and lines 10 through 15 in columns (f) and (g) .	**16** ( )		
17 Net long-term gain or (loss), combine columns (f) and (g) of line 16	**17**		

Schedule D (Form 1040) 1987

69

Name(s) as shown on Form 1040 (Do not enter name and social security number if shown on other side.)   Your social security number

Part III   Summary of Parts I and II

18	Combine lines 8 and 17, and enter the net gain or (loss) here. If result is a gain, also enter the gain on Form 1040, line 14	18	30,000

     Note: If lines 17 and 18 are net gains and your taxable income is taxed over the 28% tax rate, see Part IV below. You may be able to reduce your tax if you qualify for the alternative tax computation.

19	If line 18 is a loss, enter here and as a loss on Form 1040, line 14, the **smaller** of:		
a	The amount on line 18; **or** b $3,000 ($1,500 if married filing a separate return)	19	—

Part IV   Alternative Tax Computation
     First complete Form 1040 through line 36.

Use Part IV if both lines 17 and 18 show net gains, **AND:**

You checked filing status box	AND	Form 1040, line 36 is over:	You checked filing status box	AND	Form 1040, line 36 is over:
1		$27,000	3		$22,500
2 or 5		45,000	4		38,000

20	Enter amount from Form 1040, line 36	20	
21	Enter the smaller of the gain on line 17 or the gain on line 18	21	
22	Subtract line 21 from 20 and enter the result	22	
23	Enter: **a** $16,800 if you checked filing status box 1; **b** $28,000 if you checked filing status box 2 or 5; **c** $14,000 if you checked filing status box 3; **or d** $23,000 if you checked filing status box 4	23	
24	Enter the **greater** of line 22 or line 23	24	
25	Subtract line 24 from line 20	25	
26	Figure the amount of tax on line 24. Use the Tax Table or Tax Rate Schedules, whichever applies . . .	26	
27	Multiply line 25 by 28% (.28) and enter the result	27	
28	Add lines 26 and 27. Enter the result here and on Form 1040, line 37 and check the box for Schedule D	28	

Part V   Computation of Capital Loss Carryovers From 1987 to 1988
     (Complete this part if the loss on line 18 is more than the loss on line 19.)

29	Enter the loss shown on line 8; if none, enter zero and skip lines 30 through 33.	29	
30	Enter gain shown on line 17. If that line is blank or shows a loss, enter zero	30	
31	Subtract line 30 from line 29	31	
32	Enter the smaller of line 19 or line 31	32	
33	Subtract line 32 from line 31. This is your **short-term capital loss carryover from 1987 to 1988** .	33	
34	Enter loss from line 17; if none, enter zero and skip lines 35 through 38	34	
35	Enter gain shown on line 8. If that line is blank or shows a loss, enter zero	35	
36	Subtract line 35 from line 34	36	
37	Subtract line 32 from line 19. (**Note:** If you skipped lines 30 through 33, enter the amount from line 19.)	37	
38	Subtract line 37 from line 36. This is your **long-term capital loss carryover from 1987 to 1988** . .	38	

Part VI   Complete This Part Only If You Elect Out of the Installment Method and Report a Note or Other Obligation at Less Than Full Face Value

39	Check here if you elect out of the installment method . . . . ▶ ☐
40	Enter the face amount of the note or other obligation . . . . ▶
41	Enter the percentage of valuation of the note or other obligation . . . . ▶

Part VII   Reconciliation of Forms 1099-B for Bartering Transactions
     Complete this part if you received one or more Form(s) 1099-B or an equivalent substitute statement(s) reporting bartering income.

			Amount of bartering income from Form 1099-B or equivalent statement reported on form or schedule
42	Form 1040, line 21	42	
43	Schedule C (Form 1040)	43	
44	Schedule D (Form 1040)	44	
45	Schedule E (Form 1040)	45	
46	Schedule F (Form 1040)	46	
47	Other (identify) (if not taxable, indicate reason—attach additional sheets if necessary) ▶	47	
48	Total (add lines 42 through 47)	48	

     Note: The amount on line 48 should be the same as the total bartering income on all Forms 1099-B or equivalent statements received.

RAISING THE BASIS OF YOUR STOCK

Because owner-shareholders are not permitted to deduct losses in excess of the basis of their stock, this is a good time to discuss the basis of your stock: what it is and how to raise it.

The basis of your stock is a dollar figure that consists of the assets (property, etc.) that the shareholder contributes to the corporation both at its inception and throughout its life. Even if your corporation is a service corporation, you can still make contributions to it: at its inception, you might give the corporation some office equipment and furniture and a library. These items are valued at cost, not present value, since the IRS considers current or replacement value irrelevant.

Assets you contribute to your corporation will increase the basis of your stock. They increase the value of the outstanding shares pro rata; they do not increase the value of any Employees' Stock Ownership Plan (ESOP) shares. Depending on when the shares are issued, you may have shares at varying bases, just as though you had bought stock at varying prices.

Why do you want to increase the basis of your stock? You want to make your basis as high as possible so that when you liquidate the corporation, as much money as possible is considered a return of capital and exempt from taxes. Thus, if your stock had a basis of $10,000 and you liquidated a corporation with assets of $100,000, the $10,000 would be considered a return of capital; you would subtract it from the $100,000 and start your calculations with $90,000.

If your corporation deals in services, you can still contribute to the corporation during its life. Attractive contributions would be in areas where corporations get preferential treatment, as opposed to individuals: either cash, with which the corporation could buy stocks, or the stocks themselves, since as soon as the stocks were transferred to the corporation, their dividends would be 70 percent tax-free. But remember: once you give the cash or stock to the corporation, you cannot use the dividends yourself or take the money out of the corporation without declaring a distribution and being taxed on it.

You could also buy paintings and other works of art or antiques for your corporation to raise the basis of your stock, but you would have to use your own funds to do so. While you are increasing the basis of the stock, you are increasing the assets of your corporation at the same time; in a sense, you are adding the same quantity to both sides of a balance, so that there is actually no net change. It would be far more desirable to give the corporation money to purchase stocks or the stocks themselves, since corporations are able to shelter 70 percent of dividends from taxes and individuals are not, as explained above. If you do transfer stock to the corporation, remember that you must use your cost—not the current market price—as the basis.

In this connection, a sixty-year-old professional could incorporate and turn over his stock portfolio to his corporation, at which point his dividends would be 70 percent tax-exempt. As long as his earned income constituted 40 percent or more of his total annual income, he would not be held to be a personal holding corporation. He could then retire at sixty-five or seventy with lots of tax-free dividend accumulation and a fairly high basis on his stock, so that when his corporation was liquidated, a good part of the assets would be considered a return of capital and therefore be tax-free.

As mentioned earlier, there's a compelling reason for owner-shareholders of an S corporation to monitor the basis of their stock and to be prepared to raise it: they cannot deduct losses in excess of the basis of their stock. If they want to take full advantage of their corporation's losses to offset their personal income from other sources, their basis must be equal to or greater than their portion of the loss.

In practice, here's how it works: Startup Corporation, your new Subchapter S corporation in which you are the sole shareholder, is expecting a loss of $10,000 this year. You paid $2,000 for 100 shares (100 percent) of the stock of your new corporation. Your basis in the stock is $2,000. During the year you loaned Startup $5,000. Now you have a basis in debt of $5,000 as well as a basis in stock of $2,000. (Yes, they are two separate accounts.)

If you have a basis in both stock and debt, operating losses are applied first to your basis in stock, then to your basis in debt. In this example, $2,000 of the $10,000 operating loss is applied to your basis in stock and wipes out its value. Then only $5,000 of the remaining $8,000 loss can be used to offset your personal income from other sources because your basis in debt is only $5,000.

In order to make use of the entire $10,000 loss, rather than only $7,000, you'll have to lend Start-up $3,000. Next year, when Start-up becomes profitable, it can repay you the $3,000.

Your basis changes every year in which Startup has a profit or a loss. When Startup shows a profit, your basis rises by the amount of the profit; if Startup has a loss, your basis is reduced by the amount of the loss. You are taxed on the profit whether or not it is distributed. When you are taxed, your basis is raised. When the profit is distributed, your basis is reduced by the amount of the distribution.

DISADVANTAGES OF SUBCHAPTER S

Everything has its price. The price of Subchapter S election is sacrificing the income-splitting feature of C corporations, which can save thousands of dollars in taxes every year, and giving up lots of juicy fringe benefits.

Not all employee benefits can be deducted by your Subchapter S corporation as business expenses. The Subchapter S Revision Act differentiates between employee-shareholders owning 2 percent or less of the corporation's stock and those owning *more than 2 percent of the stock.* Obviously, you're in the latter category. Under that legislation, only those benefits received by employee-shareholders owning 2 percent or less of the corporation's stock will be deductible by the corporation as a business expense. Thus, if you elect Subchapter S status, you'll lose many tax-favored fringe benefits; among them, valuable medical and insurance plans.

Under Subchapter S, you also lose the right to borrow from your pension plan, as employee-shareholders of C corporations are permitted to do. This right can be useful and very profitable to you and to the corporation. Let's say that you want to borrow $50,000 for two years so that you can put a down payment on a house. You can borrow the money at 10 percent for two years, then pay it back with interest. Your pension fund is enriched by $10,000. (But you may not deduct the interest payment on your personal income-tax return.)

There's an even greater disadvantage. If your corporation requires a great deal of expensive equipment, a Subchapter S corporation may very well be the wrong choice. A Subchapter S corporation must report that its shareholders have earned profits even if it doesn't distribute those profits to them. If your corporation buys a new gizmo for $20,000, you still must report that $20,000 as income and pay taxes on it, even if you never see the money.

STATES' RITES

When you weigh the advantages and disadvantages of electing Subchapter S status for your new corporation, consider whether the state in which you incorporate recognizes Subchapter S status. Some states recognize Subchapter S status; some do not and treat Subchapter S corporations as C corporations or as unincorporated businesses. Whether your state does or doesn't recognize Subchapter S corporations can make a big difference in how much you pay in taxes and how many tax returns you must file.

While you probably should consult a tax adviser before electing Subchapter S status, the following list of states that do and don't recognize Subchapter S corporations will start you on the right track:

Alabama	Recognizes federal Subchapter S status. Nonresident shareholders will be taxed on their share of Subchapter S income from Alabama sources.
Alaska	Recognizes federal Subchapter S status.
Arizona	Recognizes federal Subchapter S status.
Arkansas	Recognizes federal Subchapter S status. Nonresident shareholders will be taxed on their share of Subchapter S income from Arkansas sources.
California	Recognizes federal Subchapter S status. Nonresident shareholders will be taxed on their share of Subchapter S income from California sources.
Colorado	Recognizes federal Subchapter S status. Nonresident shareholders will be taxed on their share of Subchapter S income from Colorado sources. However, the Colorado Court of Appeals has held that distributions of S corporation income to nonresident shareholders are not taxable.
Connecticut	Does not recognize Subchapter S status. Connecticut S corporations are subject to the state business (income) tax.

Delaware   Recognizes federal Subchapter S status. However, if on the last day of the corporation's fiscal year any shareholders are nonresidents, the corporation is subject to tax on the percentage of its taxable income equal to the percentage of its stock owned by nonresidents on that day.

District of Columbia   A Subchapter S corporation is treated as an unincorporated business and pays the District of Columbia unincorporated business franchise (income) tax if its gross income for a tax year is $12,000 or more. If its gross income is less than $12,000, it is treated as a partnership and files an information partnership return. It is exempt from the franchise tax.

If the Subchapter S corporation has paid the unincorporated business franchise tax, its shareholders are entitled to a deduction ("modification") on income that has been subject to the franchise tax. But if the corporation has not paid the franchise tax because its gross income was under $12,000, its shareholders are completely taxed on their Subchapter S income.

Florida   A Subchapter S corporation is not taxable, except to the extent that it is liable for federal income tax. However, Florida law defines taxable income according to a former Internal Revenue Code Section 1372(b)(1), *prior* to amendment by the Subchapter S Revision Act of 1982.

Georgia   Recognizes federal Subchapter S status. Nonresident shareholders will be taxed on their share of Subchapter S income from Georgia sources.

Hawaii   Recognizes Subchapter S status only if all shareholders are Hawaii residents.

Idaho   Recognizes federal Subchapter S status.

Illinois   Recognizes federal Subchapter S status, but substitutes a personal property replacement income tax on Illinois net income for S corporations. There are many other intricate modifications. Consult your tax adviser.

Indiana   Recognizes federal Subchapter S status. Nonresident shareholders will be taxed on their share of Subchapter S income from Indiana sources.

Iowa   Recognizes federal Subchapter S status.

Kansas   Recognizes federal Subchapter S status. Nonresident shareholders will be taxed on their share of Subchapter S income from Kansas sources.

Kentucky   Recognizes federal Subchapter S status.

Louisiana   Subchapter S corporations are taxed as though they were C corporations.

Maine   Recognizes federal Subchapter S status. Nonresident shareholders will be taxed on their share of Subchapter S income from Maine sources.

Maryland   Recognizes federal Subchapter S status. The corporation will be taxed on Maryland income attributable to each nonresident shareholder.

Massachusetts   Recognizes federal Subchapter S status. However, shareholders are taxed on their distributive share of the S corporation's items of Massachusetts income, loss, or deduction as though they had realized or incurred the item directly from the source, rather than through the S corporation. Consult your tax adviser.

Michigan   Michigan Subchapter S corporations must pay the single business tax. However, Subchapter S corporations can enjoy a special exemption equal to $12,000 times the number of qualified shareholders, up to a maximum of $48,000,

	plus a graduated special tax credit. Consult your tax adviser.
Minnesota	Recognizes federal Subchapter S status.
Mississippi	Subchapter S corporations are not subject to the Mississippi income tax on corporations, but still must file the regular corporation income-tax return and schedules, as well as partnership returns. Nonresident shareholders will be taxed on their share of Subchapter S income from Mississippi sources.
Missouri	Recognizes federal Subchapter S status.
Montana	Recognizes federal Subchapter S status. Every electing corporation must pay a minimum fee of $10.
Nebraska	Recognizes federal Subchapter S status. Nonresident shareholders will be taxed on their share of Subchapter S income from Nebraska sources, but the corporation may pay these taxes for them.
Nevada	No corporate or personal taxes are imposed.
New Hampshire	Does not recognize Subchapter S status. New Hampshire S corporations are subject to the state business profits tax.
New Jersey	Does not recognize Subchapter S status. New Jersey S corporations are subject to the corporation business tax.
New Mexico	Recognizes federal Subchapter S status.
New York	Recognizes federal Subchapter S status. Nonresident shareholders will be taxed on their share of Subchapter S income from New York sources. *However, New York City does not recognize Subchapter S status,* and S corporations are taxed as though they were C corporations.
North Carolina	Does not recognize Subchapter S status. North Carolina S corporations are taxed as though they were C corporations.

North Dakota	Recognizes federal Subchapter S status, but an S corporation may elect to be taxed as a C corporation for state income-tax purposes.
Ohio	Recognizes federal Subchapter S status. Nonresident shareholders may be entitled to claim the nonresident tax credit.
Oklahoma	Recognizes federal Subchapter S status. Nonresident shareholders or the corporation will be taxed on their share of Subchapter S income from Oklahoma sources.
Oregon	Recognizes federal Subchapter S status. Oregon Subchapter S corporations must file state corporation income and excise tax returns, but are liable only for the minimum $10 corporate excise tax. Nonresident shareholders will be taxed on their share of Subchapter S income from Oregon sources.
Pennsylvania	Recognizes federal Subchapter S status.
Rhode Island	Recognizes federal Subchapter S status. Rhode Island Subchapter S corporations are not subject to the state income tax or net worth tax on corporations, but are subject to a franchise tax (minimum $100). Nonresident shareholders or the corporation will be taxed on their share of Subchapter S income from Rhode Island sources.
South Carolina	Recognizes federal Subchapter S status.
South Dakota	Recognizes federal Subchapter S status, except for financial institutions. No corporate or personal income taxes are imposed.
Tennessee	Does not recognize Subchapter S status. Tennessee Subchapter S corporations are subject to the Tennessee excise (income) tax.
Texas	Does not recognize Subchapter S status. Texas Subchapter S corporations are subject to the Texas franchise tax. Texas does not impose a personal income tax.

Utah	Recognizes federal Subchapter S status.
Vermont	Recognizes federal Subchapter S status.
Virginia	Recognizes federal Subchapter S status. Nonresident shareholders will be taxed on their share of Subchapter S income from Virginia sources.
Washington	Does not recognize Subchapter S status. Washington Subchapter S corporations are subject to a franchise tax and gross receipts tax.
West Virginia	Recognizes federal Subchapter S status.
Wisconsin	Recognizes federal Subchapter S status, with a few minor modifications.
Wyoming	Wyoming imposes a corporate franchise tax, but not an income tax.

TRADE-OFFS

Do the advantages of a Subchapter S corporation outweigh the disadvantages? It all depends.

You Gain

- More favorable income-tax rates for members of the "perilous professions."
- Ability to offset personal income with corporate losses.
- Immediate use of corporate funds every year—no buildup of assets to be taxed upon liquidation.
- Only one tax is paid when money is taken out of the corporation. (In a C corporation, sometimes—but not always—a second tax

You Lose

- Income-splitting strategies.
- Right to invest corporate surplus in stocks whose dividends paid to your corporation are 70 percent tax-free.
- More generous corporate pension contributions.
- Right to borrow from pension fund.
- Free $50,000 group term life insurance.
- Free accident and health insurance plans.
- $5,000 death benefit paid to

may have to be paid when money is taken out of the corporation, as in liquidation.)

- employee-shareholder's estate or beneficiaries.
- Cost of meals or lodging furnished for the convenience of employer.

To clarify the pros and cons of electing Subchapter S status, let's look at two stereotypes, one of whom should choose Subchapter S status and one of whom should not. Your own situation is probably not so clear-cut as these because these examples are weighted heavily in one direction or the other. Nevertheless, these examples should guide you in making a choice. The list is far from complete, but it should point you in the right direction and help you organize questions to ask your tax adviser.

Ideal Subchapter S

- Single, few medical expenses that total less than $1,000 per year.

Ideal C Corporation

- Married, heavy medical expenses—orthodontia for one child, psychotherapy for one child. Needs gym and pool memberships and masseur for bad back. Everyone in family wears contact lenses. Medical expenses total over $10,000 per year.

- Member of a "perilous profession"—faces flat tax rate of 34 percent if doesn't elect Subchapter S.

- Not a member of a "perilous profession." Entitled to corporate tax rate of 15 percent on income under $50,000.

- Needs most of corporate income to live on so doesn't care about income splitting.

- Does not need most of corporate income to live on—plans to take advantage of income splitting and of investing corporate surplus in stocks whose dividends paid to the corporation are 70 percent tax-free.

- Profession does not require a great deal of expensive equipment.
- Indifferent to borrowing from pension fund, which is prohibited in Subchapter S corporations.

- Business requires a great deal of expensive equipment.
- Expects to borrow from pension fund in several years to buy new home.

Fortunately, you can have it both ways. You can start as a Subchapter S corporation to benefit from the flow through of your fledgling corporation's losses to offset your personal income and reduce your taxes. When your corporation flourishes and becomes profitable, you can terminate its Subchapter S status to take advantage of income-splitting strategies, greater pension contributions, medical, dental, and insurance fringe benefits, and corporate investment for dividends that are 70 percent tax-free. Finally, as your corporation matures, if it becomes extremely successful and nets $100,000 a year, you may want to reelect Subchapter S status so that your corporation doesn't face the Scylla of the accumulated earnings trap (see Chapter 1) or the Charybdis of double taxation of dividends—once as corporate earnings and once as dividends you receive from your corporation.

Because it's easy to elect and to terminate Subchapter S status but difficult to return to it, this decision should be made in consultation with your tax adviser. You may want to work out some scenarios on a computer, e.g., "If I have only $20,000 outside income, it does/doesn't pay to elect Sub S. If my outside income rises to $50,000, it does/doesn't pay to elect Sub S." For most one-person corporations, Subchapter S status is desirable at some point, and therefore its election and/or termination should be examined every year.

RETURN TO SUBCHAPTER S

In general, there is a five-year waiting period between terminating and reelecting Subchapter S status. The major exception to the rule requires the approval of the IRS District Director. How easy is it to get? Do you need a compelling reason?

In all likelihood, the District Director will ask you: How much will your corporation save because of this change? And in all likelihood, the IRS will make your corporation pay the difference in taxes before it grants your request. The IRS isn't going to give you the benefit of flip-flopping back and forth. Instead, the IRS will probably say: "It's okay if you want to change back to Subchapter S status, but you'll have to pay for the privilege."

HOW TO USE YOUR SUBCHAPTER S CORPORATION AS A FINANCIAL-PLANNING TOOL

Many financial planners are using Subchapter S corporations as sophisticated long-term tools to achieve not only tax savings but also business and family goals. Because of the impact of state and local income taxes, these can be discussed only generally here and are meant to serve as guidelines and openers for more specific planning with your tax advisers. Here are some problems faced by many successful small businesses and their profitable Subchapter S solutions:

Problem: How to avoid federal estate tax without loss of the owner's present or future control of the business.

Solution: In general, when a business owner gives or transfers corporate stock to a beneficiary in order to remove the value and growth of the donated stock from his or her gross estate, the donor also creates a potential problem: even a minor block of stock may be sufficient to swing voting control away from the donor, to his or her detriment. However, by structuring or restructuring a company as a Subchapter S corporation, business owners can create two types of common voting stock (not classes—this distinction is crucial): Type A, with ten or more votes per share; and Type B, with one vote per share. (Or Type B can even be nonvoting stock.) The owners can then give all their Type B stock to children or grandchildren and keep all the Type A stock themselves. Giving away the Type B stock removes it from the owners' taxable estates, which saves current income and eventual estate taxes. But since the Type B stock possesses very little voting power, the business owners can remain secure, in firm control of their corporation.

Problem: How to avoid paying double tax on corporate income while treating family members who work for the company and those who do not equally.

Solution: In family-owned businesses, it's very common for some members to work for the company and for some members not to.

These two groups are often at loggerheads over dividends. The family shareholders who don't work for the company want their dividends. The family shareholders who work for the company frequently don't want to receive dividends because it is often difficult for general corporations to pay out corporate earnings to stockholders without incurring a double tax on corporate income. Their refusal may preclude dividends for the other shareholders. A Subchapter S corporation can solve this problem because corporate earnings are distributed to the shareholders with only one tax on shareholders, as if they were partners.

Problem: How to turn investment income into earned income so that you can qualify for pensions and profit sharing.

Solution: Many people own income-producing securities, but despite the high income taxes they have to pay, they are not entitled to any kind of pension or profit-sharing plan because their dividends and interest are not considered to be earned income. Setting up a Subchapter S corporation to hold these securities—it could be called "My Investments, Inc."—lets these people receive the same amount as before, but now some of it can be transmuted into salary. The corporations can now pay them a reasonable salary for managing the investments and other concerns of the corporations, and these salaries mean that these people—with no real change in their activities—are now permitted the pension and profit-sharing plans that they were denied earlier.

Furthermore, through their Subchapter S corporations, these investors are able to make estate-planning gifts of stock to children or grandchildren without loss of control, as in the previous example.

These are only a few ideas to serve as a springboard. Subchapter S corporations are advantageous, but intricate. To make sure that you belong in one and that you're getting all those benefits, enlist your accountant and lawyer in developing your strategies.

6

Especially for
Women

Self-employed women, like self-employed men, can enjoy such benefits of incorporation as limited liability, increased pension benefits, minimally taxed dividend income, and medical and insurance programs.

But there are special benefits for women, too. One talented young *Vogue* photographer puts it this way: "Incorporating sets me apart from a hundred other free-lance photographers. It shows clients and prospective clients that I'm successful and financially sophisticated. It's that extra bit—that extra little touch—that helps them remember *me,* not just my work."

Nowadays, more and more women are self-employed, and with increasing financial sophistication, more women are incorporating. But very often women suffer from the legacy of the past: they are not as knowledgeable about banking and establishing credit as men are, and all too often, wives, widows, and divorcées suddenly find that they have no financial history. Quite simply, this means that lenders don't know whether or not to lend them money.

Whether you'll ever use it or not, establish a credit record immediately; you never know when you'll need it. The best way to do this is to open a checking account—*in your own name alone*—and to become known to your bank manager.

Next, ask for a line of credit: overdraft privileges for your checking account. Most banks give this a fancy name—Privilege Checking, Executive Credit, The No-Bounce Check. All it means is that if you overdraw your account, your checks will be honored—but at the same time you will have automatically borrowed money to cover them, at a hefty 12 to 18 percent. Formerly, the traditional advice on establishing credit was: "Take out a loan, make the payments promptly, and pay the final installment a little early." However, if you can show your bank manager that you have assets, you should be granted a line of credit without having to go through the rigmarole of a bank loan that you don't need.

What assets will impress a bank manager? A savings account in your name and property in your name. A savings account is particularly good because it shows that you are not a spendthrift and also that there is money at your disposal even if your income should fluctuate.

A good credit-card or charge-account history will also show that you are fiscally responsible. Like your checking and savings accounts, your credit card and charge plates should also be in your name alone.

Whatever method you use—checking account, line of credit, credit cards—always use your own name alone, even if it involves what seems like duplication and extra service charges. One of my friends who'd worked for twenty years finally decided to go into business for herself and applied for a bank loan to furnish her home office. Alas, the bank manager required her husband to cosign the loan because my friend had never built up an independent credit record—all her accounts were in joint names, and thus all the credit records were in her husband's name.

Now, if you incorporate, there's an additional reason to keep separate accounts: to prove to the IRS that there's no "corporate pocketbook" at work, that you are not lumping together your corporate and personal expenditures.

In most corporate situations, women experience the same problems as men: setting up a corporation, making it successful, investing corporate surplus profitably, etc. But there is one area in which women (and, incidentally, artists and writers who may produce only one major money-making work every two, three, or more years) are particularly vulnerable.

WOMEN AS PERSONAL HOLDING CORPORATIONS

Because women will often curtail their workload during pregnancy and for a time after their children are born, women who incorporate may frequently have years in which their corporation receives much more dividend income from the stocks the corporation has bought than earned income from the work the corporation has performed for customers and clients, and thus be in danger of being held by the IRS to be a personal holding corporation. This situation would be especially likely if a woman had accumulated around $100,000 in a corporate portfolio that was invested in high-yield stocks paying $7,000 or $8,000 a year at the time of her maternity leave.

As explained earlier, a woman in this position could easily avoid having her corporation deemed a personal holding corporation simply by selling one or more of the corporation's stocks to bring the dividend income down to 59 percent or less of the total corporate income and then by reinvesting the proceeds of the stock sales in either low-yielding growth stocks (but making sure to keep the dividend income down to 59 percent) or municipal bonds (whose income is not counted by the IRS in making these calculations), depending on how aggressive or conservative an investor she is.

When she returns to work full time and her corporation is earning enough so that it is no longer in danger of being classified as a personal holding corporation, she can—and should—reverse the procedure so that her corporation can benefit from the 70 percent tax-free dividend exclusion. She should sell the corporation's municipal bonds or growth stocks and reinvest the proceeds of the sales in high-yielding common or preferred stocks.

Now that women are finally achieving their own in the business world and are earning enough money to make it worthwhile, doesn't it make sense for a woman to incorporate?

7

Your
Employees

Up until now, we've been discussing the sometimes-idyllic situation where you are truly a one-man band: in your one-person corporation, you are everything from president down to file clerk.

But what if you have employees? Then it gets more complicated, though not necessarily more expensive.

If your corporation is able to hire what the IRS calls "independent contractors," you will not have to withhold taxes on their pay or cover them for Social Security. At the end of the year, the corporation just sends them an IRS Form 1099, which shows how much you paid them. Obviously, then, your corporation does not have to include independent contractors in its pension or profit-sharing plans because they are not considered to be the corporation's employees. (These independent contractors can set up their own Keogh plans, of course, but that's another subject for another book.)

If your corporation hires part-timers who are held by the IRS to be your employees, unless they give you a W-4 form showing that they are exempt from withholding, you will have to withhold income taxes on their salaries and furnish them with W-2 forms showing the amounts withheld. Depending upon how much they earn each quarter, the corporation may or may not have to contribute to their Social Security accounts. State regulations on contributions to workers' compensation and unemployment insurance funds vary too widely to be discussed here. The important point: unless your corporation's part-time employee completes 1,000 hours a year (an average of 20 hours a week), you do not have to include him or her in the corporation's pension or profit-sharing plans.

This means, of course, that your corporation could hire two or three part-timers instead of one full-time employee and save thousands of dollars every year by not having to contribute to employees' plans. Be aware that, because you are paying yourself much more than you are paying your employee(s), your corporate pension plan will be classified as "top-heavy" and will be subject to the accelerated vesting rules discussed several paragraphs below.

Hiring part-timers has social as well as financial benefits. Very often you can hire more intelligent and qualified people—college students, mothers, retirees—who are unable to work a full week but who perform splendidly on a part-time basis and are often delighted to work flexible hours. (I know from personal experience: I worked my way through college assisting the president of a small legal-services corporation.)

Even if you have full-time employees, though, you may not have to include them in your pension and profit-sharing plans immediately—and there are even ways to exclude them permanently.

First, there is a minimum-age requirement: an employer does not have to include anyone in its pension and profit-sharing plans (1) who is not at least 21 and (2) who has not completed at least one year of service.

Second, in a top-heavy plan, for plan years beginning after December 31, 1988, if an employer is willing to vest 100 percent of its contributions to an employee pension plan immediately, it can legally delay including that employee in the plan for 3 years. Then, of course, all employer contributions are 100 percent vested, and if the employee leaves after 4 years of employment, he or she could take 100 percent of 1 year's worth of your contributions.* Compare this with the figures shown in Section 6.4 of Appendix C, where, if the employee is included after completion of 1,000 hours, after 4 years of employment the employer's contribution is only 60 percent vested. This means that if your employee leaves after 4 years, he or she can take only 60 percent of your corporation's contribution to the pension and

---

*Vesting and eligibility rules become very complicated for plan years beginning after December 31, 1988. Consult your accountant for details and possible strategy changes.

profit-sharing plans; the remaining 40 percent reverts to the corporation. If he or she leaves before working 2 years, no funds are vested and all the corporation's contributions revert to the corporation.

These two options present an obvious trade-off. If your corporation is in an industry where people move around frequently (advertising, Wall Street, and publishing are typical examples), it might be wise to wait the 3 years and then vest 100 percent of the contributions, because the odds are that none of your employees will stay the 3 years and you won't have to make any contributions at all. On the other hand, if your corporation is in an industry where employee turnover is low, it might be best to include an employee in the plan immediately so that if he or she leaves after 3 or 4 years, only 40 or 60 percent of your corporation's contributions will be vested. What it boils down to in the case where an employee leaves after 4 years is your risking 100 percent of 1 year's contributions versus 60 percent of 4 years' contributions. Check with your lawyer and accountant before you decide.

But don't think that you can hire employees and then fire them just before their 3 years' waiting time is up and they become eligible to join your corporation's pension and profit-sharing plans. You may get away with it for the first two 3-year periods. But when the IRS audits your corporation's plan and discovers that your corporation terminates its employees as soon as they become eligible, the IRS will disqualify the plan. The plan then becomes a taxable trust, and the employer really has problems. Besides, this kind of behavior just isn't ethical.

There's still another gimmick, though, for eliminating low-paid employees from pension and profit-sharing plans. Here's how it works: the plan—called an integrated plan because it is integrated with Social Security—is constructed to cover employees earning amounts over the Social Security maximum, which is $45,000 in 1988. Under those amounts, the employer pays the Social Security tax, and above the cutoff point, the employer contributes to the pension and profit-sharing plans. Thus, if a secretary earned $20,000 in 1988, the corporation would pay only the Social Security tax on the $20,000. If the president of the corporation earned $75,000 in 1988, the corporation would pay the Social Security tax on the first $45,000 of salary and would contribute to the pension and profit-sharing plans on a base of $30,000 ($75,000 minus $45,000).

Of course, the base doesn't have to be the maximum Social Security salary. In the preceding illustration, the cutoff point could have been $20,000; then the secretary would still be excluded from the pension and profit-sharing plans and would be covered only by the Social Security tax, but the base on which the corporation would contribute to its president's pension and profit-sharing plans would rise to $55,000 ($75,000 minus $20,000). If the corporation wanted to be generous, it might make the cutoff point $15,000. Then the corporation would pay the Social Security tax on $20,000 and make a contribution based on $5,000 for the secretary, and would pay the Social Security tax on $45,000 and make a contribution based on $60,000 for the president. *Notice that because the cutoff point is less than the maximum Social Security, the secretary is getting retirement coverage on $25,000, and the president is getting retirement coverage on $105,000 ($45,000 + $60,000).* In fact, the lower you make the cutoff point, the more retirement coverage your corporation can provide for you and your employees.

The important thing to note is that the Social Security level is a maximum; your corporation could not make the cutoff point $50,000—unless the Social Security maximum had risen to $50,000 by that time.

Again, the constant refrain: consult a lawyer or accountant before you decide how to cover (or not to cover) your employees. Good employees should be rewarded somehow; you *do* want them to stay, don't you?

8

"Free"
Insurance

As a key employee of your corporation, you can get "free" life insurance and disability insurance. Workers' compensation, a third form of insurance, is available *only* to employees; sole proprietors are ineligible. By "free" insurance, I mean that the insurance premiums are fully deductible by the corporation and reduce its pretax income, while at the same time they are not treated by the IRS as income to the insured. This "free" insurance may be worth $1,000 a year.

The "free" life insurance—sometimes called §79 insurance—is limited to one-year renewable term policies of up to $50,000 face value as group insurance in groups of ten people or more. However, smaller groups—including a "group" of one—can qualify for similar renewable term policies that get similar tax treatment from the IRS. It is possible to discriminate on an employee's class basis in choosing the face value for these policies; a common choice would be for officer/employees to have $50,000 policies and for other employees to have $10,000 policies.

If additional life-insurance coverage above $50,000 is desired, the IRS insists that the employee pay taxes on what is called "imputed income." This is a figure per $1,000 of coverage that is based solely on the age of the employee; it is not a percentage of the annual premium. The following table shows annual premiums and imputed income as of January 1, 1988:

Age	Approximate Annual Premium Per Additional $50,000*	Annual Imputed Income Per $50,000
30–34	$ 72.00	$ 54.00
35–39	102.00	66.00
40–44	156.00	102.00
45–49	246.00	174.00
50–54	384.00	288.00
55–59	612.00	450.00
60–64	922.00	702.00

*For dividend-paying insurance company. Companies that do not pay dividends may charge premiums 50 percent–75 percent lower.

Since, at all ages, the imputed income is less than the premium for the additional insurance, it pays for the corporation to pay for the additional insurance and for the shareholder/employee to accept the imputed income. A $200,000 policy may save you $500–$1,000 a year.

But as important as life insurance is, many people worry far more about disability. There are many people who don't need life insurance; they have no family to protect. However, they all need disability insurance: some form of income protection to provide for them if they are unable to work because of illness or injury. Disability insurance premiums, too, are fully deductible by the corporation and are not considered by the IRS to be income to the insured.

It is difficult to set up hard-and-fast guidelines about insurance coverage—especially disability insurance coverage. There are too many variables: riskiness of work, riskiness of life-style, extent of medical insurance coverage, living expenses, escalating medical costs, etc. This is an area that really needs individual treatment and frequent examination and revision. However, as a general rule, it may make sense to arrange for generous—if not maximum—coverage. What little extra the corporation may pay for your being overinsured against possible disability is certainly worth the price in terms of peace of mind. Besides, the premiums are paid out of pretax dollars, so they're less expensive than they may seem and may even pull your corporation down from the 25 percent bracket into the 15 percent bracket.

9

Medical
Benefits

First, the bad news. Prior to the Tax Reform Act of 1976, employees of corporations (but not individual proprietors) were able to take a sick-pay exclusion (and, in effect, receive tax-free income) when they were absent from work due to illness or injury. The Tax Reform Act has virtually put an end to these benefits for corporate employees, except in the case of permanent and total disability.

There's more bad news. Employees of Subchapter S corporations are not entitled to the medical benefits in this chapter. These perks are only for employees of C corporations.

Now, the good news. Employees of C corporations can still enjoy "free" medical insurance and payment of medical expenses and drugs for themselves and their families. They are "free" in that the corporation can write off the payments as a business expense, but they are not held by the IRS to be income to the individuals receiving them.

Although the IRS calls them "medical reimbursement plans," your corporation can actually pay your medical bills for you and your family directly, rather than reimbursing you for your medical expenses. While legally this plan can be informal and unwritten (especially if you are the sole employee and stockholder) and can consist of the understanding that the corporation will pay all medical bills, in actual practice, where the IRS is concerned, a formal written corporate resolution of the type shown later in this chapter carries much more weight.

In a one-person corporation, that one officer/stockholder/employee unquestionably provides significant services as an employee and can be covered, along with his or her family. In larger corporations, it has been held that medical reimbursement plans must benefit employees, rather than stockholders as such. The basis of the plan must be the employer-employee relationship, not the stockholder relationship. Of course, covered employees can also be stockholders, and, in fact, many closely held corporations limit participation in their medical reimbursement plans to officers who are also stockholders. If these officers contribute substantial services as employees, the medical reimbursement plan will resist challenge.

In a one-person reimbursement plan, the corporation can—and should—arrange to reimburse 100 percent of medical expenses. In a larger corporation, thought must be given to the total medical expenses among the plan's participants; it may be wise to set a limit on the amount of reimbursement per eligible employee. It may also be advisable to set up a medical care reimbursement plan for stockholder/employees and to provide a more limited plan—or just Blue Cross/Blue Shield—for ordinary employees.

Following is a sample medical care reimbursement plan and minutes of a meeting of the board of directors approving the plan. As in other areas of corporate life, remember that your plan can be amended as situations change: as the corporation covers an increasing number of employees, it may be wise to lower the reimbursement limit per employee.

(NAME OF YOUR CORPORATION) MEDICAL REIMBURSEMENT PLAN

ARTICLE I   Benefits

The Corporation shall reimburse all eligible employees for expenses incurred by themselves and their dependents, as defined in IRC S152, as amended, for medical care, as defined in IRC S213(d), as amended, subject to the conditions and limitations as hereinafter set forth. It is the intention of the Corporation that the benefits payable to eligible employees hereunder shall be excluded from their gross income pursuant to IRC S105, as amended.

ARTICLE II Eligibility

All corporate officers employed on a full-time basis at the date of inception of this Plan, including those who may be absent due to illness or injury on said date, are eligible employees under the Plan. A corporate officer shall be considered employed on a full-time basis if said officer customarily works at least seven months in each year and twenty hours in each week. Any person hereafter becoming an officer of the Corporation employed on a full-time basis shall be eligible under this Plan.

ARTICLE III Limitations

(a) The Corporation shall reimburse any eligible employee (without limitation) (no more than $_____) in any fiscal year for medical care expenses.

(b) Reimbursement or payment provided under this Plan shall be made by the Corporation only in the event and to the extent that such reimbursement or payment is not provided under any insurance policy(ies), whether owned by the Corporation or the employee, or under any other health and accident or wage-continuation plan. In the event that there is such an insurance policy or plan in effect providing for reimbursement in whole or in part, then to the extent of the coverage under such policy or plan, the Corporation shall be relieved of any and all liability hereunder.

ARTICLE IV Submission of Proof

Any eligible employee applying for reimbursement under this Plan shall submit to the Corporation, at least quarterly, all bills for medical care, including premium notices for accident or health insurance, for verification by the Corporation prior to payment. Failure to comply herewith may, at the discretion of the Corporation, terminate such eligible employee's right to said reimbursement.

ARTICLE V Discontinuation

This Plan shall be subject to termination at any time by vote of the board of directors of the Corporation; provided, however, that medical care expenses incurred prior to such termination shall be reimbursed or paid in accordance with the terms of this Plan.

ARTICLE VI   Determination

The president shall determine all questions arising from the administration and interpretation of the Plan except where reimbursement is claimed by the president. In such case, determination shall be made by the board of directors.

MINUTES OF SPECIAL MEETING OF DIRECTORS
OF
(NAME OF YOUR CORPORATION)

A special meeting of the board of directors of (name of your corporation) was held on (date) at (time) at (address where meeting was held).

All of the directors being present, the meeting was called to order by the chairman. The chairman advised that the meeting was called to approve and adopt a medical care expense reimbursement plan. A copy of the plan was presented to those present and upon motion duly made, seconded, and unanimously carried, it was

RESOLVED, that the "Medical Care Reimbursement Plan" presented to the meeting is hereby approved and adopted, that a copy of the Plan shall be appended to these minutes, and that the proper officers of the corporation are hereby authorized to take whatever action is necessary to implement the Plan, and it is further

RESOLVED, that the signing of these minutes by the directors shall constitute full ratification thereof and waiver of notice of the meeting by the signatories.

There being no further business to come before the meeting, upon motion duly made, seconded, and unanimously carried, the meeting was adjourned.

_____
Secretary

_____   _____
Chairman   Director

_____   _____
Director   Director

The advantages of your corporation's paying all your medical bills are enormous. If you were to pay your medical bills yourself, as a sole proprietor (or if your corporation hadn't adopted the medical reimbursement plan), the totals would be reduced by 7.5 percent of your adjusted gross income, as shown below. The dollar amount of these reductions can be quite sizable and in many cases can completely wipe out your medical deductions. Even the $150 you could always deduct in earlier years has been done away with.

However, a corporation is not subject to the 7.5 percent reductions; every penny of medical expense counts.

Let's look at some simple Schedule A returns. We'll assume that Entrepreneur's adjusted gross income is $20,000 and Worldly Wise's adjusted gross income is $40,000. We'll give them identical medical expenses:

Medicine and drugs	$1,500.00
Doctors, dentists, etc.	900.00
Other (eyeglasses)	300.00
Transportation to doctors	300.00
	$3,000.00

Entrepreneur's medical deductions have been slashed by 50 percent: from $3,000 to $1,500. If he is in the 25 percent tax bracket, his medical deductions are now worth only $225 in tax dollars. If his medical insurance cost $1,000, the adjustment would be worth only $63 in tax dollars.

Poor Worldly Wise has fared even worse. His medical deductions have dwindled to zero. If his medical insurance cost $1,000, the adjustment would be worth only $95 in tax dollars.

But your corporation is not subject to that 7.5 percent reduction. The total medical expenditures remain at $3,000, and consequently their value in tax dollars is much greater:

Corporate Income	Tax Bracket as Percentage	Dollar Value of $3,000 Deduction
$ 0–$50,000	15%	$ 450
$50,000–$75,000	25	750
$75,000+	34	1,020

Amazing, isn't it!

SCHEDULES A&B
(Form 1040)

Department of the Treasury
Internal Revenue Service   (X)

OMB No. 1545-0074

1987

Attachment
Sequence No. 07

Schedule A—Itemized Deductions

(Schedule B is on back)

▶ Attach to Form 1040. ▶ See Instructions for Schedules A and B (Form 1040).

Name(s) as shown on Form 1040

ENTREPRENGUR

Your social security number

000 : 00 : 0000

Medical and Dental Expenses (Do not include expenses reimbursed or paid by others.) (See Instructions on page 21.)	1a	Prescription medicines and drugs, insulin, doctors, dentists, nurses, hospitals, insurance premiums you paid for medical and dental care, etc.	1a	2,400 —	
	b	Transportation and lodging	1b	300 —	
	c	Other (list—include hearing aids, dentures, eyeglasses, etc.) ▶ EYEGLASSES	1c	300 —	
	2	Add lines 1a through 1c, and enter the total here	2	3,000 —	
	3	Multiply the amount on Form 1040, line 31, by 7.5% (.075)	3	1,500 —	
	4	Subtract line 3 from line 2. If zero or less, enter -0-. Total medical and dental ▶	4	1,500 —	

SCHEDULES A&B
(Form 1040)

Department of the Treasury
Internal Revenue Service   (X)

OMB No. 1545-0074

1987

Attachment
Sequence No. 07

Schedule A—Itemized Deductions

(Schedule B is on back)

▶ Attach to Form 1040. ▶ See Instructions for Schedules A and B (Form 1040).

Name(s) as shown on Form 1040

WORLDLY WISE

Your social security number

000 : 00 : 0000

Medical and Dental Expenses (Do not include expenses reimbursed or paid by others.) (See Instructions on page 21.)	1a	Prescription medicines and drugs, insulin, doctors, dentists, nurses, hospitals, insurance premiums you paid for medical and dental care, etc.	1a	2,400 —	
	b	Transportation and lodging	1b	300 —	
	c	Other (list—include hearing aids, dentures, eyeglasses, etc.) ▶ EYEGLASSES	1c	300 —	
	2	Add lines 1a through 1c, and enter the total here	2	3,000 —	
	3	Multiply the amount on Form 1040, line 31, by 7.5% (.075)	3	3,000 —	
	4	Subtract line 3 from line 2. If zero or less, enter -0-. Total medical and dental ▶	4	0	

10

All about ERISA: Tax-Sheltered Pension and Profit-Sharing Plans

ERISA—the Employees' Retirement Income Security Act—is one of the most complicated and confusing pieces of legislation ever to be enacted. Even lawyers and accountants have trouble interpreting it, so if you find this chapter difficult to understand, you're not alone. There is a lot of paperwork to file with the IRS and the Labor Department (in some cases, the Labor Department will be satisfied with the IRS form), but the results are worth it. Your corporation will be able to put away for you, its (sole) employee, up to 25 percent of your annual compensation, even including bonuses, if you like—up to $30,000. Furthermore, *you* can add up to 10 percent of your annual compensation to this retirement fund as what is called a Voluntary Contribution, as long as you don't exceed the 25 percent/$30,000 limitations. And if you choose a defined-benefit plan, you can contribute even more.

The simplest, cheapest, and easiest-to-adopt plans are the money-purchase and profit-sharing plans, both of which are classified as defined-contribution plans.

DEFINED-CONTRIBUTION PLANS

Defined-contribution plans are just what they sound like: a set contribution that is made every year. The contribution is defined as a percentage of the employee's annual compensation.

MONEY-PURCHASE PLAN

A money-purchase plan is a defined-contribution plan with a specific contribution formula. Unlike a profit-sharing plan, which is also a defined-contribution plan, contributions to a money-purchase plan must be made *each year, whether or not the employer has a profit.* The annual contribution is based on a stated percentage of the employee's compensation. The contribution can range from less than 1 percent to 25 percent of compensation if the money-purchase plan is used alone. The money-purchase plan can also be combined with a profit-sharing plan or a defined-benefit plan, as explained later in this chapter.

Example: The employer agrees to contribute 10 percent of each employee's compensation each year. The contributions and earnings thereon are accumulated until the employee retires or leaves the employer. The benefit that the employee will receive depends on the amount to his or her credit and whether or not the terminated participant has a vested interest. An employee is always fully vested at normal retirement age, and usually at death or retirement because of disability. The rate of vesting depends on provisions in the plan. (A more thorough discussion of vesting is found in Chapter 7, "Your Employees," and in Appendix C, the "Model Profit-Sharing Plan.")

PROFIT-SHARING PLAN

As its name implies, a profit-sharing plan is a defined-contribution plan in which contributions are made only in years in which the employer shows a profit. Contributions can range from less than 1 percent to 15 percent of compensation. Furthermore, there are unwritten IRS assumptions (which come to light if the employer's tax return is audited) that contributions not only be a percentage of the employee's compensation but also not exceed a certain percentage of the employer's profit. Thus, even though the employer has a profit for the year, contributions to an employee profit-sharing plan probably should not exceed 60 percent of the employer's profits. After all, the IRS doesn't want 80 or 90 percent of the employer's profits being eaten up by retirement-plan contributions; it wants some profits left over so the employer can pay income tax on them. Thus, in wording a Trust Agreement (sample shown in Appendix D) and an Adoption

Agreement (sample shown in Appendix E), to be discussed later in this chapter, the employer should construct limits on profit-sharing contributions first on the basis of the corporation's profits and second on the basis of the desired contribution as a percentage of compensation.

Example: The employer's Adoption Agreement could say: "So long as retirement-plan contributions are less than 60 percent of net profits, contributions to employee profit-sharing plans shall be made on the basis of 15 percent of compensation. If retirement-plan contributions are in excess of 60 percent of net profits, contributions to employee profit-sharing plans shall be reduced to 10 percent of compensation," or words to that effect. The simplest wording, with the greatest flexibility, is: "The employer shall contribute such amount to the profit-sharing plan as annually determined by its board of directors."

If the employer provides both a money-purchase plan and a profit-sharing plan, the maximum annual additions to an individual account cannot exceed the lesser of 25 percent of compensation or $30,000. Since the profit-sharing contribution maximum is 15 percent, most employers choose a combination of a 15 percent (remember: this is a flexible maximum, meaning 0 to 15 percent) profit-sharing plan and a 10 percent money-purchase plan.

If you are thinking of choosing defined-contribution plans, it pays to investigate the pros and cons of money-purchase and profit-sharing plans. If you choose the money-purchase plan for a maximum contribution of 25 percent, your corporation doesn't have to show a profit in order to be entitled to make that 25 percent contribution. In the first few years of a new corporation's existence, this may be an important advantage, since under a money-purchase plan it could make contributions that it could not make if it were bound by profit-sharing-plan regulations. The corporation would have to borrow the money to make the initial contributions, but both it and the employee would have the benefit of those contributions.

On the other hand, the set-percentage contribution (not a set amount because raises in employee salaries automatically increase the contributions) feature of the money-purchase plan is also a liability: as long as it remains in effect, the corporation is locked into a fixed liability. It must make contributions every year. There are no options under the money-purchase plan, and this plan's lack of flexibility can be quite detrimental to many corporations when management realizes that a fixed liability of what may run into thousands of dollars a year for many years has been created.

Profit-sharing plans offer the flexibility of determining contributions that money-purchase plans lack, but are limited to a maximum of 15 percent, compared to the money-purchase plan's maximum of 25 percent. Many corporate employers try to optimize the benefits of both plans by adopting profit-sharing plans that permit them to contribute 15 percent and 10 percent money-purchase plans for the total of 25 percent. In this way they can effectively choose contributions from a mandatory 10 percent to the full permitted 25 percent each year. And, of course, many corporations choose only the 15 percent profit-sharing plan option, rather than the combined 25 percent.

Generally speaking, the 25 percent money-purchase plan can be compared to the forced-saving element of Christmas Club bank accounts; the combined 10 percent money-purchase plan and 15 percent profit-sharing plan can be compared to an ordinary savings account, where the amount of money saved depends entirely upon the saver, with no element of coercion or penalty for not saving. If you feel that you are psychologically oriented to saving by yourself, the combined 10 percent money-purchase plan and 15 percent profit-sharing plan will offer you greater flexibility. If, however, you need a spur to put away retirement funds every year, the 25 percent money-purchase plan is probably better for you; otherwise, you might find that your corporation is putting away only the mandatory 10 percent in the money-purchase plan.

Setting up the profit-sharing plan is fairly easy. If the Model Profit-Sharing Plan shown in Appendix C suits your purposes, use it. It already has been approved by the IRS. You'll also need to file the new IRS Form 5307, Short Form Application for Determination for Employee Benefit Plan. Otherwise, your lawyer will have to draw up a profit-sharing plan and submit it to the IRS for approval. It's a good idea to draw up the plan and submit it shortly after you incorporate; the IRS has a very large backlog of plans to approve, stemming from corporations' necessity to rewrite plans to conform to ERISA, and you want IRS approval before your corporation files its taxes and makes its retirement-plan contribution the following April. You will need to have your lawyer draw up a money-purchase plan, which is somewhat more complicated.

Both Appendix D, the "Trust Agreement," and, in some cases, Appendix E, the "Adoption Agreement," are integral parts of Appendix C, the "Model Profit-Sharing Plan." The Model Profit-Sharing Plan sets the rules and regulations that bind your corporation; the Trust Agreement goes further in discussing the areas your corporation is empowered to invest in and the means by which investments will be made and funds administered; the Adoption Agreement, while usually used by mutual funds, can be used effectively by your corporation to nail down exactly which employees are covered, how contributions are calculated, how vesting is accomplished, and many other important details.

There is one refinement on the defined-contribution plan that was discussed in Chapter 7, "Your Employees": the defined-contribution plan that is integrated with Social Security contributions and is thus called the integrated defined-contribution plan.

INTEGRATED DEFINED-CONTRIBUTION PLAN

Under this type of defined-contribution plan, the employer can choose to cover employees earning amounts above the Social Security maximum ($45,000 in 1988). If this option is chosen, the employer pays only the Social Security tax for employees who are earning $45,000 or less and contributes 5.7 percent of salaries over $45,000 to the defined-contribution plan. The 5.7 percent figure is set by regulations issued by the Secretary of the Treasury. It is an actuarial value of the 7.5 percent the employer contributes for Social Security. As explained earlier, a base lower than the Social Security maximum (presently $45,000) may be chosen, but not a base higher than that figure.

The 5.7 percent contribution can be increased only if a percentage is contributed for the excluded taxable wage base.

Example: If a corporation's president earns $65,000 and employees who earn $45,000 or less are covered only by Social Security, the corporation can contribute $1,140 to the president's retirement account (5.7 percent $\times$ $20,000). If, however, the corporation contributes 3 percent to the retirement fund of employees earning $45,000 or less, then it can contribute $4,515 to the president's account (3 percent $\times$ $20,000 plus 8.7 percent $\times$ $45,000).

Thus, for each percent contributed for the amount below the

taxable wage base or any base below that which is chosen by the employer, the employer can add 1 percent to the 5.7 percent above the taxable wage base or the base that is chosen by the employer.

Be aware that these contribution rules may change for plan years beginning after December 31, 1988. Congress wants to limit the disparity between contribution percentages for higher- and lower-paid employees to 5 percent or less—it's now 5.7 percent. However, at press time, new legislation in the form of a Technical Corrections Act of 1988 had not yet been passed.

Now we get to the hard part: the defined-benefit plans.

DEFINED-BENEFIT PLANS

The benefits in these plans are usually stated as an annual amount. The amount could be (a) a percentage of compensation; (b) a fixed dollar amount; (c) a dollar amount per month times the number of years of service; or (d) an annual percentage of compensation multiplied by years of service.

When the benefit is a percentage of compensation, compensation is usually defined as the average of the highest 3 or 5 *consecutive* years of compensation multiplied by years of service.

Examples of types of defined-benefit plans:

a. percentage of compensation—If the highest average compensation during years of participation is $50,000, the annual benefit at normal retirement age (normally age 65) would be $15,000 per year if the percentage was 30 percent.

b. fixed dollar amount—$1,000 per month.

c. dollar amount per month times number of years of service—If the monthly figure is $10 per year of service, someone with 20 years of service would receive $200 per month; someone with 10 years of service would receive $100 per month.

d. annual percentage of compensation times years of service—If the plan provides 1 percent of compensation each year times years of service, for a participant who worked for 25 years at an average compensation of $50,000, his benefit would be 25 percent (1 percent × 25) of $50,000, for an annual benefit of $12,500.

The benefit in a defined-benefit plan is limited to the lesser of $94,023 in 1988, increased annually by a cost-of-living adjustment, or 100 percent of compensation based on a straight-life annuity. This limit is decreased for a benefit that is payable to an individual with less than 10 years of service at normal retirement age. A minimum benefit of $10,000 can be provided; it, too, is reduced for less than 10 years of service.

An employer can provide both a defined-benefit plan and a defined-contribution plan covering the same employees. In addition to the statutory limits of each plan, the prior combined limit of 1.4 (140 percent has been reduced by the Tax Equity and Fiscal Responsibility Act (TEFRA) to 1.0 (100 percent). However, the mechanical application of this reduction is tricky, and under certain circumstances, the effective rate may range up to 1.25 (125 percent). If you are interested in a defined-benefit plan, get more information from your accountant or tax lawyer.

Unlike the defined-contribution plans, where determining the contribution is as simple as calculating a percentage, the defined-benefit plans require the work of an actuary, since they are based on such individual factors as the participants' ages, the number of years to work before normal retirement age, and the retirement benefits desired. If your corporation chooses a defined-benefits plan through a bank or insurance company—usually in the form of an annuity—these institutions will prepare all the actuarial work and all the filing with the IRS. They usually have a master plan that has already been approved by the IRS and that your corporation can adopt simply by your signing your name as president of the corporation.

(Incidentally, in all these plans, if you are a one-person corporation, you can be plan administrator, trustee, and fiduciary. You needn't have any other person acting in any capacity in supervising the plan.)

401(K) PLANS

A 401(k) plan, also known as a "cash or deferred arrangement" (CODA), is a nonforfeitable, immediately vesting deferred-compensation plan set up as a qualified profit-sharing or stock-bonus plan. Under the 401(k) plan, participating employees elect to defer both the receipt and *taxation* of a portion of their compensation by having their employer pay it into a trust set up under the plan. The corporation can also match the employees' contributions by making a contribution of up to 25 percent of the employees' contributions.

These elective deferrals are subject to limitations. The maximum amount an employee can contribute to the plan in a tax year is $7,000, increased yearly by a cost-of-living adjustment. (The maximum contribution for 1988 is $7,313.) Be aware that this amount is included in the $30,000 defined-contribution limitations; if you choose to contribute $7,313 to a 401(k) plan, your corporation will be limited to a maximum defined contribution of $22,687.

Distributions from a 401(k) plan are generally prohibited until age 59½, although hardship withdrawals may be permitted in specified situations. Loans from the plan are permitted. There are some antidiscrimination rules and length-of-service restrictions, but they don't apply to one-person corporations and they are not onerous for small corporations to comply with.

Here's an example of how a 401(k) plan works. You plan to pay yourself a salary of $37,000 this year but would like to defer $7,000. This deferral is permitted because $7,000 is less than 25 percent of $37,000.

While your corporation is permitted to deduct $37,000 from your salary, it can deduct only $2,250 for your pension-fund contribution because your $7,000 401(k) contribution is counted as part of the $9,250 25 percent contribution your corporation could make. You will be paid a salary of $30,000 and will pay federal and local income taxes on that amount. (You do have to pay Social Security tax on the entire $37,000.) If you are a single New York City taxpayer, your deferral of $7,000 would save you a total of almost $3,500 in federal, state, and city income taxes in just one year.

Essentially, it's a trade-off. Without the 401(k) plan, you'd receive and pay income taxes on a salary of $37,000. However, your corporation would be able to take a deduction of $37,000 for your salary and $9,250 for your defined-contribution pension fund, for a total of $46,250. With the 401(k) plan, you'd receive and pay income taxes on a salary of $30,000, but your corporation would be permitted to take a deduction of only $39,250: $37,000 for your salary and $2,250 for your pension plan. Based on individual and corporate state and city income taxes, a 401(k) plan may be more or less attractive to you in terms of the tax savings it offers. Play with some spread sheets, then consult your tax adviser to determine whether a 401(k) plan would be profitable for you.

HOW AND WHAT TO INVEST IN

While most corporations wait until the end of the year or the following April to make contributions to their retirement funds, it's often better to make periodic contributions during the year to take advantage of more months of tax-preferred accumulation.

If you are a one-person or husband-and-wife corporation, your universe of investment choices is nearly boundless. Although the Tax Equity and Fiscal Responsibility Act has removed antiques, works of art, gemstones, jewelry, rare books, stamps, and coins from the list of permitted investments, your corporation can invest in stocks, bonds, mutual funds, and real estate—in fact, any investment that "a prudent man might reasonably make." Legally, this concept, which is called the prudent-man rule, governs most investments that are made on behalf of other people or institutions.

If your corporation includes outsiders, it would be wisest to stick to securities—stocks, bonds, and mutual funds. When retirement or other benefits have to be paid, it's much easier to sell shares of stock, bonds, or mutual funds than it is to figure out who owns what part of the real estate and to sell it quickly but profitably; or to try to divide a shopping center or to sell it, pay out the benefits, and reinvest the remainder in another shopping center.

Regardless of what investment vehicles are purchased, make sure that they are registered in the name of the corporation's retirement funds, as follows:

John Smith & Co., Inc. Retirement Fund—Profit-Sharing Plan
Jane Smith & Co., Inc. Retirement Fund—Money-Purchase Plan
Smith & Associates, Inc. Retirement Fund—Defined-Benefits Plan

If stocks and bonds are purchased, your corporation will probably have to furnish the brokerage house where it has an account with corporate resolutions appointing the brokerage house as its broker and with copies of whichever retirement plans are being used.

If a mutual fund is chosen, your corporation will have to furnish it with whatever documents it requires: usually copies of the retirement plans being used, a sample of which is shown in Appendix C, and a Trust Agreement, and an Adoption Agreement, samples of which are shown in Appendix D and Appendix E.

Do not feel that your corporation must stick to only one type of investment. If the Trust Agreement permits, your corporation can invest in a combination of stocks, bonds, mutual funds, and real estate, choosing according to market conditions—or according to whim, for that matter.

WHAT IF THE RETIREMENT PLANS HAVE PROFITS OR LOSSES?

In a defined-contribution plan, the gains and losses are divided among all the participants, based on the account balance of each participant as a ratio to the total of all participants' balances. Simply put, profits and losses are prorated according to the size of each participant's account.

In a defined-benefit plan, once again, the situation is a little more complicated. As explained earlier, the employer's contribution each year is based on actuarial calculations and includes an assumption that the fund will earn a stated percentage each year. If the fund does not earn the stated percentage, the employer's contribution will be greater the following year to bring it up to the required balance. Conversely, if the fund earns more than the stated percentage, the next annual employer contribution will be lower. This will assure that when an employee is ready to retire, there is enough in the fund to provide his or her benefits. To ensure that the employer will make its annual contribution, ERISA provides an excise tax penalty of 5 percent each year if the minimum funding standard is not met.

Before choosing any ERISA plan, discuss all the options with your lawyer and your accountant. These plans are very tricky, and an entire book could easily be written about any of the plans. This chapter is merely an overview. Get more information before you decide. But remember: if you decide to change your plan, you can. You don't have to be saddled with a bad choice. All it will take is the money to have another retirement plan drawn up and the time to have the IRS approve it.

11

But I Already Have a Keogh Plan!

If you have a Keogh plan at the time that you incorporate, you have three major choices: you can switch it to an ERISA account at the same institution (bank, insurance company, mutual fund); you can discontinue it and invest your ERISA funds elsewhere, in which case the Keogh plan is frozen until you retire, when you will collect from both the Keogh plan and your corporate retirement fund; or, under certain circumstances, you can transfer it.

If you choose the first option—a transfer to an ERISA account at the same institution—your paperwork will be minimal. Just write to the bank, insurance company, or mutual fund, notifying them of your incorporation and your desire to continue the investment program, but using the more generous contribution allowances permitted to corporations. Give the institution your new Employer Identification Number. You will be sent some forms to fill out to effect the transfer, and you will be told what to do.

If you choose the second option—discontinuing the Keogh and investing your ERISA funds elsewhere—just keep on collecting and filing the material you are sent by the Keogh plan institution every year. You will need it to calculate your tax liability on your pension when you retire. You would set up your corporate pension and profit-sharing plans as shown in Chapter 10, "All about ERISA," just as though you had never had a Keogh plan.

The last option—transferring your Keogh plan—is the most complicated, but by no means impossible. The Internal Revenue Code permits you to roll over an existing Keogh plan to a corporate pension and profit-sharing plan.*

If you are transferring from one mutual fund to another, there are a number of steps to take involving the old Keogh plan mutual fund and the new ERISA mutual fund. First, you will want to get credit for your final contribution to the Keogh plan in your last year as sole proprietor. Accordingly, when you file your income tax return, you would send your Keogh contribution to the custodian bank and deduct the contribution on IRS Form 5500–K.

Then, at some point during your first corporate year, but as soon as possible, you would apply to the new mutual fund you had chosen, either directly or through its custodian bank, and file the necessary forms to set up an ERISA plan with the fund. You would probably send a token check of $100 or $500 just to start the plan; the balance, of course, would be contributed in April of the following year or whenever the corporation's tax returns were filed. Having established an ERISA plan with a new mutual fund, you could then write to the Keogh custodian bank and the ERISA custodian bank to effect the transfer, using the following letters or similar wording:

ABC Bank as Custodian for
  DEF Mutual Fund
Address
To whom it may concern:
    Please transfer the funds in my DEF mutual fund Keogh plan account *directly* to GHI Bank as custodian for my ERISA account with the JKL mutual fund. My ERISA account number is _____.

                                        Very truly yours,

cc: GHI Bank as Custodian
    for JKL Mutual Fund

Strategy: If you have chosen a defined-benefit plan and have enough money to fund it, you will get bigger tax deductions and retire with more money if you freeze your old Keogh plan and start from zero with your new corporate defined-benefit plan, rather than rolling over your Keogh plan.

GHI Bank as Custodian for
  JKL Mutual Fund
Address
To whom it may concern:

  Please accept, as custodian of the JKL mutual fund, the funds being transferred from ABC Bank as custodian of my Keogh plan account with the DEF mutual fund and use the funds to immediately purchase shares of the JKL mutual fund for my ERISA account number _____.

Very truly yours,

cc: ABC Bank as Custodian
    for DEF Mutual Fund

  In this way, when your Keogh custodian bank liquidates your mutual fund, rather than sending you a check for the proceeds that you would then send to the ERISA custodian bank to purchase new shares for your ERISA account, it sends a check directly to your new custodian bank.

  These details may sound very picky, but they're extremely important. At all costs, you must avoid what the IRS calls "constructive use" of the funds, which would invalidate your Keogh plan and subject you to taxes and penalties. In fact, if you should receive the liquidating check from the Keogh custodian bank by mistake, *do not endorse it.* This would be constructive use. Don't even think of endorsing it and sending the new ERISA custodian bank your own corporate check. The safest procedure is to return the check to the Keogh custodian bank with another letter explaining what happened and what you want the bank to do.

  Let's take a slightly more complicated case: transferring your Keogh plan funds to a brokerage house so that you can buy your own securities for your corporate retirement fund. First, of course, you would need a trust agreement that had been approved by the IRS; the one shown in Appendix D, designed to permit all prudent-man investments (stocks, bonds, mutual funds, real estate, etc.), might be suitable.

  With the IRS approval, you would open a brokerage account for your corporate retirement fund; this would be a completely separate account from your corporate account, if any. Then you would write to the Keogh custodian bank and to your brokerage house to effect the transfer of your Keogh funds, using the following letters or similar wording:

ABC Bank as Custodian for
  DEF Mutual Fund
Address
To whom it may concern:
    Please transfer the funds in my DEF mutual fund Keogh plan account *directly* to GHI brokerage house to be deposited to the (name of your corporation) Retirement Fund. The account number is _____.

Very truly yours,

cc: GHI Brokerage House

GHI Brokerage House
Address
To whom it may concern:
    Please accept the funds being transferred from ABC Bank as custodian of my Keogh plan account and deposit them in the (name of your corporation) Retirement Fund. The account number is _____.

Very truly yours,

cc: ABC Bank as Custodian
    for DEF Mutual Fund

Again, as in the previous case, under no circumstances should the liquidating check from the Keogh custodian bank come to you; if it should, return it. It's easier than trying to explain to the IRS that even though the check was sent to you, you didn't really have constructive use of the funds.

12

Fabulous
ESOP

For many corporations, an ESOP (Employees' Stock Ownership Plan) is an even better choice than the other ERISA profit-sharing plans discussed in Chapter 10, "All about ERISA." As a profit-sharing plan, of course, it can be combined with either a money-purchase plan or a defined-benefits plan, if desired. Although this plan, created by Louis Kelso, a California lawyer, is used most frequently by large corporations whose stock is traded publicly and has actual value, an ESOP can benefit a one-person corporation. Its use has been approved by the Los Angeles division of the IRS, and many major accounting firms are recommending ESOPs for their one-person general business and professional corporations.

The beauty of an ESOP is that your corporation generates tax deductions at the corporate level *without its having to contribute any actual money to the plan.* It's all playing games with paper, in a sense—a one-person-corporation ESOP is designed for people who really aren't concerned with retirement benefits . . . because there are no *direct* benefits under the plan.

An ESOP is just a way of generating legitimate "cashless" deductions at the corporate level, not of really providing retirement benefits. Hopefully, your retirement benefits will be funded by your 10 percent money-purchase contribution or your defined-benefit contribution, by the corporation's accumulated profits, and by all the cumulative tax savings of having a cashless deduction. Your corporation might have accumulated a write-off of $100,000 over a period of 20 years. In a sense, the tax savings that your corporation is realizing fund your retirement benefit because you would be entitled to all the assets of your corporation at liquidation, and the assets would be increased by all your tax savings on money you never even had to contribute.

HOW AN ESOP WORKS

That's the philosophy behind ESOPs. Now let's see how an ESOP actually works in a one-person corporation.

With an ESOP, your corporation would continually contribute its own stock to the ESOP and receive tax deductions for the value of the stock without making any cash expenditure for it. The stock would be beneficially owned by the sole stockholder, so both before and after the contributions began, the stockholder would own 100 percent of the stock. The net effect would be that the corporation would be getting tax deductions without really dispersing the ownership of its stock at all or spending any money.

Let's say that our stockholder has 100 shares—all the issued and outstanding shares of the corporation. The first step would be a corporate resolution authorizing the corporation to issue 400 additional shares, for a total of 500 shares (authorized but unissued). In conjunction with this, let's say that our stockholder is earning a salary of $20,000. Since the ESOP belongs to the broad category of profit-sharing plans, the corporation can deduct up to 15 percent of his or her compensation ($3,000). The corporation can then contribute stock equal to $3,000.

But how does this stock acquire value? *This has nothing to do with either par value, discussed in Chapter 2, or basis value, discussed in Chapter 5.* In effect, the corporation can assign the ESOP stock a reasonable value based on its net worth and then give the stock to the sole stockholder. In the case of donating $3,000 of stock, let's say each share of stock has a value of $100. Then the stockholder would donate 30 shares to the ESOP, but of course he would still be the beneficial owner and control 100 percent of the stock. If, after a number of years, he had issued all the authorized stock (all the 400 shares), he would simply make another corporate resolution (amending the Certificate of Incorporation, if necessary in his state), authorizing and issuing more stock.

This is how the arithmetic looks:

If the corporate gross income is	$40,000	
	−20,000	salary
	$20,000	
	−3,000	ESOP contribution
	$17,000	
	−2,000	money-purchase contribution
	$15,000	corporate net
	−2,250	federal taxes
	$12,750	net corporate profit

And so it would go each year, the ESOP contribution and the money-purchase or defined-benefit contribution increasing only when the stockholder's salary was increased.

WHAT HAPPENS AT RETIREMENT?

At retirement, the value of the stock that is distributed to the stockholder as beneficiary of the ESOP will be taxable. If you choose an ESOP, you will have to get a lump-sum distribution for more favorable tax treatment (discussed thoroughly in Chapter 15, "Retire with the Biggest Tax Break Possible"). But for all this time, your corporation has not paid tax on the "paper" contributions to the ESOP, so you have had use of these funds at the corporate level for all these years.

An ESOP is often preferable to other profit-sharing plans because the corporation can take a deduction without spending any of its money. In other profit-sharing plans, the corporation actually would have to pay the $3,000 in cash to a trustee, who would then invest it. With an ESOP the $3,000 is just written off on the books, and in this case, the $450 saved in taxes (15 percent × $3,000) remains in the corporation.

The advantages of an ESOP are even greater as your corporation becomes more profitable and its tax bracket increases. If you're entitled to contribute $15,000 worth of stock and your corporation is in the 34 percent bracket, the corporation is saving $5,100 in taxes each year without having to make any $15,000 contribution. The $5,100 saved in taxes each year would compound to over $200,000 in corporate assets at the end of 20 years and would be an asset of the corporation, translating into a higher liquidating value when you liquidated the corporation. And remember that all this time, the corporation hasn't spent a penny—it's just issued paper to a trust, of which you are the trustee.

PRESENT TAX STATUS OF ESOPS

As mentioned earlier, ESOPs have been approved by the Los Angeles division of the IRS. There hasn't been any litigation on ESOPs yet, but the intent of Congress is to encourage ESOPs, so the legislative climate is favorable. You may be gambling on future legislation's closing up ESOPs for one-person corporations, but so far the Senate Finance Committee is behind the ESOP program and doesn't seem likely to move to close up the loopholes.

To set up an ESOP, you or your accountant must apply to the IRS for an Application for a Determination Letter; this is a standard form that is self-explanatory. In a one-person corporation, the form is really a formality.

If you think the ESOP is the profit-sharing plan for you, consult your lawyer or accountant and get an opinion. As with so many other one-person corporations, an ESOP may be fabulous for you, too.

13

Investing Your Corporate Surplus

Let's hope you're running a successful business or you're a successful professional. After contributing to corporate pension and profit-sharing plans and paying taxes, your corporation still has a surplus. Despite the great stock-market meltdown of October 1987, you should be able to invest that surplus profitably. Investing in common and preferred stocks, whose dividends paid to your corporation are 70 percent tax-free, is a major benefit of forming a general business (C) corporation.

For the most part, investing your corporate surplus (after-tax profits) depends on the following variables:

1. how aggressive an investor you are;
2. the length of time before your retirement;
3. how much money you can invest each year.

The first two factors are closely interrelated; if you are 30 years old and plan to retire in 35 years, you can afford to assume more risks than if you are 50 and plan to retire in 10 years.

But this is the classic textbook approach to investment planning. In real life there are supercautious 23-year-olds and crapshooting 53-year-olds. While bearing the classic investment strategies in mind, always take only the amount of risk you feel comfortable with.

Perhaps the most important variable—in terms of its limiting your choices—is the last one: how much money you can invest every year.

This amount will determine what kind of professional investment management help you can expect. After all, if you can invest $10,000 a year, your choices are much wider than if you can invest $1,000 a year.

Up until the time that your corporate portfolio reaches $25,000 to $50,000, it's virtually impossible to get any kind of professional management for your investments. About the best you can do is buy a mutual fund (preferably a no-load fund with a good track record); choose a good broker with excellent research capabilities; or subscribe to one or more investment services, do your own research, and have your orders executed by a discount broker so that you save on commissions.

At $25,000 to $50,000, some banks will manage your portfolio on a pooled-trust basis, combining your portfolio with those of other investors with the same investment goals and creating, in effect, a mini-mutual fund. The fees for this service vary, but generally run about 1 to 2 percent per year—tax deductible, of course. When your portfolio reaches anywhere from $100,000 to $200,000, many banks will manage your portfolio as a separate portfolio.

When your corporation does get big enough for a bank to handle its investment, there is one major advantage—apart from professional investment advice—that a bank can offer. As an institution (as banks are known in the investment community), a bank has access to the negotiated commission market because its trading volume is so much greater than any individual's. These commissions can range from about 20 percent to about 50 percent of individual commissions, or a discount of from 50 percent to 80 percent. If your corporation invests or trades heavily, this may be an important consideration for you.

In order to get the best executions of orders for its clients, a bank will often use different brokers for different orders or will use what is called the "fourth market" (trading between the institutions themselves, as opposed to trading on the stock exchanges). This "shopping around" is aimed at getting both the best prices and the smallest commissions.

Banks do offer economies of size. The question you must answer for yourself is: are the bank's fees worth the savings in executions and commissions?

Without exception, all the professional investment analysts and money managers I interviewed emphasized the necessity of common stocks in a corporate portfolio. Not only are their dividends 70 percent tax-free at the corporate level, but also they are one of the most powerful hedges against long-term inflationary pressures. Even at the present low inflationary levels of economic recovery, the rate of inflation is still higher than the interest rate of AA-rated bonds, after taxes; and no one can predict long-term trends, except that inflation at one level or another is certain to be with us. Common stocks can help protect the investor against that inflation and erosion of his or her purchasing power. Over a period of years, common stocks have outperformed bonds and other money-market instruments (e.g., commercial paper) and preferred stocks. And dividends on stocks owned by your corporation are 70 percent tax-free, whereas interest on bonds is fully taxed.

Another advantage of common stocks over bonds is less obvious, but by no means less real. The stock market is far more liquid than the bond market: stocks are traded more frequently and in smaller quantities than bonds, so a buy order for 100 shares—or even less—is less likely to raise the price you pay, and a sell order for 100 shares or less is less likely to lower the price you receive. In contrast, the bond market deals with much greater numbers and dollar amounts: an "average" order is usually for 25 or 50 bonds ($25,000 or $50,000 face value). Orders from smaller investors for 1, 5, or 10 bonds are penalized at both ends: they pay more for the bonds when they buy them and receive less for the bonds when they sell them. Small orders tend to have a disproportionately large effect on bond prices, both up and down, but always to the disadvantage of the small investor.

Preferred stocks are a hybrid, but in this respect they seem more like bonds: their liquidity is very limited, and they offer no protection against inflation. All they do offer, like common stocks, is the 70 percent dividend exclusion.

The stocks shown in the portfolio that follows are not to be construed as being recommendations; they are merely high-quality, high-yielding stocks suitable for corporate investment. The preferred stocks are at least BBB+-rated by Standard & Poor's Corporation; the common stocks are characterized by low P/E (price/earnings) ratio and good to high yield, combined with moderate growth.

REPRESENTATIVE CORPORATE PORTFOLIO

Standard & Poor's Rating	Preferred Stocks	Price 7/28/88	Dividend	Yield	Income from 100 Shares
A−	Alabama Power	94	$9.44	10.04%	$ 944
BBB+	Boston Edison 8.88% cum. pfd.	85	8.88	10.45	888
A	Public Service Electric & Gas $7.40 pfd.	74	7.40	10.00	740
					$2,572
	Common Stocks				
A−	Detroit Edison	14	1.68	12.00	168
A−	Eastern Utilities	24⅝	2.40	9.75	240
B+	Public Service of Colorado	21⅝	2.00	9.24	200
A+	Texas Utilities	28	2.80	10.00	280
					$ 888
					$3,460

The purpose of such a high-yield portfolio is the compounding of dividends, 70 percent of which are totally excluded from taxes, and 30 percent of which are taxed at 15 percent if net corporate income is less than $50,000, 25 percent if net corporate income is between $50,000 and $75,000, and 34 percent if net corporate income is greater than $75,000.

The table below shows the actual percentage that is taxed and the percentage of dividend income that your corporation retains:

Net Corporate Income	Tax Bracket	Percentage of Dividend Taxed	Effective Tax Rate	Percentage of Dividend Retained
Under $50,000	15%	30%	4.5%	95.5%
$50,000–$75,000	25	30	7.5	92.5
Over $75,000	34	30	10.2	89.8

Even at the highest corporate tax brackets, dividends received by your corporation are more than 89 percent tax-free!

To illustrate this point, let's assume a portfolio consisting of 100 shares of each security. The annual income from the portfolio would be $3,460.

If the owner of the portfolio was a sole proprietor in the 33 percent bracket, he would have to pay $1,142 in taxes on his dividend income, and could keep only $2,318.

Dividend income	$3,460
Tax rate	×.33
Tax	$1,142
Net dividend income	$2,318

However, if his corporation owned the portfolio, the taxes are *eleven times* lower if his corporation is in the 15 percent bracket and *more than six times lower* if his corporation is in the 25 percent bracket.

	Assuming 15 Percent Bracket Net Corp. Taxable Income Under $50M	Assuming 25 Percent Bracket Net Corp. Taxable Income $50M–$75M
Dividend Income	$3,460	$3,460
Less 70 percent exclusion	2,422	2,422
	$1,038	$1,038
Tax rate	×.15	×.25
Tax	$ 156	$ 260
Net dividend income	$3,304	$3,200
Amount saved from individual tax	$ 986	$ 882
Percent saved from individual tax	86%*	77%*

*In 1986 these percentages were 94 percent and 93 percent, respectively. These percentages are slightly lower because the dividend-exclusion percentage was reduced from 85 percent in 1986 to 70 percent in 1988. These percentages are especially impressive because they are compared with individual tax rates that were reduced by the Tax Reform Act of 1986.

Furthermore, if we project this unchanged portfolio for five or ten years, it is easy to see how the more than $750 saved each year on the corporate stock portfolio alone can compound itself to more than $5,000 or $10,000. And if we go further and conceive of this portfolio as a unit, with an additional unit purchased each year, so that at the end of five years there are 500 shares each and at the end of ten years there are 1,000 shares each, the savings are truly staggering.

The only thing we would have to worry about is that the portfolio income would not exceed 60 percent of total corporate income in any year, so that the corporation would not be construed by the IRS as a personal holding corporation, as discussed more fully in Chapter 1 and Chapter 6.

HOW AND WHEN YOUR CORPORATION DECLARES DIVIDENDS

So far we've talked about your corporation's *receiving* dividends from other corporations: dividends that are 70 percent tax-free. But what about your corporation's *paying* dividends to its stockholder(s)? In general, of course, you want to keep dividend income from common and preferred stocks in the corporation; if you draw the dividends out for your own use, you will be taxed on them. Furthermore, they won't be able to accumulate at minimal tax rates.

You may be much better off taking the money as a raise in salary or as a special year-end bonus. The raise or bonus may enable your corporation to contribute more to your pension fund, and the amount of the raise or bonus will be taxed only once (to you) rather than twice (to your corporation and to you), as dividends are taxed.

However, there are always times or special occasions that may warrant taking money out of the corporation, and this necessitates the corporation's declaring a dividend to the stockholders. A meeting of the board of directors of the corporation is called, and someone proposes that a dividend of X dollars per share be paid on a certain date to all stockholders who owned stock on a certain earlier date. The proposal is turned into a motion and voted on. When it is approved, as it is certain to be, it is recorded as Minutes of a Special Meeting of the Board of Directors and entered into the corporation's minute book. Then, on the payment date, the corporation gives or sends the dividend checks to its stockholders. Dividends do not have to be paid on a regular basis; it is thus wiser to declare each dividend as a special dividend.

TREATMENT OF CAPITAL GAINS

Up to now, I've emphasized dividends because dividend payments to corporations are 70 percent tax-free. Bond interest is taxed as though it were ordinary income: at 15 percent, 25 percent, or up to 34 percent, depending upon your corporation's tax bracket. Capital gains on the sale of securities your corporation owns are also taxed as though they were ordinary income: at 15 percent, 25 percent, or up to 34 percent. There is no longer any distinction between long-term and short-term capital gains, although there is congressional pressure to restore favorable treatment for long-term gains.

OTHER CORPORATE INVESTMENTS

Your corporation can make other investments besides stocks, bonds, mutual funds, and other securities. It can invest in real estate, antiques, art, gemstones or jewelry, or, in fact, anything of value that is tangible and not likely to depreciate in value. Your investment universe consists of anything and everything that would be selected by "a prudent man." (A company car would be a corporate possession, but would not be considered a prudent corporate investment because of its depreciability. A 1936 Rolls-Royce, however, would certainly qualify as an investment.)

If you are more comfortable with English furniture or Ming porcelain, nineteenth-century photographs or Old Master drawings, Lalique or Fabergé jewelry or just plain old diamonds or emeralds, set or unset, feel free to invest in them. Just make sure that you are paying for them with a corporate check and that they are insured in the name of the corporation. Antiques and art that are owned by the corporation must stay clearly on corporate territory: they may be displayed in your office, but not in your home. However, if your office is in your home, you do have more leeway about where to place them.

SUMMING UP

This chapter, like the rest of this book, has been written primarily for the one-person or husband-and-wife corporation. If you are part of a larger, nonfamily corporation, think carefully about investing in the more unusual corporate investments. They will be harder to liquidate, and this may generate problems. They will certainly be less divisible than stocks, bonds, or mutual fund shares, and they will surely be more difficult to value.

14

Putting It All Together

It's often said that one picture is worth 10,000 words. Let's look, then, at three pictures. Following are tax returns for three businesses at three different income levels, both as corporations and as sole proprietorships. To simplify matters, the individuals are assumed to be single and will take what amounts to the standard deduction, now included in the tax tables. Otherwise, at their income levels, they would lose most or all of their medical deduction.

First, there is George Gordon, a real estate broker whose earnings are $45,000 a year, with dividend income of $6,000 and medical expenses of $2,000. George prefers to retain as much corporate income as possible, so his corporation pays him a salary of $16,000 a year. His corporate return and his employee tax return, followed by his tax return as a sole proprietor, are shown on pages 127–37.

By accepting the low salary, George saves over 54 percent in taxes: $13,305 as a sole proprietor versus a total of $6,160; $3,652 in corporate taxes and $2,508 in employee income taxes.

Geoffrey Fourmyle, a technical writer, has chosen a higher salary of $26,000, although his gross income is also $45,000 and his dividends are also $6,000. His medical expenses are $4,000. By taking the higher salary, however, he cuts his tax saving to 42 percent: $12,206 as a sole proprietor versus a total of $7,134; $1,994 in corporate taxes and $5,140 in employee income taxes. He is sheltering less of his income at the preferential corporate rate; thus, his tax savings are smaller. See pages 138–48 for his tax returns.

Last, there is Tiffany Field, a successful designer who earned $100,000 last year and had dividend income of $10,000 and medical expenses of $6,000. By taking a salary of $40,000, she cuts her total tax bill from a maximum tax of $30,290 as a sole proprietor to $16,491, for a saving of $13,799 in just one year. If Tiffany took a higher salary, her corporate contribution would continue to rise; at $50,000, her corporation could contribute $12,500. However, she would be sheltering less income at low corporate rates. In this return, take special notice of the $10,000 dividend income. Tiffany's corporation was able to shelter $8,000 of it (see line 29(b) page 149), and was taxed on $2,000, for a tax liability of only $300. (In 1988 she can shelter $7,000 and will be taxed on $3,000, for a tax liability of only $450. If Tiffany owned the stock herself, she would be taxed on the full $10,000, for a tax liability of approximately $3,300, eleven times greater than the corporate tax in 1987. For her tax returns, see pages 149–59.

Let's summarize the tax savings of incorporation shown on the sample returns this way:

Name	Corporate Income Taxes*	Employee Income Taxes	Employee SS Taxes	Total	Sole Proprietor Tax	Amount Saved	Percent Saved
Gordon	$3,652	$1,364	$1,144	$6,160	$13,305	$7,145	54%
Fourmyle	1,994	3,281	1,859	7,134	12,206	5,072	42
Field	6,141	8,305	2,045	16,491	30,290	13,799	46

*Includes real cost to corporation of Social Security tax.

Form **1120**	**U.S. Corporation Income Tax Return**	OMB No. 1545-0123
Department of the Treasury Internal Revenue Service	For calendar 1987 or tax year beginning .... , 1987, ending .... , 19 .... ▶ For Paperwork Reduction Act Notice, see page 1 of the instructions.	**1987**

Check if a—		Use IRS label. Other-wise please print or type.	Name **GEORGE GORDON + Co., Inc.**	**D** Employer identification number **00-0000000**
A Consolidated return ☐			Number and street **350 FIFTH AVENUE**	**E** Date incorporated **1/1/81**
B Personal Holding Co. ☐			City or town, state, and ZIP code **NEW YORK, NY 10118**	**F** Total assets (See Specific Instructions.)
C Business Code No. (See the list in the instructions.) **5777**				Dollars **100,248** Cents

G Check applicable boxes: (1) ☐ Initial return (2) ☐ Final return (3) ☐ Change in address

Income				
	1a Gross receipts or sales .... **b** Less returns and allowances .... Balance ▶		**1c**	
	2 Cost of goods sold and/or operations (Schedule A)		**2**	
	3 Gross profit (line 1c less line 2)		**3**	
	4 Dividends (Schedule C)		**4**	6,000
	5 Interest		**5**	
	6 Gross rents		**6**	
	7 Gross royalties		**7**	
	8 Capital gain net income (attach separate Schedule D)		**8**	
	9 Net gain or (loss) from Form 4797, line 18, Part II (attach Form 4797)		**9**	
	10 Other income (see instructions—attach schedule)		**10**	45,000
	11 TOTAL income—Add lines 3 through 10 and enter here ▶		**11**	51,000

Deductions (See Instructions for limitations on deductions)				
	12 Compensation of officers (Schedule E)		**12**	16,000
	13a Salaries and wages .... **b** Less jobs credit .... Balance ▶		**13c**	
	14 Repairs		**14**	
	15 Bad debts (see instructions)		**15**	
	16 Rents		**16**	3,000
	17 Taxes **Soc. Sec.**		**17**	1,144
	18 Interest		**18**	
	19 Contributions (see instructions for 10% limitation)		**19**	
	20 Depreciation (attach Form 4562)	**20** 1,000		
	21 Less depreciation claimed in Schedule A and elsewhere on return	**21a** 0	**21b**	1,000
	22 Depletion		**22**	
	23 Advertising		**23**	
	24 Pension, profit-sharing, etc., plans		**24**	4,000
	25 Employee benefit programs **MEDICAL**		**25**	2,000
	26 Other deductions (attach schedule) **PHONES + POSTAGE**		**26**	1,191
	27 TOTAL deductions—Add lines 12 through 26 and enter here ▶		**27**	28,335
	28 Taxable income before net operating loss deduction and special deductions (line 11 less line 27)		**28**	22,665
	29 Less: **a** Net operating loss deduction (see instructions)	**29a**		
	b Special deductions (Schedule C)	**29b** 4,800	**29c**	4,800
	30 Taxable income (line 28 less line 29c)		**30**	17,865
	31 TOTAL TAX (Schedule J)		**31**	2,680

Tax and Payments				
	32 Payments: **a** 1986 overpayment credited to 1987			
	b 1987 estimated tax payments	2,400		
	c Less 1987 refund applied for on Form 4466	( )		
	d Tax deposited with Form 7004			
	e Credit from regulated investment companies (attach Form 2439)			
	f Credit for Federal tax on gasoline and special fuels (attach Form 4136)		**32**	2,400
	33 Enter any PENALTY for underpayment of estimated tax—check ▶ ☐ if Form 2220 is attached		**33**	
	34 TAX DUE—If the total of lines 31 and 33 is larger than line 32, enter AMOUNT OWED		**34**	280
	35 OVERPAYMENT—If line 32 is larger than the total of lines 31 and 33, enter AMOUNT OVERPAID		**35**	
	36 Enter amount of line 35 you want: Credited to 1988 estimated tax ▶ Refunded ▶		**36**	

Please Sign Here	Under penalties of perjury, I declare that I have examined this return, including accompanying schedules and statements, and to the best of my knowledge and belief, it is true, correct, and complete. Declaration of preparer (other than taxpayer) is based on all information of which preparer has any knowledge.		
	▶ Signature of officer	3/15/88 Date	▶ PRESIDENT Title

Paid Preparer's Use Only	Preparer's signature ▶	Date	Check if self-employed ☐	Preparer's social security number
	Firm's name (or yours, if self-employed) and address ▶		E.I. No. ▶ ZIP code ▶	

Schedule A   Cost of Goods Sold and/or Operations (See instructions for line 2, page 1.)

1 Inventory at beginning of year		**1**	
2 Purchases		**2**	
3 Cost of labor		**3**	
4a Additional section 263A costs (see instructions)		**4a**	
b Other costs (attach schedule)		**4b**	
5 Total—Add lines 1 through 4b		**5**	
6 Inventory at end of year		**6**	
7 Cost of goods sold and/or operations—Line 5 less line 6. Enter here and on line 2, page 1		**7**	

8a Check all methods used for valuing closing inventory:

    (i) ☐ Cost   (ii) ☐ Lower of cost or market as described in Regulations section 1.471-4 (see instructions)

    (iii) ☐ Writedown of "subnormal" goods as described in Regulations section 1.471-2(c) (see instructions)

    (iv) ☐ Other (Specify method used and attach explanation.) ▶

   b Check if the LIFO inventory method was adopted this tax year for any goods (if checked, attach Form 970) . . . . . ☐

   c If the LIFO inventory method was used for this tax year, enter percentage (or amounts) of closing inventory computed under LIFO   **8c**

   d Do the rules of section 263A (with respect to property produced or acquired for resale) apply to the corporation? . . ☐ Yes ☐ No

   e Was there any change (other than for section 263A purposes) in determining quantities, cost, or valuations between opening and closing inventory? If "Yes," attach explanation . . . . ☐ Yes ☐ No

Schedule C   Dividends and Special Deductions (See Schedule C instructions.)

	(a) Dividends received	(b) %	(c) Special deductions: multiply (a) x (b)
1 Domestic corporations subject to section 243(a) deduction (other than debt-financed stock)	6,000	see instructions	4,800
2 Debt-financed stock of domestic and foreign corporations (section 246A)		see instructions	
3 Certain preferred stock of public utilities		see instructions	
4 Foreign corporations and certain FSCs subject to section 245 deduction		see instructions	
5 Wholly owned foreign subsidiaries and FSCs subject to 100% deduction (sections 245(b) and (c))		100	
6 Total—Add lines 1 through 5. See instructions for limitation			
7 Affiliated groups subject to the 100% deduction (section 243(a)(3))		100	
8 Other dividends from foreign corporations not included in lines 4 and 5			
9 Income from controlled foreign corporations under subpart F (attach Forms 5471)			
10 Foreign dividend gross-up (section 78)			
11 IC-DISC or former DISC dividends not included in lines 1 and/or 2 (section 246(d))			
12 Other dividends			
13 Deduction for dividends paid on certain preferred stock of public utilities (see instructions)			
14 Total dividends—Add lines 1 through 12. Enter here and on line 4, page 1 ▶	6,000		
15 Total deductions—Add lines 6, 7, and 13. Enter here and on line 29b, page 1 . . . . . . ▶			4,800

Schedule E   Compensation of Officers (See instructions for line 12, page 1.)

Complete Schedule E only if total receipts (line 1a, plus lines 4 through 10, of page 1, Form 1120) are $150,000 or more.

(a) Name of officer	(b) Social security number	(c) Percent of time devoted to business	Percent of corporation stock owned		(f) Amount of compensation
			(d) Common	(e) Preferred	
		%	%	%	
		%	%	%	
		%	%	%	
		%	%	%	
		%	%	%	
		%	%	%	
		%	%	%	
Total compensation of officers—Enter here and on line 12, page 1.					

Schedule J	**Tax Computation** (See instructions.)

1 Check if you are a member of a controlled group (see sections 1561 and 1563) . . . . ▶ ☐

2 If line 1 is checked, see instructions. If your tax year includes June 30, 1987, complete both a and b below.
   Otherwise, complete only b.

a (i) $ .... (ii) $ .... (iii) $ .... (iv) $ ....

b (i) $ .... (ii) $ ....

3	Income tax (see instructions to figure the tax; enter this tax or alternative tax from Schedule D, whichever is less). Check if from Schedule D ▶ ☐	**3**	2,680
4a	Foreign tax credit (attach Form 1118)	**4a**	
b	Possessions tax credit (attach Form 5735) . . .	**b**	
c	Orphan drug credit (attach Form 6765)	**c**	
d	Credit for fuel produced from a nonconventional source (see instructions)	**d**	
e	General business credit. Enter here and check which forms are attached ☐ Form 3800 ☐ Form 3468 ☐ Form 5884 ☐ Form 6478 ☐ Form 6765 ☐ Form 8586 .	**e**	
5	Total—Add lines 4a through 4e	**5**	0
6	Line 3 less line 5	**6**	2,680
7	Personal holding company tax (attach Schedule PH (Form 1120)) . .	**7**	0
8	Tax from recomputing prior-year investment credit (attach Form 4255) .	**8**	0
9a	Alternative minimum tax (see instructions—attach Form 4626) . .	**9a**	0
b	Environmental tax (see instructions—attach Form 4626) . . .	**9b**	0
10	Total tax—Add lines 6 through 9b. Enter here and on line 31, page 1	**10**	2,680

Additional Information (See instruction F.)

		Yes	No
H	Did the corporation claim a deduction for expenses connected with:		
(1)	An entertainment facility (boat, resort, ranch, etc.)? . . .		✓
(2)	Living accommodations (except employees on business)? . .		✓
(3)	Employees attending conventions or meetings outside the North American area? (See section 274(h).)		✓
(4)	Employees' families at conventions or meetings? . . .		✓
	If "Yes," were any of these conventions or meetings outside the North American area? (See section 274(h).)		
(5)	Employee or family vacations not reported on Form W-2? .		✓
I (1)	Did the corporation at the end of the tax year own, directly or indirectly, 50% or more of the voting stock of a domestic corporation? (For rules of attribution, see section 267(c).) . .		✓
	If "Yes," attach a schedule showing: (a) name, address, and identifying number; (b) percentage owned; (c) taxable income or (loss) before NOL and special deductions of such corporation for the tax year ending with or within your tax year; (d) highest amount owed by the corporation to such corporation during the year; and (e) highest amount owed to the corporation by such corporation during the year.		
(2)	Did any individual, partnership, corporation, estate, or trust at the end of the tax year own, directly or indirectly, 50% or more of the corporation's voting stock? (For rules of attribution, see section 267(c).) If "Yes," complete (a) through (d) . . .	✓	
(a)	Attach a schedule showing name, address and identifying number. Enter percentage owned ▶ 100 %		
(b)	Was the owner of such voting stock a person other than a U.S. person? (See instructions.) **Note:** If "Yes," the corporation may have to file Form 5472.		✓
	If "Yes," enter owner's country ▶		
(c)	Enter highest amount owed by the corporation to such owner during the year ▶		
(d)	Enter highest amount owed to the corporation by such owner during the year ▶		
	Note: For purposes of I(1) and I(2), "highest amount owed" includes loans and accounts receivable/payable.		

		Yes	No
J	Refer to the list in the instructions and state the principal:		
	Business activity ▶ REAL ESTATE		
	Product or service ▶ SALES		
K	Was the corporation a U.S. shareholder of any controlled foreign corporation? (See sections 951 and 957.)		✓
	If "Yes," attach Form 5471 for each such corporation.		
L	At any time during the tax year, did the corporation have an interest in or a signature or other authority over a financial account in a foreign country (such as a bank account, securities account, or other financial account)?		✓
	(See instruction F and filing requirements for form TD F 90-22.1.)		
	If "Yes," enter name of foreign country ▶		
M	Was the corporation the grantor of, or transferor to, a foreign trust which existed during the current tax year, whether or not the corporation has any beneficial interest in it?		✓
	If "Yes," the corporation may have to file Forms 3520, 3520-A, or 926.		
N	During this tax year, did the corporation pay dividends (other than stock dividends and distributions in exchange for stock) in excess of the corporation's current and accumulated earnings and profits? (See sections 301 and 316.).		✓
	If "Yes," file Form 5452. If this is a consolidated return, answer here for parent corporation and on Form 851, Affiliations Schedule, for each subsidiary.		
O	During this tax year did the corporation maintain any part of its accounting/tax records on a computerized system? . . .		✓
P	Check method of accounting:		
	(1) ☐ Cash (2) ☐ Accrual		
	(3) ☐ Other (specify) ▶		
Q	Check this box if the corporation issued publicly offered debt instruments with original issue discount . . . . . ☐		
	If so, the corporation may have to file Form 8281.		
R	Enter the amount of tax-exempt interest received or accrued during the tax year ▶		
S	If you are a member of a controlled group, enter the amount of taxable income for the entire group ▶		

Form 1120 (1987)

Page **4**

Schedule L — Balance Sheets

Assets	Beginning of tax year (a)	(b)	End of tax year (c)	(d)
1 Cash		5,333		14,581
2 Trade notes and accounts receivable				
a Less allowance for bad debts				
3 Inventories				
4 Federal and state government obligations				
5 Other current assets (attach schedule)				
6 Loans to stockholders		4,000		
7 Mortgage and real estate loans				
8 Other investments (attach schedule) (STOCK)		60,000		72,000
9 Buildings and other depreciable assets	6,667		6,667	
a Less accumulated depreciation		6,667	1,000	5,667
10 Depletable assets				
a Less accumulated depletion				
11 Land (net of any amortization)				
12 Intangible assets (amortizable only)				
a Less accumulated amortization				
13 Other assets (attach schedule)		2,250		8,000
14 Total assets		78,250		100,248
Liabilities and Stockholders' Equity				
15 Accounts payable		8,250		8,000
16 Mortgages, notes, bonds payable in less than 1 year				
17 Other current liabilities (attach schedule)				
18 Loans from stockholders				
19 Mortgages, notes, bonds payable in 1 year or more				
20 Other liabilities (attach schedule)				2,263
21 Capital stock: a preferred stock				
b common stock	10,000	10,000	10,000	10,000
22 Paid-in or capital surplus		10,000		10,000
23 Retained earnings—Appropriated (attach schedule)				
24 Retained earnings—Unappropriated		50,000		69,985
25 Less cost of treasury stock		( )		( )
26 Total liabilities and stockholders' equity		78,250		100,248

Schedule M-1 — Reconciliation of Income per Books With Income per Return

You are not required to complete this schedule if the total assets on line 14, column (d), of Schedule L are less than $25,000.

1 Net income per books	19,985	7 Income recorded on books this year not included in this return (itemize)	
2 Federal income tax	2,680	a Tax-exempt interest $	
3 Excess of capital losses over capital gains			
4 Income subject to tax not recorded on books this year (itemize)			
		8 Deductions in this tax return not charged against book income this year (itemize)	
5 Expenses recorded on books this year not deducted in this return (itemize)		a Depreciation $	
a Depreciation $		b Contributions carryover $	
b Contributions carryover $			
		9 Total of lines 7 and 8	
6 Total of lines 1 through 5	22,665	10 Income (line 28, page 1)—line 6 less line 9	22,665

Schedule M-2 — Analysis of Unappropriated Retained Earnings per Books (line 24, Schedule L)

You are not required to complete this schedule if the total assets on line 14, column (d), of Schedule L are less than $25,000.

1 Balance at beginning of year	50,000	5 Distributions: a Cash	
2 Net income per books	19,985	b Stock	
3 Other increases (itemize)		c Property	
		6 Other decreases (itemize)	
		7 Total of lines 5 and 6	
4 Total of lines 1, 2, and 3	69,985	8 Balance at end of year (line 4 less line 7)	69,985

Form **1040** Department of the Treasury—Internal Revenue Service **1987**
U.S. Individual Income Tax Return

For the year Jan.–Dec. 31, 1987, or other tax year beginning _____, 1987, ending _____, 19___ | OMB No 1545-0074

Label Use IRS label. Otherwise, please print or type.	Your first name and initial (if joint return, also give spouse's name and initial) **GEORGE** **GORDON** Last name **Your social security number** 000 00 0000
	Present home address (number and street or rural route). (If you have a P.O. Box, see page 6 of Instructions.) **350 FIFTH AVENUE** **Spouse's social security number**
	City, town or post office, state, and ZIP code **NEW YORK NY 10118** For Privacy Act and Paperwork Reduction Act Notice, see Instructions.

Presidential Election Campaign ▶ Do you want $1 to go to this fund? ✔ Yes ☐ No | **Note:** Checking "Yes" will not change your tax or reduce your refund.
If joint return, does your spouse want $1 to go to this fund? ☐ Yes ☐ No

Filing Status

Check only one box.

1. ✔ Single
2. ☐ Married filing joint return (even if only one had income)
3. ☐ Married filing separate return. Enter spouse's social security no. above and full name here. _____
4. ☐ Head of household (with qualifying person). (See page 7 of Instructions.) If the qualifying person is your child but not your dependent, enter child's name here. _____
5. ☐ Qualifying widow(er) with dependent child (year spouse died ▶ 19___). (See page 7 of Instructions.)

Exemptions

(See Instructions on page 7.)

Caution: If you can be claimed as a dependent on another person's tax return (such as your parents' return), do not check box 6a. But be sure to check the box on line 32b on page 2.

6a ✔ Yourself   6b ☐ Spouse

No. of boxes checked on 6a and 6b ▶	1

c Dependents

(1) Name (first, initial, and last name)	(2) Check if under age 5	(3) If age 5 or over, dependent's social security number	(4) Relationship	(5) No. of months lived in your home in 1987

No. of children on 6c who lived with you ▶
No. of children on 6c who didn't live with you due to divorce or separation ▶
No. of parents listed on 6c ▶
No. of other dependents listed on 6c ▶

If more than 7 dependents, see Instructions on page 7.

d If your child didn't live with you but is claimed as your dependent under a pre-1985 agreement, check here . . ▶ ☐

e Total number of exemptions claimed (also complete line 35) . . . .

Add numbers entered in boxes above ▶	1

Income

Please attach Copy B of your Forms W-2, W-2G, and W-2P here.

If you do not have a W-2, see page 6 of Instructions.

7	Wages, salaries, tips, etc. *(attach Form(s) W-2)*	**7** 16,000
8	**Taxable** interest income *(also attach Schedule B if over $400)* . . .	**8**
9	Tax-exempt interest income (see page 10). DON'T include on line 8	**9**
10	Dividend income *(also attach Schedule B if over $400)*	**10**
11	Taxable refunds of state and local income taxes, if any, from worksheet on page 11 of Instructions.	**11**
12	Alimony received	**12**
13	Business income or (loss) *(attach Schedule C)*	**13**
14	Capital gain or (loss) *(attach Schedule D)*	**14**
15	Other gains or (losses) *(attach Form 4797)*	**15**
16a	Pensions, IRA distributions, annuities, and rollovers. Total received	16a	
b	Taxable amount (see page 11)	**16b**
17	Rents, royalties, partnerships, estates, trusts, etc. *(attach Schedule E)*	**17**
18	Farm income or (loss) *(attach Schedule F)*	**18**
19	Unemployment compensation (insurance) (see page 11)	**19**
20a	Social security benefits (see page 12)	20a	
b	Taxable amount, if any, from the worksheet on page 12	**20b**
21	Other income (list type and amount—see page 12)	**21**
22	Add the amounts shown in the far right column for lines 7, 8, and 10–21. This is your **total income** ▶	**22** 16,000

Please attach check or money order here.

Adjustments to Income

(See Instructions on page 12.)

23	Reimbursed employee business expenses from Form 2106 . .	**23**	
24a	Your IRA deduction, from applicable worksheet on page 13 or 14	**24a** 2,000	
b	Spouse's IRA deduction, from applicable worksheet on page 13 or 14	**24b**	
25	Self-employed health insurance deduction, from worksheet on page 14	**25**	
26	Keogh retirement plan and self-employed SEP deduction . . .	**26**	
27	Penalty on early withdrawal of savings	**27**	
28	Alimony paid (recipient's last name _____ and social security no. _____).	**28**	
29	Add lines 23 through 28. These are your **total adjustments** . . . . ▶	**29** 2,000

Adjusted Gross Income

30 Subtract line 29 from line 22. This is your **adjusted gross income.** If this line is less than $15,432 and a child lived with you, see "Earned Income Credit" (line 56) on page 18 of the Instructions. If you want IRS to figure your tax, see page 15 of the Instructions . . . ▶ | **30**   14,000

131

Form 1040 (1987)

Page **2**

Tax Computation	31	Amount from line 30 (adjusted gross income)	31	14,000
	32a	Check if: ☐ **You** were 65 or over ☐ Blind; ☐ **Spouse** was 65 or over ☐ Blind.		
		Add the number of boxes checked and enter the total here . . . ▶	32a	
	b	If you can be claimed as a dependent on another person's return, check here . . ▶	32b ☐	
	c	If you are married filing a separate return and your spouse itemizes deductions, or you are a dual-status alien, see page 15 and check here . . . . ▶	32c ☐	
	33a	**Itemized deductions.** See page 15 to see if you should itemize. If you don't itemize, enter zero. If you do itemize, attach Schedule A, enter the amount from Schedule A, line 26, **AND** skip line 33b .	33a	0
Caution: ◀ If you checked any box on line 32a, b, or c **and** you don't itemize, see page 16 for the amount to enter on line 33b.	**b**	**Standard deduction.** Read **Caution** to left. If it applies, see page 16 for the amount to enter. If **Caution** doesn't apply and your filing status from page 1 is: { Single or Head of household, enter $2,540 Married filing jointly or Qualifying widow(er), enter $3,760 Married filing separately, enter $1,880 }	33b	2,540
	34	Subtract line 33a or 33b, whichever applies, from line 31. Enter the result here	34	11,460
	35	Multiply $1,900 by the total number of exemptions claimed on line 6e or see chart on page 16 .	35	1,900
	36	**Taxable income.** Subtract line 35 from line 34. Enter the result (but not less than zero) .	36	9,560
		Caution: If under age 14 and you have more than $1,000 of investment income, check here ▶☐ and see page 16 to see if you have to use Form 8615 to figure your tax.		
	37	Enter tax. Check if from ☑ Tax Table, ☐ Tax Rate Schedules, ☐ Schedule D, or ☐ Form 8615	37	1,364
	38	Additional taxes (see page 16). Check if from ☐ Form 4970 or ☐ Form 4972	38	0
	39	Add lines 37 and 38. Enter the total . . . . ▶	39	1,364

Credits (See Instructions on page 17.)	40	Credit for child and dependent care expenses (attach Form 2441)	40	
	41	Credit for the elderly or for the permanently and totally disabled (attach Schedule R)	41	
	42	Add lines 40 and 41. Enter the total	42	
	43	Subtract line 42 from line 39. Enter the result (but not less than zero) .	43	
	44	Foreign tax credit (attach Form 1116)	44	
	45	General business credit. Check if from ☐ Form 3800, ☐ Form 3468, ☐ Form 5884, ☐ Form 6478, ☐ Form 6765, or ☐ Form 8586 .	45	
	46	Add lines 44 and 45. Enter the total	46	
	47	Subtract line 46 from line 43. Enter the result (but not less than zero) . ▶	47	1,364

Other Taxes (Including Advance EIC Payments)	48	Self-employment tax (attach Schedule SE)	48	
	49	Alternative minimum tax (attach Form 6251)	49	
	50	Tax from recapture of investment credit (attach Form 4255)	50	
	51	Social security tax on tip income not reported to employer (attach Form 4137) .	51	
	52	Tax on an IRA or a qualified retirement plan (attach Form 5329)	52	
	53	Add lines 47 through 52. This is your **total tax** . . . . ▶	53	1,364

Payments Attach Forms W-2, W-2G, and W-2P to front.	54	Federal income tax withheld (including tax shown on Form(s) 1099)	54	1,250
	55	1987 estimated tax payments and amount applied from 1986 return	55	
	56	Earned income credit (see page 18)	56	
	57	Amount paid with Form 4868 (extension request)	57	
	58	Excess social security tax and RRTA tax withheld (see page 19)	58	
	59	Credit for Federal tax on gasoline and special fuels (attach Form 4136)	59	
	60	Regulated investment company credit (attach Form 2439) . .	60	
	61	Add lines 54 through 60. These are your **total payments** . . . . . . ▶	61	1,250

Refund or Amount You Owe	62	If line 61 is larger than line 53, enter amount **OVERPAID**	62	
	63	Amount of line 62 to be **REFUNDED TO YOU** . . . . ▶	63	
	64	Amount of line 62 to be applied to your 1988 estimated tax . . ▶	64	
	65	If line 53 is larger than line 61, enter **AMOUNT YOU OWE.** Attach check or money order for full amount payable to "Internal Revenue Service." Write your social security number, daytime phone number, and "1987 Form 1040" on it . . . . Check ▶ ☐ if Form 2210 (2210F) is attached. See page 20. **Penalty: $**	65	114

Please Sign Here

Under penalties of perjury, I declare that I have examined this return and accompanying schedules and statements, and to the best of my knowledge and belief, they are true, correct, and complete. Declaration of preparer (other than taxpayer) is based on all information of which preparer has any knowledge.

Your signature	Date 4/15/88	Your occupation REAL ESTATE BROKER
Spouse's signature (if joint return, BOTH must sign)	Date	Spouse's occupation

Paid Preparer's Use Only

Preparer's signature ▶	Date	Check if self-employed ☐	Preparer's social security no.
Firm's name (or yours if self-employed) and address ▶		E.I. No.	
		ZIP code	

132

Form **1040** Department of the Treasury—Internal Revenue Service 19**87**

U.S. Individual Income Tax Return

For the year Jan.-Dec. 31, 1987, or other tax year beginning _____, 1987, ending _____ 19___ | OMB No 1545-0074

Label Use IRS label. Otherwise, please print or type.	Your first name and initial (if joint return, also give spouse's name and initial) GEORGE Last name GORDON
	Your social security number 000 00 0000
	Present home address (number and street or rural route). (If you have a P.O. Box, see page 6 of Instructions.) 350 FIFTH AVENUE
	Spouse's social security number
	City, town or post office, state, and ZIP code NEW YORK NY 10118
	For Privacy Act and Paperwork Reduction Act Notice, see Instructions.

Presidential Election Campaign ▶

Do you want $1 to go to this fund? Yes ☐ No ✔

If joint return, does your spouse want $1 to go to this fund?. Yes ☐ No ☐

Note: Checking "Yes" will not change your tax or reduce your refund.

Filing Status

Check only one box.

1 ✔ Single
2 ☐ Married filing joint return (even if only one had income)
3 ☐ Married filing separate return. Enter spouse's social security no. above and full name here. _____
4 ☐ Head of household (with qualifying person). (See page 7 of Instructions.) If the qualifying person is your child but not your dependent, enter child's name here. _____
5 ☐ Qualifying widow(er) with dependent child (year spouse died ▶ 19___). (See page 7 of Instructions.)

Exemptions

(See Instructions on page 7.)

Caution: If you can be claimed as a dependent on another person's tax return (such as your parents' return), do not check box 6a. But be sure to check the box on line 32b on page 2.

		No. of boxes checked on 6a and 6b ▶	**1**

6a ☐ Yourself 6b ☐ Spouse

c Dependents

(1) Name (first, initial, and last name)	(2) Check if under age 5	(3) If age 5 or over, dependent's social security number	(4) Relationship	(5) No. of months lived in your home in 1987

If more than 7 dependents, see Instructions on page 7.

No. of children on 6c who lived with you ▶

No. of children on 6c who didn't live with you due to divorce or separation ▶

No. of parents listed on 6c ▶

No. of other dependents listed on 6c ▶

d If your child didn't live with you but is claimed as your dependent under a pre-1985 agreement, check here . ▶ ☐

e Total number of exemptions claimed (also complete line 35)

Add numbers entered in boxes above ▶ **1**

Income

Please attach Copy B of your Forms W-2, W-2G, and W-2P here.

If you do not have a W-2, see page 6 of Instructions.

7	Wages, salaries, tips, etc. (attach Form(s) W-2)	7	
8	**Taxable** interest income (also attach Schedule B if over $400)	8	
9	Tax-exempt interest income (see page 10). DON'T include on line 8 9		
10	Dividend income (also attach Schedule B if over $400)	10	6,000
11	Taxable refunds of state and local income taxes, if any, from worksheet on page 11 of Instructions .	11	
12	Alimony received	12	
13	Business income or (loss) (attach Schedule C)	13	35,809
14	Capital gain or (loss) (attach Schedule D)	14	
15	Other gains or (losses) (attach Form 4797)	15	
16a	Pensions, IRA distributions, annuities, and rollovers. Total received 16a		
b	Taxable amount (see page 11)	16b	
17	Rents, royalties, partnerships, estates, trusts, etc. (attach Schedule E) .	17	
18	Farm income or (loss) (attach Schedule F)	18	
19	Unemployment compensation (insurance) (see page 11)	19	
20a	Social security benefits (see page 12) 20a		
b	Taxable amount, if any, from the worksheet on page 12	20b	
21	Other income (list type and amount—see page 12)	21	
22	Add the amounts shown in the far right column for lines 7, 8, and 10-21. This is your **total income** ▶	22	41,709

Please attach check or money order here.

Adjustments to Income

(See Instructions on page 12.)

23	Reimbursed employee business expenses from Form 2106 . .	23	
24a	Your IRA deduction, from applicable worksheet on page 13 or 14	24a	
b	Spouse's IRA deduction, from applicable worksheet on page 13 or 14	24b	
25	Self-employed health insurance deduction, from worksheet on page 14 .	25	
26	Keogh retirement plan and self-employed SEP deduction . . .	26	
27	Penalty on early withdrawal of savings	27	
28	Alimony paid (recipient's last name _____ and social security no. _____)	28	
29	Add lines 23 through 28. These are your **total adjustments** . . . . . ▶	29	O

Adjusted Gross Income

30 Subtract line 29 from line 22. This is your **adjusted gross income.** If this line is less than $15,432 and a child lived with you, see "Earned Income Credit" (line 56) on page 18 of the instructions. If you want IRS to figure your tax, see page 15 of the Instructions . . . ▶ | 30 | 41,709

133

Tax Computation	**31**	Amount from line 30 (adjusted gross income)	**31**	41,709
	32a	Check if: ☐ **You** were 65 or over ☐ Blind; ☐ **Spouse** was 65 or over ☐ Blind.		
		Add the number of boxes checked and enter the total here . . . . ▶ | **32a** |		
	b	If you can be claimed as a dependent on another person's return, check here . . ▶ **32b** ☐		
	c	If you are married filing a separate return and your spouse itemizes deductions, or you are a dual-status alien, see page 15 and check here . . . . . ▶ **32c** ☐		
Caution: If you checked any box on line 32a, b, or c and you don't itemize, see page 16 for the amount to enter on line 33b.	**33a**	**Itemized deductions.** See page 15 to see if you should itemize. If you don't itemize, enter zero. If you do itemize, attach Schedule A, enter the amount from Schedule A, line 26, **AND** skip line 33b .	**33a**	0
◀ **b**		**Standard deduction.** Read **Caution** to left. If it applies, see page 16 for the amount to enter. If **Caution** doesn't apply and your filing status from page 1 is: { Single or Head of household, enter $2,540 / Married filing jointly or Qualifying widow(er), enter $3,760 } / Married filing separately, enter $1,880	**33b**	2,540
	34	Subtract line 33a or 33b, whichever applies, from line 31. Enter the result here	**34**	39,169
	35	Multiply $1,900 by the total number of exemptions claimed on line 6e or see chart on page 16 .	**35**	1,900
	36	**Taxable income.** Subtract line 35 from line 34. Enter the result (but not less than zero)	**36**	37,269
		Caution: If under age 14 and you have more than $1,000 of investment income, check here ▶☐ and see page 16 to see if you have to use Form 8615 to figure your tax.		
	37	Enter tax. Check if from ☑Tax Table, ☐ Tax Rate Schedules, ☐ Schedule D, or ☐ Form 8615	**37**	8,900
	38	Additional taxes (see page 16). Check if from ☐ Form 4970 or ☐ Form 4972	**38**	
	39	Add lines 37 and 38. Enter the total . . . . ▶	**39**	8,900
Credits (See Instructions on page 17.)	**40**	Credit for child and dependent care expenses (attach Form 2441) **40**		
	41	Credit for the elderly or for the permanently and totally disabled (attach Schedule R) **41**		
	42	Add lines 40 and 41. Enter the total	**42**	
	43	Subtract line 42 from line 39. Enter the result (but not less than zero)	**43**	
	44	Foreign tax credit (attach Form 1116) **44**		
	45	General business credit. Check if from ☐ Form 3800, ☐ Form 3468, ☐ Form 5884, ☐ Form 6478, ☐ Form 6765, or ☐ Form 8586 **45**		
	46	Add lines 44 and 45. Enter the total	**46**	
	47	Subtract line 46 from line 43. Enter the result (but not less than zero) . . . . . ▶	**47**	8,900
Other Taxes (Including Advance EIC Payments)	**48**	Self-employment tax (attach Schedule SE)	**48**	4,405
	49	Alternative minimum tax (attach Form 6251)	**49**	
	50	Tax from recapture of investment credit (attach Form 4255)	**50**	
	51	Social security tax on tip income not reported to employer (attach Form 4137) . . .	**51**	
	52	Tax on an IRA or a qualified retirement plan (attach Form 5329)	**52**	
	53	Add lines 47 through 52. This is your **total tax** . . . . ▶	**53**	13,305
Payments Attach Forms W-2, W-2G, and W-2P to front.	**54**	Federal income tax withheld (including tax shown on Form(s) 1099) **54**		
	55	1987 estimated tax payments and amount applied from 1986 return **55** 13,000		
	56	Earned income credit (see page 18) **56**		
	57	Amount paid with Form 4868 (extension request) **57**		
	58	Excess social security tax and RRTA tax withheld (see page 19) **58**		
	59	Credit for Federal tax on gasoline and special fuels (attach Form 4136) **59**		
	60	Regulated investment company credit (attach Form 2439) . . . **60**		
	61	Add lines 54 through 60. These are your **total payments** . . . . ▶	**61**	13,000
Refund or Amount You Owe	**62**	If line 61 is larger than line 53, enter amount **OVERPAID** . . . . ▶	**62**	
	63	Amount of line 62 to be **REFUNDED TO YOU** . . . . ▶	**63**	
	64	Amount of line 62 to be applied to your 1988 estimated tax . ▶ | **64** |		
	65	If line 53 is larger than line 61, enter **AMOUNT YOU OWE.** Attach check or money order for full amount payable to "Internal Revenue Service." Write your social security number, daytime phone number, and "1987 Form 1040" on it	**65**	305
		Check ▶ ☐ if Form 2210 (2210F) is attached. See page 20. **Penalty: $**		

Please Sign Here

Under penalties of perjury, I declare that I have examined this return and accompanying schedules and statements, and to the best of my knowledge and belief, they are true, correct, and complete. Declaration of preparer (other than taxpayer) is based on all information of which preparer has any knowledge.

Your signature	Date 4/15/88	Your occupation REAL ESTATE BROKER
Spouse's signature (if joint return, BOTH must sign)	Date	Spouse's occupation

Paid Preparer's Use Only

Preparer's signature ▶	Date	Check if self-employed ☐	Preparer's social security no.
Firm's name (or yours if self-employed) and address ▶		E.I. No.	
		ZIP code	

SCHEDULE C
(Form 1040)

Department of the Treasury
Internal Revenue Service

Profit or (Loss) From Business or Profession
(Sole Proprietorship)
Partnerships, Joint Ventures, etc., Must File Form 1065.
▶ Attach to Form 1040, Form 1041, or Form 1041S. ▶ See Instructions for Schedule C (Form 1040).

OMB No 1545 0074

1987

Attachment
Sequence No **09**

Name of proprietor: GEORGE GORDON

Social security number (SSN): 000 : 00 : 0000

A Principal business or profession, including product or service (see Instructions): REAL ESTATE BROKER

B Principal business code
(from Part IV) ▶ | 5 | 7 | 7 | 7 |

C Business name and address ▶ GEORGE GORDON
350 FIFTH AVENUE New York NY 10118

D Employer ID number (Not SSN)

E Method(s) used to value closing inventory:
(1) ☐ Cost (2) ☐ Lower of cost or market (3) ☐ Other (attach explanation)

		Yes	No
F Accounting method (1) ☑ Cash (2) ☐ Accrual (3) ☐ Other (specify) ▶			
G Was there any change in determining quantities, costs, or valuations between opening and closing inventory? (If "Yes," attach explanation.)			✓
H Are you deducting expenses for an office in your home?			✓
I Did you file **Form 941** for this business for any quarter in 1987?			✓
J Did you "materially participate" in the operation of this business during 1987? (If "No," see Instructions for limitations on losses.)		✓	
K Was this business in operation at the end of 1987?		✓	

L How many months was this business in operation during 1987? ▶ 12

M If this schedule includes a loss, credit, deduction, income, or other tax benefit relating to a tax shelter required to be registered, check here. ▶ ☐
If you check this box, you **MUST** attach Form 8271

Part I Income

1a Gross receipts or sales	1a	
b Less: Returns and allowances	1b	
c Subtract line 1b from line 1a and enter the balance here	1c	
2 Cost of goods sold and/or operations (from Part III, line 8)	2	
3 Subtract line 2 from line 1c and enter the **gross profit** here	3	45,000
4 Other income (including windfall profit tax credit or refund received in 1987)	4	
5 Add lines 3 and 4. This is the **gross income** ▶	5	45,000

Part II Deductions

6 Advertising			**23** Repairs		
7 Bad debts from sales or services (see Instructions.)			**24** Supplies (not included in Part III)		
8 Bank service charges			**25** Taxes		
9 Car and truck expenses			**26** Travel, meals, and entertainment:		
10 Commissions			**a** Travel		450
11 Depletion			**b** Total meals and entertainment		
12 Depreciation and section 179 deduction from Form 4562 (not included in Part III)	1,000		**c** Enter 20% of line 26b subject to limitations (see Instructions)		
13 Dues and publications			**d** Subtract line 26c from 26b		
14 Employee benefit programs			**27** Utilities and telephone		491
15 Freight (not included in Part III)			**28a** Wages		
16 Insurance			**b** Jobs credit		
17 Interest:			**c** Subtract line 28b from 28a		
a Mortgage (paid to financial institutions)			**29** Other expenses (list type and amount):		
b Other			Postage		100
18 Laundry and cleaning			Books + subscriptions		50
19 Legal and professional services			....		
20 Office expense	100		....		
21 Pension and profit-sharing plans	4,000				
22 Rent on business property	3,000				

30 Add amounts in columns for lines 6 through 29. These are the **total deductions** ▶	30	9,191

31 Net profit or (loss). Subtract line 30 from line 5. If a profit, enter here and on Form 1040, line 13, and on Schedule SE, line 2 (or line 5 of Form 1041 or Form 1041S). If a loss, you **MUST** go on to line 32. | 31 | 35,809 |

32 If you have a loss, you **MUST** answer this question: "Do you have amounts for which you are not at risk in this business?" (See Instructions.) ☐ Yes ☐ No
If "Yes," you **MUST** attach Form 6198. If "No," enter the loss on Form 1040, line 13, and on Schedule SE, line 2 (or line 5 of Form 1041 or Form 1041S).

For Paperwork Reduction Act Notice, see Form 1040 Instructions.

Schedule C (Form 1040) 1987

SCHEDULE SE
(Form 1040)

Department of the Treasury
Internal Revenue Service

Computation of Social Security Self-Employment Tax

▶ See Instructions for Schedule SE (Form 1040).

▶ Attach to Form 1040.

OMB No. 1545-0074

1987

Attachment
Sequence No 18

Name of person with **self-employment** income (as shown on social security card)

GEORGE GORDON

Social security number of person
with **self-employment** income ▶ 000 : 00 : 0000

A If your only self-employment income was from earnings as a minister, member of a religious order, or Christian Science practitioner, AND you filed Form 4361, then DO NOT file Schedule SE. Instead, write "Exempt-Form 4361" on Form 1040, line 48. However, if you filed Form 4361, but have $400 or more of other earnings subject to self-employment tax, continue with Part I and check here ▶ ☐

B If you filed Form 4029 and have received IRS approval, DO NOT file Schedule SE. Write "Exempt-Form 4029" on Form 1040, line 48.

C If your only earnings subject to self-employment tax are wages from an electing church or church-controlled organization that is exempt from employer social security taxes and you are not a minister or a member of a religious order, skip lines 1–8. Enter zero on line 9. Continue with line 11a.

Part I Regular Computation of Net Earnings From Self-Employment

1	Net farm profit (or loss) from Schedule F (Form 1040), line 37, and farm partnerships, Schedule K-1 (Form 1065), line 14a	**1**		
2	Net profit (or loss) from Schedule C (Form 1040), line 31, and Schedule K-1 (Form 1065), line 14a (other than farming). (See Instructions for other income to report.) Employees of an electing church or church-controlled organization DO NOT enter your Form W-2 wages on line 2. See the Instructions	**2**	35,809	

Part II Optional Computation of Net Earnings From Self-Employment (See "Who Can Use Schedule SE" in the Instructions.)

See Instructions for limitations. Generally, this part may be used **only** if you meet any of the following tests:

A Your **gross farm income**[1] was not more than $2,400; **or**

B Your **gross farm income**[1] was more than $2,400 and your **net** farm profits[2] were **less** than $1,600; **or**

C Your **net** nonfarm profits[3] were less than $1,600 and your **net** nonfarm profits[3] were also **less** than two-thirds (⅔) of your **gross** nonfarm income.[4]

Note: If line 2 above is two-thirds (⅔) or more of your gross nonfarm income[4], or, if line 2 is $1,600 or more, you may **not** use the optional method.

[1]From Schedule F (Form 1040), line 12, and Schedule K-1 (Form 1065), line 14b.   [3]From Schedule C (Form 1040), line 31, and Schedule K-1 (Form 1065), line 14a.
[2]From Schedule F (Form 1040), line 37, and Schedule K-1 (Form 1065), line 14a.   [4]From Schedule C (Form 1040), line 5, and Schedule K-1 (Form 1065), line 14c.

3	Maximum income for optional methods	**3**	$1,600	00
4	Farm Optional Method—If you meet test A or B above, enter the **smaller of:** two-thirds (⅔) of gross farm income from Schedule F (Form 1040), line 12, and farm partnerships, Schedule K-1 (Form 1065), line 14b; or $1,600	**4**		
5	Subtract line 4 from line 3	**5**		
6	Nonfarm Optional Method—If you meet test C above, enter the **smallest of:** two-thirds (⅔) of gross nonfarm income from Schedule C (Form 1040), line 5, and Schedule K-1 (Form 1065), line 14c (other than farming); or $1,600; or, if you elected the farm optional method, the amount on line 5 . . .	**6**		

Part III Computation of Social Security Self-Employment Tax

7	Enter the amount from Part I, line 1, **or,** if you elected the farm optional method, Part II, line 4	**7**		
8	Enter the amount from Part I, line 2, **or,** if you elected the nonfarm optional method, Part II, line 6 . .	**8**	35,809	
9	Add lines 7 and 8. If less than $400, do not file this schedule. (Exception: If you are an employee of an electing church or church-controlled organization and the total of lines 7 and 8 is less than $400, enter zero and complete the rest of this schedule.) . . .	**9**	35,809	
10	The largest amount of combined wages and self-employment earnings subject to social security or railroad retirement tax (tier 1) for 1987 is	**10**	$43,800	00
11a	Total social security wages and tips from Forms W-2 and railroad retirement compensation (tier 1). **Note:** Medicare qualified government employees whose wages are only subject to the 1.45% medicare (hospital insurance benefits) tax and employees of church or church-controlled organizations should **not** include those wages on this line. (See Instructions.)	**11a**			
b	Unreported tips subject to social security tax from Form 4137, line 9, or to railroad retirement tax (tier 1)	**11b**			
c	Add lines 11a and 11b	**11c**	0	
12a	Subtract line 11c from line 10. (If zero or less, enter zero.)	**12a**	43,800	
b	Enter your medicare qualified government wages if you are required to use the worksheet in Part III of the Instructions . . .	**12b**			
c	Enter your Form W-2 wages of $100 or more from an electing church or church-controlled organization . . .	**12c**			
d	Add lines 9 and 12c	**12d**	35,809	
13	Enter the smaller of line 12a or line 12d	**13**	35,809	
	If line 13 is $43,800, enter $5,387.40 on line 14. Otherwise, multiply line 13 by .123 and enter the result on line 14.		×.123	
14	Self-employment tax. Enter this amount on Form 1040, line 48	**14**	4,405	

For Paperwork Reduction Act Notice, see Form 1040 Instructions.

Schedule SE (Form 1040) 1987

Form **4562**

Department of the Treasury
Internal Revenue Service

Depreciation and Amortization

▶ See separate instructions.
▶ Attach this form to your return.

OMB No. 1545-0172

1987

Attachment
Sequence No. **67**

Name(s) as shown on return

GEORGE   GORDON

Identifying number

000-00-0000

Business or activity to which this form relates

REAL ESTATE BROKERAGE

Part I **Depreciation** (Do not use this part for automobiles, certain other vehicles, computers, and property used for entertainment, recreation, or amusement. Instead, use Part III.)

Section A.—Election To Expense Depreciable Assets Placed in Service During This Tax Year (Section 179)

(a) Description of property	(b) Date placed in service	(c) Cost	(d) Expense deduction
1			

2 Listed property—Enter total from Part III, Section A, column (h) · · · · · · ·

3 Total (add lines 1 and 2, but do not enter more than $10,000) · · · · · · ·

4 Enter the amount, if any, by which the cost of all section 179 property placed in service during this tax year is more than $200,000 · · ·

5 Subtract line 4 from line 3. If result is less than zero, enter zero. (See instructions for other limitations) · ·

Section B.—Depreciation

(a) Class of property	(b) Date placed in service	(c) Basis for depreciation (Business use only—see instructions)	(d) Recovery period	(e) Method of figuring depreciation	(f) Deduction
6 Accelerated Cost Recovery System (ACRS) (see instructions): *For assets placed in service ONLY during tax year beginning in 1987*					
a 3-year property					
b 5-year property					
c 7-year property					
d 10-year property					
e 15-year property					
f 20-year property					
g Residential rental property					
h Nonresidential real property					

7 Listed property—Enter total from Part III, Section A, column (g). · · · · · · ·

8 ACRS deduction for assets placed in service prior to 1987 (see instructions) · · · · · · · | | | | | | 1,000

Section C.—Other Depreciation

9 Property subject to section 168(f)(1) election (see instructions) · · · · · · ·

10 Other depreciation (see instructions) · · · · · · · · · · · · · ·

Section D.—Summary

11 Total (add deductions on lines 5 through 10). Enter here and on the Depreciation line of your return (Partnerships and S corporations—Do NOT include any amounts entered on line 5.) · · · · · · ·

12 For assets above placed in service during the current year, enter the portion of the basis attributable to additional section 263A costs. (See instructions for who must use.) · ·

Part II **Amortization**

(a) Description of property	(b) Date acquired	(c) Cost or other basis	(d) Code section	(e) Amortization period or percentage	(f) Amortization for this year
1 Amortization for property placed in service only during tax year beginning in 1987					
2 Amortization for property placed in service prior to 1987 · · · · · · ·					

3 Total. Enter here and on Other Deductions or Other Expenses line of your return · · · · · · · ·

See Paperwork Reduction Act Notice on page 1 of the separate instructions.

Form **4562** (1987)

Form **1120**		**U.S. Corporation Income Tax Return**		OMB No. 1545-0123
Department of the Treasury Internal Revenue Service		For calendar 1987 or tax year beginning .... , 1987, ending .... , 19 .... ▶ For Paperwork Reduction Act Notice, see page 1 of the instructions.		**1987**

Check if a—		**Use IRS label. Other- wise please print or type.**	Name	GEOFFREY FOURMYLE & Co., INC.		**D** Employer identification number 00-0000000
A Consolidated return ☐			Number and street	5217 CERES BOULEVARD		**E** Date incorporated 1/1/87
B Personal Holding Co. ☐			City or town, state, and ZIP code	SAN FRANCISCO CA 94701		**F** Total assets (See Specific Instructions.)
C Business Code No. (See the list in the instructions.) 7980						

G Check applicable boxes. (1) ☐ Initial return (2) ☐ Final return (3) ☐ Change in address		Dollars	Cents
		67,148	

Income	1a	Gross receipts or sales	b Less returns and allowances .... Balance ▶		1c	
	2	Cost of goods sold and/or operations (Schedule A)			2	
	3	Gross profit (line 1c less line 2)			3	
	4	Dividends (Schedule C)			4	6,000
	5	Interest			5	
	6	Gross rents			6	
	7	Gross royalties			7	
	8	Capital gain net income (attach separate Schedule D)			8	
	9	Net gain or (loss) from Form 4797, line 18, Part II (attach Form 4797)			9	
	10	Other income (see instructions—attach schedule)			10	45,000
	11	TOTAL income—Add lines 3 through 10 and enter here ▶			11	51,000
Deductions (See Instructions for limitations on deductions)	12	Compensation of officers (Schedule E)			12	26,000
	13a	Salaries and wages .... b Less jobs credit .... Balance ▶			13c	
	14	Repairs			14	
	15	Bad debts (see instructions)			15	
	16	Rents			16	3,000
	17	Taxes Soc. Sec.			17	1,859
	18	Interest			18	
	19	Contributions (see instructions for 10% limitation)			19	
	20	Depreciation (attach Form 4562)	20	1,000		
	21	Less depreciation claimed in Schedule A and elsewhere on return	21a	0	21b	1,000
	22	Depletion			22	
	23	Advertising			23	
	24	Pension, profit-sharing, etc., plans			24	6,500
	25	Employee benefit programs MEDICAL			25	4,000
	26	Other deductions (attach schedule)			26	1,079
	27	TOTAL deductions—Add lines 12 through 26 and enter here ▶			27	43,438
	28	Taxable income before net operating loss deduction and special deductions (line 11 less line 27)			28	7,562
	29	Less: a Net operating loss deduction (see instructions)	29a			
		b Special deductions (Schedule C)	29b	4,800	29c	4,800
	30	Taxable income (line 28 less line 29c)			30	2,762
	31	TOTAL TAX (Schedule J)			31	414
Tax and Payments	32	Payments: a 1986 overpayment credited to 1987				
	b	1987 estimated tax payments	400			
	c	Less 1987 refund applied for on Form 4466	( )			
	d	Tax deposited with Form 7004				
	e	Credit from regulated investment companies (attach Form 2439)				
	f	Credit for Federal tax on gasoline and special fuels (attach Form 4136)			32	400
	33	Enter any PENALTY for underpayment of estimated tax—check ▶ ☐ if Form 2220 is attached			33	
	34	TAX DUE—If the total of lines 31 and 33 is larger than line 32, enter AMOUNT OWED			34	14
	35	OVERPAYMENT—If line 32 is larger than the total of lines 31 and 33, enter AMOUNT OVERPAID			35	
	36	Enter amount of line 35 you want: Credited to 1988 estimated tax ▶ Refunded ▶			36	

Please Sign Here	Under penalties of perjury, I declare that I have examined this return, including accompanying schedules and statements, and to the best of my knowledge and belief, it is true, correct, and complete. Declaration of preparer (other than taxpayer) is based on all information of which preparer has any knowledge.		
	▶ Signature of officer	3/15/88 Date	▶ PRESIDENT Title

Paid Preparer's Use Only	Preparer's signature ▶		Date	Check if self-employed ☐	Preparer's social security number
	Firm's name (or yours, if self-employed) and address ▶			E.I. No. ▶	
				ZIP code ▶	

Form 1120 (1987)

Schedule A Cost of Goods Sold and/or Operations (See instructions for line 2, page 1.)

1 Inventory at beginning of year	1	
2 Purchases	2	
3 Cost of labor	3	
4a Additional section 263A costs (see instructions)	4a	
b Other costs (attach schedule)	4b	
5 Total—Add lines 1 through 4b	5	
6 Inventory at end of year	6	
7 Cost of goods sold and/or operations—Line 5 less line 6. Enter here and on line 2, page 1	7	

8 a Check all methods used for valuing closing inventory:

(i) ☐ Cost (ii) ☐ Lower of cost or market as described in Regulations section 1.471-4 (see instructions)

(iii) ☐ Writedown of "subnormal" goods as described in Regulations section 1.471-2(c) (see instructions)

(iv) ☐ Other (Specify method used and attach explanation.) ▶ _____

b Check if the LIFO inventory method was adopted this tax year for any goods (if checked, attach Form 970) . . . ☐

c If the LIFO inventory method was used for this tax year, enter percentage (or amounts) of closing inventory computed under LIFO . . . . | 8c | |

d Do the rules of section 263A (with respect to property produced or acquired for resale) apply to the corporation? . . ☐ Yes ☐ No

e Was there any change (other than for section 263A purposes) in determining quantities, cost, or valuations between opening and closing inventory? If "Yes," attach explanation . . . . ☐ Yes ☐ No

Schedule C Dividends and Special Deductions (See Schedule C instructions.)

	(a) Dividends received	(b) %	(c) Special deductions: multiply (a) × (b)
1 Domestic corporations subject to section 243(a) deduction (other than debt-financed stock).	6,000	see instructions	4,800
2 Debt-financed stock of domestic and foreign corporations (section 246A)		see instructions	
3 Certain preferred stock of public utilities		see instructions	
4 Foreign corporations and certain FSCs subject to section 245 deduction		see instructions	
5 Wholly owned foreign subsidiaries and FSCs subject to 100% deduction (sections 245(b) and (c)) . .		100	
6 Total—Add lines 1 through 5. See instructions for limitation			
7 Affiliated groups subject to the 100% deduction (section 243(a)(3))		100	
8 Other dividends from foreign corporations not included in lines 4 and 5			
9 Income from controlled foreign corporations under subpart F (attach Forms 5471) . .			
10 Foreign dividend gross-up (section 78)			
11 IC-DISC or former DISC dividends not included in lines 1 and/or 2 (section 246(d)) .			
12 Other dividends			
13 Deduction for dividends paid on certain preferred stock of public utilities (see instructions)			4,800
14 Total dividends—Add lines 1 through 12. Enter here and on line 4, page 1. . . ▶	6,000		
15 Total deductions—Add lines 6, 7, and 13. Enter here and on line 29b, page 1 . . . . ▶			4,800

Schedule E Compensation of Officers (See instructions for line 12, page 1.)

Complete Schedule E only if total receipts (line 1a, plus lines 4 through 10, of page 1, Form 1120) are $150,000 or more.

(a) Name of officer	(b) Social security number	(c) Percent of time devoted to business	Percent of corporation stock owned		(f) Amount of compensation
			(d) Common	(e) Preferred	
		%	%	%	
		%	%	%	
		%	%	%	
		%	%	%	
		%	%	%	
		%	%	%	
		%	%	%	
Total compensation of officers—Enter here and on line 12, page 1					

Schedule J Tax Computation (See instructions.)

1 Check if you are a member of a controlled group (see sections 1561 and 1563) . . . . ▶ ☐

2 If line 1 is checked, see instructions. If your tax year includes June 30, 1987, complete both a and b below. Otherwise, complete only b.

a (i) $ _____ (ii) $ _____ (iii) $ _____ (iv) $ _____

b (i) $ _____ (ii) $ _____

3 Income tax (see instructions to figure the tax; enter this tax or alternative tax from Schedule D, whichever is less). Check if from Schedule D ▶ ☐ . . . . | **3** | 414

		4a	
4a	Foreign tax credit (attach Form 1118) . . .	**4a**	
b	Possessions tax credit (attach Form 5735) . .	**b**	
c	Orphan drug credit (attach Form 6765) . .	**c**	
d	Credit for fuel produced from a nonconventional source (see instructions) .	**d**	
e	General business credit. Enter here and check which forms are attached ☐ Form 3800 ☐ Form 3468 ☐ Form 5884 ☐ Form 6478 ☐ Form 6765 ☐ Form 8586	**e**	

5 Total—Add lines 4a through 4e . . . . | **5** | 0

6 Line 3 less line 5 . . . . | **6** | 414

7 Personal holding company tax (attach Schedule PH (Form 1120)) . . . | **7** | 0

8 Tax from recomputing prior-year investment credit (attach Form 4255) . . | **8** | 0

9a Alternative minimum tax (see instructions—attach Form 4626) . . . | **9a** | 0

b Environmental tax (see instructions—attach Form 4626) . . . . | **9b** | 0

10 Total tax—Add lines 6 through 9b. Enter here and on line 31, page 1 | **10** | 414

Additional Information (See instruction F.)

	Yes	No
H Did the corporation claim a deduction for expenses connected with:		
(1) An entertainment facility (boat, resort, ranch, etc.)? . . .		✓
(2) Living accommodations (except employees on business)? . .		✓
(3) Employees attending conventions or meetings outside the North American area? (See section 274(h).)		✓
(4) Employees' families at conventions or meetings? . . .		✓
If "Yes," were any of these conventions or meetings outside the North American area? (See section 274(h).)		✓
(5) Employee or family vacations not reported on Form W-2? . .		✓
I (1) Did the corporation at the end of the tax year own, directly or indirectly, 50% or more of the voting stock of a domestic corporation? (For rules of attribution, see section 267(c).) . .		✓

If "Yes," attach a schedule showing: (a) name, address, and identifying number; (b) percentage owned; (c) taxable income or (loss) before NOL and special deductions of such corporation for the tax year ending with or within your tax year; (d) highest amount owed by the corporation to such corporation during the year; and (e) highest amount owed to the corporation by such corporation during the year.

(2) Did any individual, partnership, corporation, estate, or trust at the end of the tax year own, directly or indirectly, 50% or more of the corporation's voting stock? (For rules of attribution, see section 267(c).) If "Yes," complete (a) through (d) . . . ✓

(a) Attach a schedule showing name, address and identifying number. Enter percentage owned ▶ 099-00-0000 100%

(b) Was the owner of such voting stock a person other than a U.S. person? (See instructions.) **Note:** If "Yes," the corporation may have to file Form 5472. . . . ✓

If "Yes," enter owner's country ▶ _____

(c) Enter highest amount owed by the corporation to such owner during the year ▶ _____

(d) Enter highest amount owed to the corporation by such owner during the year ▶ _____

Note: For purposes of I(1) and I(2), "highest amount owed" includes loans and accounts receivable/payable.

	Yes	No
J Refer to the list in the instructions and state the principal: Business activity ▶ _____ Product or service ▶ _____		
K Was the corporation a U.S. shareholder of any controlled foreign corporation? (See sections 951 and 957.) . . .		✓
If "Yes," attach Form 5471 for each such corporation.		
L At any time during the tax year, did the corporation have an interest in or a signature or other authority over a financial account in a foreign country (such as a bank account, securities account, or other financial account)?		✓
(See instruction F and filing requirements for form TD F 90-22.1.) If "Yes," enter name of foreign country ▶ _____		
M Was the corporation the grantor of, or transferor to, a foreign trust which existed during the current tax year, whether or not the corporation has any beneficial interest in it? . . .		✓
If "Yes," the corporation may have to file Forms 3520, 3520-A, or 926.		
N During this tax year, did the corporation pay dividends (other than stock dividends and distributions in exchange for stock) in excess of the corporation's current and accumulated earnings and profits? (See sections 301 and 316.).		✓
If "Yes," file Form 5452. If this is a consolidated return, answer here for parent corporation and on Form 851, Affiliations Schedule, for each subsidiary.		
O During this tax year did the corporation maintain any part of its accounting/tax records on a computerized system? . . .		✓
P Check method of accounting: (1) ☐ Cash (2) ☐ Accrual (3) ☐ Other (specify) ▶ _____		
Q Check this box if the corporation issued publicly offered debt instruments with original issue discount . . . ☐ If so, the corporation may have to file Form 8281.		
R Enter the amount of tax-exempt interest received or accrued during the tax year ▶ _____		
S If you are a member of a controlled group, enter the amount of taxable income for the entire group ▶ _____		

Schedule L — Balance Sheets

Assets	Beginning of tax year (a)	(b)	End of tax year (c)	(d)
1 Cash				1,481
2 Trade notes and accounts receivable				
a Less allowance for bad debts				
3 Inventories				
4 Federal and state government obligations				
5 Other current assets (attach schedule)				
6 Loans to stockholders		INCORPORATED 1/1/87		
7 Mortgage and real estate loans				
8 Other investments (attach schedule)				60,000
9 Buildings and other depreciable assets			6,667	
a Less accumulated depreciation			1,000	5,667
10 Depletable assets				
a Less accumulated depletion				
11 Land (net of any amortization)				—
12 Intangible assets (amortizable only)				
a Less accumulated amortization				
13 Other assets (attach schedule)				
14 Total assets				67,148
Liabilities and Stockholders' Equity				
15 Accounts payable				
16 Mortgages, notes, bonds payable in less than 1 year				
17 Other current liabilities (attach schedule)		INITIAL		
18 Loans from stockholders		RETURN		
19 Mortgages, notes, bonds payable in 1 year or more				
20 Other liabilities (attach schedule)				
21 Capital stock: a preferred stock				
b common stock				10,000
22 Paid-in or capital surplus				50,000
23 Retained earnings—Appropriated (attach schedule)				
24 Retained earnings—Unappropriated				7,148
25 Less cost of treasury stock		( )		( )
26 Total liabilities and stockholders' equity				67,148

Schedule M-1 — Reconciliation of Income per Books With Income per Return

You are not required to complete this schedule if the total assets on line 14, column (d), of Schedule L are less than $25,000.

1 Net income per books	7,148	7 Income recorded on books this year not included in this return (itemize)	
2 Federal income tax	414	a Tax-exempt interest $	
3 Excess of capital losses over capital gains			
4 Income subject to tax not recorded on books this year (itemize)		8 Deductions in this tax return not charged against book income this year (itemize)	
5 Expenses recorded on books this year not deducted in this return (itemize)		a Depreciation $	
a Depreciation $		b Contributions carryover $	
b Contributions carryover $			
		9 Total of lines 7 and 8	
6 Total of lines 1 through 5	7,562	10 Income (line 28, page 1)—line 6 less line 9	7,562

Schedule M-2 — Analysis of Unappropriated Retained Earnings per Books (line 24, Schedule L)

You are not required to complete this schedule if the total assets on line 14, column (d), of Schedule L are less than $25,000.

1 Balance at beginning of year	0	5 Distributions: a Cash	
2 Net income per books	7,148	b Stock	
3 Other increases (itemize)		c Property	
		6 Other decreases (itemize)	
		7 Total of lines 5 and 6	
4 Total of lines 1, 2, and 3	7,148	8 Balance at end of year (line 4 less line 7)	7,148

Form **1040** Department of the Treasury—Internal Revenue Service

U.S. Individual Income Tax Return 1987

	For the year Jan.–Dec. 31, 1987, or other tax year beginning , 1987, ending , 19	OMB No 1545-0074

Label

Use IRS label. Otherwise, please print or type.

Your first name and initial (if joint return, also give spouse's name and initial) GEOFFREY — Last name FOURMYLE

Your social security number 000 00 0000

Present home address (number and street or rural route) (If you have a P.O. Box, see page 6 of instructions.)
5217 CERES BOULEVARD

Spouse's social security number

City, town or post office, state, and ZIP code
SAN FRANCISCO, CA 94701

For Privacy Act and Paperwork Reduction Act Notice, see Instructions.

Presidential Election Campaign ▶

Do you want $1 to go to this fund? . . . . Yes ☐ / No ✓

If joint return, does your spouse want $1 to go to this fund? . Yes ☐ / No ☐

Note: Checking "Yes" will not change your tax or reduce your refund.

Filing Status

Check only one box.

1 ✓ Single
2 ☐ Married filing joint return (even if only one had income)
3 ☐ Married filing separate return. Enter spouse's social security no. above and full name here. ___
4 ☐ Head of household (with qualifying person). (See page 7 of Instructions.) If the qualifying person is your child but not your dependent, enter child's name here. ___
5 ☐ Qualifying widow(er) with dependent child (year spouse died ▶ 19). (See page 7 of Instructions.)

Exemptions

(See Instructions on page 7.)

If more than 7 dependents, see Instructions on page 7.

Caution: If you can be claimed as a dependent on another person's tax return (such as your parents' return), do not check box 6a. But be sure to check the box on line 32b on page 2.

6a ✓ Yourself   6b ☐ Spouse

c Dependents (1) Name (first, initial, and last name)	(2) Check if under age 5	(3) If age 5 or over, dependent's social security number	(4) Relationship	(5) No. of months lived in your home in 1987

No. of boxes checked on 6a and 6b ▶ 1

No. of children on 6c who lived with you ▶

No. of children on 6c who didn't live with you due to divorce or separation ▶

No. of parents listed on 6c ▶

No. of other dependents listed on 6c ▶

d If your child didn't live with you but is claimed as your dependent under a pre-1985 agreement, check here . ▶ ☐

e Total number of exemptions claimed (also complete line 35) . . . .

Add numbers entered in boxes above ▶ 1

Income

Please attach Copy B of your Forms W-2, W-2G, and W-2P here.

If you do not have a W-2, see page 6 of Instructions.

Please attach check or money order here.

7	Wages, salaries, tips, etc. (attach Form(s) W-2)	7	26,000
8	**Taxable** interest income (also attach Schedule B if over $400) . . .	8	
9	Tax-exempt interest income (see page 10). DON'T include on line 8	9	
10	Dividend income (also attach Schedule B if over $400)	10	
11	Taxable refunds of state and local income taxes, if any, from worksheet on page 11 of Instructions. .	11	
12	Alimony received	12	
13	Business income or (loss) (attach Schedule C)	13	
14	Capital gain or (loss) (attach Schedule D)	14	
15	Other gains or (losses) (attach Form 4797)	15	
16a	Pensions, IRA distributions, annuities, and rollovers. Total received 16a		
b	Taxable amount (see page 11)	16b	
17	Rents, royalties, partnerships, estates, trusts, etc. (attach Schedule E)	17	
18	Farm income or (loss) (attach Schedule F)	18	
19	Unemployment compensation (insurance) (see page 11)	19	
20a	Social security benefits (see page 12) 20a		
b	Taxable amount, if any, from the worksheet on page 12	20b	
21	Other income (list type and amount—see page 12)	21	
22	Add the amounts shown in the far right column for lines 7, 8, and 10–21. This is your **total income** ▶	22	26,000

Adjustments to Income

(See Instructions on page 12.)

23	Reimbursed employee business expenses from Form 2106 . .	23		
24a	Your IRA deduction, from applicable worksheet on page 13 or 14 .	24a	1,800	
b	Spouse's IRA deduction, from applicable worksheet on page 13 or 14 .	24b		
25	Self-employed health insurance deduction, from worksheet on page 14	25		
26	Keogh retirement plan and self-employed SEP deduction . . .	26		
27	Penalty on early withdrawal of savings	27		
28	Alimony paid (recipient's last name and social security no. ___) .	28		
29	Add lines 23 through 28. These are your **total adjustments** . . . . . . ▶	29		1,800

Adjusted Gross Income

30	Subtract line 29 from line 22. This is your **adjusted gross income.** If this line is less than $15,432 and a child lived with you, see "Earned Income Credit" (line 56) on page 18 of the Instructions. If you want IRS to figure your tax, see page 15 of the Instructions . . . . ▶	30	24,200

142

	31	Amount from line 30 (adjusted gross income)	**31**	24,200

Tax Compu- tation

32a Check if: ☐ You were 65 or over   ☐ Blind;   ☐ **Spouse** was 65 or over   ☐ Blind.

Add the number of boxes checked and enter the total here . . . . . ▶ | **32a** |

b If you can be claimed as a dependent on another person's return, check here . . ▶ **32b** ☐

c If you are married filing a separate return and your spouse itemizes deductions, or you are a dual-status alien, see page 15 and check here . . . . . . ▶ **32c** ☐

33a **Itemized deductions.** See page 15 to see if you should itemize. If you don't itemize, enter zero. If you do itemize, attach Schedule A, enter the amount from Schedule A, line 26, **AND** skip line 33b . | **33a** | 0

Caution: ◀—— **b** **Standard deduction.** Read Caution to left. If it applies, see page 16 for the amount to enter.

If you checked any box on line 32a, b, or c **and** you don't itemize, see page 16 for the amount to enter on line 33b.

If **Caution** doesn't apply and your filing status from page 1 is: { Single or Head of household, enter $2,540 Married filing jointly or Qualifying widow(er), enter $3,760 Married filing separately, enter $1,880 } . . | **33b** | 2,540

34 Subtract line 33a or 33b, whichever applies, from line 31. Enter the result here . . . . . | **34** | 21,660

35 Multiply $1,900 by the total number of exemptions claimed on line 6e or see chart on page 16 . | **35** | 1,900

36 **Taxable income.** Subtract line 35 from line 34. Enter the result (but not less than zero) . . | **36** | 19,760

Caution: If under age 14 and you have more than $1,000 of investment income, check here ▶☐ and see page 16 to see if you have to use Form 8615 to figure your tax.

37 Enter tax. Check if from ☑ Tax Table, ☐ Tax Rate Schedules, ☐ Schedule D, or ☐ Form 8615 | **37** | 3,281

38 Additional taxes (see page 16). Check if from ☐ Form 4970 or ☐ Form 4972 . . . . . | **38** |

39 Add lines 37 and 38. Enter the total . . . . ▶ | **39** | 3,281

Credits
(See Instructions on page 17.)

40 Credit for child and dependent care expenses *(attach Form 2441)* | **40** |

41 Credit for the elderly or for the permanently and totally disabled *(attach Schedule R)* . . . . | **41** |

42 Add lines 40 and 41. Enter the total . . . . | **42** |

43 Subtract line 42 from line 39. Enter the result (but not less than zero) . . . . . . | **43** |

44 Foreign tax credit *(attach Form 1116)* . . . . . . | **44** |

45 General business credit. Check if from ☐ Form 3800, ☐ Form 3468, ☐ Form 5884, ☐ Form 6478, ☐ Form 6765, or ☐ Form 8586 . | **45** |

46 Add lines 44 and 45. Enter the total . . . . | **46** |

47 Subtract line 46 from line 43. Enter the result (but not less than zero) . . . . ▶ | **47** | 3,281

Other Taxes
(Including Advance EIC Payments)

48 Self-employment tax *(attach Schedule SE)* . . . . | **48** |

49 Alternative minimum tax *(attach Form 6251)* . . . . | **49** |

50 Tax from recapture of investment credit *(attach Form 4255)* . . . . | **50** |

51 Social security tax on tip income not reported to employer *(attach Form 4137)* | **51** |

52 Tax on an IRA or a qualified retirement plan *(attach Form 5329)* . . . | **52** |

53 Add lines 47 through 52. This is your **total tax** . . . . | **53** | 3,281

Payments

Attach Forms W-2, W-2G, and W-2P to front.

54 Federal income tax withheld (including tax shown on Form(s) 1099) | **54** | 3,200

55 1987 estimated tax payments and amount applied from 1986 return | **55** |

56 Earned income credit (see page 18) . . . . | **56** |

57 Amount paid with Form 4868 (extension request) . . . . . | **57** |

58 Excess social security tax and RRTA tax withheld (see page 19) | **58** |

59 Credit for Federal tax on gasoline and special fuels *(attach Form 4136)* | **59** |

60 Regulated investment company credit *(attach Form 2439)* . . . | **60** |

61 Add lines 54 through 60. These are your **total payments** . . . . ▶ | **61** | 3,200

Refund or Amount You Owe

62 If line 61 is larger than line 53, enter amount **OVERPAID** . . . . | **62** |

63 Amount of line 62 to be **REFUNDED TO YOU** . . . . ▶ | **63** |

64 Amount of line 62 to be applied to your 1988 estimated tax . . . ▶ | **64** |

65 If line 53 is larger than line 61, enter **AMOUNT YOU OWE.** Attach check or money order for full amount payable to "Internal Revenue Service." Write your social security number, daytime phone number, and "1987 Form 1040" on it . . . . | **65** | 81

Check ▶ ☐ if Form 2210 (2210F) is attached. See page 20.   **Penalty:** $

Please Sign Here

Under penalties of perjury, I declare that I have examined this return and accompanying schedules and statements, and to the best of my knowledge and belief, they are true, correct, and complete. Declaration of preparer (other than taxpayer) is based on all information of which preparer has any knowledge.

Your signature	Date 4/15/88	Your occupation TECHNICAL WRITER
Spouse's signature (if joint return, BOTH must sign)	Date	Spouse's occupation

Paid Preparer's Use Only

Preparer's signature ▶	Date	Check if self-employed ☐	Preparer's social security no.
Firm's name (or yours if self-employed) and address		E.I. No.	
		ZIP code	

Form **1040** Department of the Treasury—Internal Revenue Service 1987

U.S. Individual Income Tax Return 1987

For the year Jan.–Dec. 31, 1987, or other tax year beginning , 1987, ending , 19 | OMB No 1545-0074

Label	Your first name and initial (if joint return, also give spouse's name and initial) **GEOFFREY** Last name **FOURMYLE**	Your social security number **000 00 0000**
Use IRS label. Otherwise, please print or type.	Present home address (number and street or rural route). (If you have a P.O. Box, see page 6 of Instructions.) **5217 CERES BOULEVARD**	Spouse's social security number
	City, town or post office, state, and ZIP code **SAN FRANCISCO CA 94701**	For Privacy Act and Paperwork Reduction Act Notice, see Instructions.

Presidential Election Campaign ▶ Do you want $1 to go to this fund? . . . . Yes ☐ No ✓ | **Note:** Checking "Yes" will not change your tax or reduce your refund.
If joint return, does your spouse want $1 to go to this fund? . . Yes ☐ No ☐

Filing Status

Check only one box.

1 ✓ Single
2 ☐ Married filing joint return (even if only one had income)
3 ☐ Married filing separate return. Enter spouse's social security no. above and full name here.
4 ☐ Head of household (with qualifying person). (See page 7 of Instructions.) If the qualifying person is your child but not your dependent, enter child's name here.
5 ☐ Qualifying widow(er) with dependent child (year spouse died ▶ 19). (See page 7 of instructions.)

Exemptions

(See Instructions on page 7.)

Caution: If you can be claimed as a dependent on another person's tax return (such as your parents' return), do not check box 6a. But be sure to check the box on line 32b on page 2.

		No. of boxes checked on 6a and 6b ▶ **1**
6a ☐ Yourself	6b ☐ Spouse	

c Dependents

(1) Name (first, initial, and last name)	(2) Check if under age 5	(3) If age 5 or over, dependent's social security number	(4) Relationship	(5) No. of months lived in your home in 1987
	:	:		
	:	:		
	:	:		
	:	:		
	:	:		

No. of children on 6c who lived with you ▶
No. of children on 6c who didn't live with you due to divorce or separation ▶
No. of parents listed on 6c ▶
No. of other dependents listed on 6c ▶

If more than 7 dependents, see Instructions on page 7.

d If your child didn't live with you but is claimed as your dependent under a pre-1985 agreement, check here . ▶ ☐

Add numbers entered in boxes above ▶ **1**

e Total number of exemptions claimed (also complete line 35) . . . . ▶

Income

Please attach Copy B of your Forms W-2, W-2G, and W-2P here.

If you do not have a W-2, see page 6 of Instructions.

7	Wages, salaries, tips, etc. (attach Form(s) W-2)	7	
8	Taxable interest income (also attach Schedule B if over $400)	8	
9	Tax-exempt interest income (see page 10). DON'T include on line 8 [9]		
10	Dividend income (also attach Schedule B if over $400) .	10	6,000
11	Taxable refunds of state and local income taxes, if any, from worksheet on page 11 of Instructions .	11	
12	Alimony received	12	
13	Business income or (loss) (attach Schedule C).	13	33,421
14	Capital gain or (loss) (attach Schedule D)	14	
15	Other gains or (losses) (attach Form 4797)	15	
16a	Pensions, IRA distributions, annuities, and rollovers. Total received [16a]	16a	
b	Taxable amount (see page 11)	16b	
17	Rents, royalties, partnerships, estates, trusts, etc. (attach Schedule E) .	17	
18	Farm income or (loss) (attach Schedule F)	18	
19	Unemployment compensation (insurance) (see page 11)	19	
20a	Social security benefits (see page 12) [20a]	20a	
b	Taxable amount, if any, from the worksheet on page 12	20b	
21	Other income (list type and amount—see page 12)	21	
22	Add the amounts shown in the far right column for lines 7, 8, and 10–21. This is your **total income** ▶	22	39,421

Please attach check or money order here.

Adjustments to Income

(See Instructions on page 12.)

23	Reimbursed employee business expenses from Form 2106 . .	23	
24a	Your IRA deduction, from applicable worksheet on page 13 or 14	24a	
b	Spouse's IRA deduction, from applicable worksheet on page 13 or 14 . .	24b	
25	Self-employed health insurance deduction, from worksheet on page 14 .	25	
26	Keogh retirement plan and self-employed SEP deduction . . .	26	
27	Penalty on early withdrawal of savings	27	
28	Alimony paid (recipient's last name _____ and social security no. _____) .	28	
29	Add lines 23 through 28. These are your **total adjustments** . . . ▶	29	

Adjusted Gross Income

30 Subtract line 29 from line 22. This is your **adjusted gross income**. If this line is less than $15,432 and a child lived with you, see "Earned Income Credit" (line 56) on page 18 of the Instructions. If you want IRS to figure your tax, see page 15 of the Instructions . . . ▶ | 30 | 39,421

Tax Compu-tation	**31**	Amount from line 30 (adjusted gross income)	**31**	39,421
	32a	Check if: ☐ **You** were 65 or over ☐ Blind; ☐ **Spouse** was 65 or over ☐ Blind.		
		Add the number of boxes checked and enter the total here . . . . . ▶ │32a│		
	b	If you can be claimed as a dependent on another person's return, check here . . ▶ 32b ☐		
	c	If you are married filing a separate return and your spouse itemizes deductions, or you are a dual-status alien, see page 15 and check here . . . . ▶ 32c ☐		
	33a	**Itemized deductions.** See page 15 to see if you should itemize. If you don't itemize, enter zero. If you do itemize, attach Schedule A, enter the amount from Schedule A, line 26, **AND** skip line 33b .	**33a**	0
Caution: If you checked any box on line 32a, b, or c and you don't itemize, see page 16 for the amount to enter on line 33b.	**b**	**Standard deduction.** Read **Caution** to left. If it applies, see page 16 for the amount to enter. If **Caution** doesn't { Single or Head of household, enter $2,540 } apply and your filing { Married filing jointly or Qualifying widow(er), enter $3,760 } status from page 1 is: { Married filing separately, enter $1,880 }	**33b**	2,540
	34	Subtract line 33a **or** 33b, whichever applies, from line 31. Enter the result here	**34**	36,881
	35	Multiply $1,900 by the total number of exemptions claimed on line 6e or see chart on page 16 .	**35**	1,900
	36	**Taxable income.** Subtract line 35 from line 34. Enter the result (but not less than zero) . .	**36**	34,981
		Caution: If under age 14 and you have more than $1,000 of investment income, check here ▶☐ and see page 16 to see if you have to use Form 8615 to figure your tax.		
	37	Enter tax. Check if from ☑ Tax Table, ☐ Tax Rate Schedules, ☐ Schedule D, or ☐ Form 8615	**37**	8,095
	38	Additional taxes (see page 16). Check if from ☐ Form 4970 or ☐ Form 4972	**38**	
	39	Add lines 37 and 38. Enter the total . . . . ▶	**39**	8,095
Credits (See Instructions on page 17.)	**40**	Credit for child and dependent care expenses (attach Form 2441)	40		
	41	Credit for the elderly or for the permanently and totally disabled (attach Schedule R)	41		
	42	Add lines 40 and 41. Enter the total	**42**	
	43	Subtract line 42 from line 39. Enter the result (but not less than zero)	**43**	
	44	Foreign tax credit (attach Form 1116)	44		
	45	General business credit. Check if from ☐ Form 3800, ☐ Form 3468, ☐ Form 5884, ☐ Form 6478, ☐ Form 6765, or ☐ Form 8586 .	45		
	46	Add lines 44 and 45. Enter the total	**46**	
	47	Subtract line 46 from line 43. Enter the result (but not less than zero) . . . . . ▶	**47**	8,095
Other Taxes (Including Advance EIC Payments)	**48**	Self-employment tax (attach Schedule SE)	**48**	4,111
	49	Alternative minimum tax (attach Form 6251)	**49**	
	50	Tax from recapture of investment credit (attach Form 4255)	**50**	
	51	Social security tax on tip income not reported to employer (attach Form 4137) . . .	**51**	
	52	Tax on an IRA or a qualified retirement plan (attach Form 5329)	**52**	
	53	Add lines 47 through 52. This is your **total tax** . . . . ▶	**53**	12,206
Payments Attach Forms W-2, W-2G, and W-2P to front.	**54**	Federal income tax withheld (including tax shown on Form(s) 1099)	54		
	55	1987 estimated tax payments and amount applied from 1986 return	55	12,000	
	56	Earned income credit (see page 18)	56		
	57	Amount paid with Form 4868 (extension request) . . .	57		
	58	Excess social security tax and RRTA tax withheld (see page 19)	58		
	59	Credit for Federal tax on gasoline and special fuels (attach Form 4136)	59		
	60	Regulated investment company credit (attach Form 2439) .	60		
	61	Add lines 54 through 60. These are your **total payments** . . . . ▶	**61**	
Refund or Amount You Owe	**62**	If line 61 is larger than line 53, enter amount **OVERPAID** . . . . ▶	**62**	
	63	Amount of line 62 to be **REFUNDED TO YOU** . . . . ▶	**63**	
	64	Amount of line 62 to be applied to your 1988 estimated tax . . ▶ │ 64 │		
	65	If line 53 is larger than line 61, enter **AMOUNT YOU OWE.** Attach check or money order for full amount payable to "Internal Revenue Service." Write your social security number, daytime phone number, and "1987 Form 1040" on it	**65**	206
		Check ▶ ☐ if Form 2210 (2210F) is attached. See page 20. **Penalty: $**		

Please Sign Here

Under penalties of perjury, I declare that I have examined this return and accompanying schedules and statements, and to the best of my knowledge and belief, they are true, correct, and complete. Declaration of preparer (other than taxpayer) is based on all information of which preparer has any knowledge.

Your signature	Date 4/15/88	Your occupation TECHNICAL WRITER
Spouse's signature (if joint return, BOTH must sign)	Date	Spouse's occupation

Paid Preparer's Use Only

Preparer's signature	Date	Check if self-employed ☐	Preparer's social security no.
Firm's name (or yours if self-employed) and address		E.I. No.	
		ZIP code	

SCHEDULE C (Form 1040)	Profit or (Loss) From Business or Profession (Sole Proprietorship)	OMB No 1545-0074
Department of the Treasury Internal Revenue Service	Partnerships, Joint Ventures, etc., Must File Form 1065. ▶ Attach to Form 1040, Form 1041, or Form 1041S. ▶ See Instructions for Schedule C (Form 1040).	**1987** Attachment Sequence No 09

Name of proprietor		Social security number (SSN)
GEOFFREY FOURMYLE		000 00 0000

A Principal business or profession, including product or service (see Instructions)
TECHNICAL WRITER

B Principal business code (from Part IV) ▶ 7 8 8 0

C Business name and address ▶ GEOFFREY FOURMYLE 5217 CERES BOULEVARD SAN FRANCISCO CA 94701

D Employer ID number (Not SSN)

E Method(s) used to value closing inventory:
(1) ☐ Cost   (2) ☐ Lower of cost or market   (3) ☐ Other (attach explanation)

F Accounting method: (1) ☑ Cash   (2) ☐ Accrual   (3) ☐ Other (specify) ▶

	Yes	No
G Was there any change in determining quantities, costs, or valuations between opening and closing inventory? (If "Yes," attach explanation.)		✓
H Are you deducting expenses for an office in your home?		✓
I Did you file **Form 941** for this business for any quarter in 1987?		✓
J Did you "materially participate" in the operation of this business during 1987? (If "No," see Instructions for limitations on losses.)	✓	
K Was this business in operation at the end of 1987?	✓	

L How many months was this business in operation during 1987? ▶ 12

M If this schedule includes a loss, credit, deduction, income, or other tax benefit relating to a tax shelter required to be registered, check here. ▶☐
If you check this box, you **MUST** attach **Form 8271**

Part I   Income

1a Gross receipts or sales	**1a**	
b Less: Returns and allowances	**1b**	
c Subtract line 1b from line 1a and enter the balance here	**1c**	
2 Cost of goods sold and/or operations (from Part III, line 8)	**2**	
3 Subtract line 2 from line 1c and enter the **gross profit** here	**3**	45,000
4 Other income (including windfall profit tax credit or refund received in 1987)	**4**	
5 Add lines 3 and 4. This is the **gross income** ▶	**5**	45,000

Part II   Deductions

6 Advertising			**23** Repairs		
7 Bad debts from sales or services (see Instructions.)			**24** Supplies (not included in Part III)		
8 Bank service charges			**25** Taxes		
9 Car and truck expenses			**26** Travel, meals, and entertainment:		
10 Commissions			**a** Travel		250
11 Depletion			**b** Total meals and entertainment		
12 Depreciation and section 179 deduction from Form 4562 (not included in Part III)	1,000		**c** Enter 20% of line 26b subject to limitations (see Instructions)		
13 Dues and publications	100		**d** Subtract line 26c from 26b		
14 Employee benefit programs			**27** Utilities and telephone		729
15 Freight (not included in Part III)			**28a** Wages		
16 Insurance			**b** Jobs credit		
17 Interest:			**c** Subtract line 28b from 28a		
a Mortgage (paid to financial institutions)			**29** Other expenses (list type and amount):		
b Other			....		
18 Laundry and cleaning			....		
19 Legal and professional services			....		
20 Office expense			....		
21 Pension and profit-sharing plans	6,500				
22 Rent on business property	3,000				

30 Add amounts in columns for lines 6 through 29. These are the **total deductions** ▶	**30**	11,579
31 Net profit or (loss). Subtract line 30 from line 5. If a profit, enter here and on Form 1040, line 13, and on Schedule SE, line 2 (or line 5 of Form 1041 or Form 1041S). If a loss, you **MUST** go on to line 32	**31**	33,421

32 If you have a loss, you **MUST** answer this question: "Do you have amounts for which you are not at risk in this business?" (See Instructions.) ☐ Yes ☐ No
If "Yes," you **MUST** attach **Form 6198**. If "No," enter the loss on Form 1040, line 13, and on Schedule SE, line 2 (or line 5 of Form 1041 or Form 1041S).

For Paperwork Reduction Act Notice, see Form 1040 Instructions.

Schedule C (Form 1040) 1987

GLBF FORM 2856 - CALL (616) 243-6267

<table>
<tr><td>SCHEDULE SE
(Form 1040)
Department of the Treasury
Internal Revenue Service</td><td align="center">Computation of Social Security Self-Employment Tax
▶ See Instructions for Schedule SE (Form 1040).
▶ Attach to Form 1040.</td><td>OMB No. 1545-0074
1987
Attachment
Sequence No. 18</td></tr>
</table>

Name of person with **self-employment** income (as shown on social security card) GEOFFREY FOURMYLE	Social security number of person with **self-employment** income ▶ 000 : 00 : 0000

A If your only self-employment income was from earnings as a minister, member of a religious order, or Christian Science practitioner, AND you filed Form 4361, then DO NOT file Schedule SE. Instead, write "Exempt-Form 4361" on Form 1040, line 48. However, if you filed Form 4361, but have $400 or more of other earnings subject to self-employment tax, continue with Part I and check here ▶ ☐

B If you filed Form 4029 and have received IRS approval, DO NOT file Schedule SE. Write "Exempt-Form 4029" on Form 1040, line 48.

C If your only earnings subject to self-employment tax are wages from an electing church or church-controlled organization that is exempt from employer social security taxes and you are not a minister or a member of a religious order, skip lines 1–8. Enter zero on line 9. Continue with line 11a.

Part I   **Regular Computation of Net Earnings From Self-Employment**

1	Net farm profit (or loss) from Schedule F (Form 1040), line 37, and farm partnerships, Schedule K-1 (Form 1065), line 14a	**1**	
2	Net profit (or loss) from Schedule C (Form 1040), line 31, and Schedule K-1 (Form 1065), line 14a (other than farming). (See Instructions for other income to report.) Employees of an electing church or church-controlled organization DO NOT enter your Form W-2 wages on line 2. See the Instructions . .	**2**	33,421

Part II   **Optional Computation of Net Earnings From Self-Employment** (See "Who Can Use Schedule SE" in the Instructions.)

See Instructions for limitations. Generally, this part may be used **only** if you meet any of the following tests:

A Your **gross** farm income[1] was not more than $2,400; **or**

B Your **gross** farm income[1] was more than $2,400 and your **net** farm profits[2] were **less** than $1,600; **or**

C Your **net** nonfarm profits[3] were less than $1,600 and your **net** nonfarm profits[3] were also **less** than two-thirds (⅔) of your **gross** nonfarm income.[4]

Note: If line 2 above is two-thirds (⅔) or more of your gross nonfarm income[4], or, if line 2 is $1,600 or more, you may not use the optional method.
[1]From Schedule F (Form 1040), line 12, and Schedule K-1 (Form 1065), line 14b.   [3]From Schedule C (Form 1040), line 31, and Schedule K-1 (Form 1065), line 14a.
[2]From Schedule F (Form 1040), line 37, and Schedule K-1 (Form 1065), line 14a.   [4]From Schedule C (Form 1040), line 5, and Schedule K-1 (Form 1065), line 14c.

3	Maximum income for optional methods	**3**	$1,600	00
4	Farm Optional Method—If you meet test A or B above, enter the **smaller of:** two-thirds (⅔) of gross farm income from Schedule F (Form 1040), line 12, and farm partnerships, Schedule K-1 (Form 1065), line 14b; or $1,600	**4**		
5	Subtract line 4 from line 3	**5**		
6	Nonfarm Optional Method—If you meet test C above, enter the **smallest of:** two-thirds (⅔) of gross nonfarm income from Schedule C (Form 1040), line 5, and Schedule K-1 (Form 1065), line 14c (other than farming); or $1,600; or, if you elected the farm optional method, the amount on line 5 .	**6**		

Part III   **Computation of Social Security Self-Employment Tax**

7	Enter the amount from Part I, line 1 **or,** if you elected the farm optional method, Part II, line 4 . . .	**7**		
8	Enter the amount from Part I, line 2, **or,** if you elected the nonfarm optional method, Part II, line 6 .	**8**	33,421	
9	Add lines 7 and 8. If less than $400, do not file this schedule. (Exception: If you are an employee of an electing church or church-controlled organization and the total of lines 7 and 8 is less than $400, enter zero and complete the rest of this schedule.) . . .	**9**	33,421	
10	The largest amount of combined wages and self-employment earnings subject to social security or railroad retirement tax (tier 1) for 1987 is	**10**	$43,800	00
11a	Total social security wages and tips from Forms W-2 and railroad retirement compensation (tier 1). **Note:** Medicare qualified government employees whose wages are only subject to the 1.45% medicare (hospital insurance benefits) tax and employees of certain church or church-controlled organizations should **not** include those wages on this line. (See Instructions.) **11a**			
	b Unreported tips subject to social security tax from Form 4137, line 9, or to railroad retirement tax (tier 1) **11b**			
	c Add lines 11a and 11b	**11c**	0	
12a	Subtract line 11c from line 10. (If zero or less, enter zero.)	**12a**	43,800	
	b Enter your medicare qualified government wages if you are required to use the worksheet in Part III of the Instructions . . . **12b**			
	c Enter your Form W-2 wages of $100 or more from an electing church or church-controlled organization . . . **12c**			
	d Add lines 9 and 12c	**12d**	33,421	
13	Enter the smaller of line 12a or line 12d	**13**	33,421	
	If line 13 is $43,800, enter $5,387.40 on line 14. Otherwise, multiply line 13 by .123 and enter the result on line 14		×.123	
14	Self-employment tax. Enter this amount on Form 1040, line 48	**14**	4,111	

For Paperwork Reduction Act Notice, see Form 1040 Instructions.   Schedule SE (Form 1040) 1987

GLBF FORM 2896 - CALL (616) 243-6267

Form 4562

Department of the Treasury
Internal Revenue Service

Depreciation and Amortization

▶ See separate instructions.
▶ Attach this form to your return.

OMB No 1545-0172

1987

Attachment
Sequence No. **67**

Name(s) as shown on return

GEOFFREY FOURMYLE

Identifying number

000-00-0000

Business or activity to which this form relates

TECHNICAL WRITER

Part I **Depreciation** (Do not use this part for automobiles, certain other vehicles, computers, and property used for entertainment, recreation, or amusement. Instead, use Part III.)

Section A.—Election To Expense Depreciable Assets Placed in Service During This Tax Year (Section 179)

(a) Description of property	(b) Date placed in service	(c) Cost	(d) Expense deduction
1			

2 Listed property—Enter total from Part III, Section A, column (h) .

3 Total (add lines 1 and 2, but do not enter more than $10,000) .

4 Enter the amount, if any, by which the cost of all section 179 property placed in service during this tax year is more than $200,000 .

5 Subtract line 4 from line 3. If result is less than zero, enter zero. (See instructions for other limitations) .

Section B.—Depreciation

(a) Class of property	(b) Date placed in service	(c) Basis for depreciation (Business use only—see instructions)	(d) Recovery period	(e) Method of figuring depreciation	(f) Deduction
6 Accelerated Cost Recovery System (ACRS) (see instructions): *For assets placed in service ONLY during tax year beginning in 1987*					
a 3-year property					
b 5-year property					
c 7-year property					
d 10-year property					
e 15-year property					
f 20-year property					
g Residential rental property					
h Nonresidential real property					

7 Listed property—Enter total from Part III, Section A, column (g) .

8 ACRS deduction for assets placed in service prior to 1987 (see instructions) .   1,000

Section C.—Other Depreciation

9 Property subject to section 168(f)(1) election (see instructions) .

10 Other depreciation (see instructions) .

Section D.—Summary

11 Total (add deductions on lines 5 through 10). Enter here and on the Depreciation line of your return (Partnerships and S corporations—Do NOT include any amounts entered on line 5.) .

12 For assets above placed in service during the current year, enter the portion of the basis attributable to additional section 263A costs. (See instructions for who must use.) .

Part II **Amortization**

(a) Description of property	(b) Date acquired	(c) Cost or other basis	(d) Code section	(e) Amortization period or percentage	(f) Amortization for this year
1 Amortization for property placed in service only during tax year beginning in 1987					
2 Amortization for property placed in service prior to 1987 .					
3 Total. Enter here and on Other Deductions or Other Expenses line of your return .					

See Paperwork Reduction Act Notice on page 1 of the separate instructions.

Form **4562** (1987)

Form 1120 — U.S. Corporation Income Tax Return

Department of the Treasury
Internal Revenue Service

For calendar 1987 or tax year beginning _____, 1987, ending _____, 19____

▶ For Paperwork Reduction Act Notice, see page 1 of the instructions.

OMB No. 1545-0123

1987

Check if a—
A Consolidated return ☐
B Personal Holding Co. ☐
C Business Code No. (See the list in the instructions.) **7880**

Use IRS label. Other-wise please print or type.

Name: TIFFANY FIELD + CO., INC.
Number and street: 795 FIFTH AVENUE
City or town, state, and ZIP code: NEW YORK, NY 10021

D Employer identification number: 00-0000000
E Date incorporated: 1/1/87
F Total assets (See Specific Instructions.)

Dollars: 109,552 | Cents:

G Check applicable boxes. (1) ☐ Initial return (2) ☐ Final return (3) ☐ Change in address

Income

1a Gross receipts or sales _____ b Less returns and allowances _____ Balance ▶	1c	
2 Cost of goods sold and/or operations (Schedule A)	2	
3 Gross profit (line 1c less line 2)	3	
4 Dividends (Schedule C)	4	10,000
5 Interest	5	
6 Gross rents	6	
7 Gross royalties	7	
8 Capital gain net income (attach separate Schedule D)	8	
9 Net gain or (loss) from Form 4797, line 18, Part II (attach Form 4797)	9	
10 Other income (see instructions—attach schedule)	10	100,000
11 TOTAL income—Add lines 3 through 10 and enter here ▶	11	110,000

Deductions (See instructions for limitations on deductions)

12 Compensation of officers (Schedule E)	12	40,000
13a Salaries and wages _____ b Less jobs credit _____ Balance ▶	13c	
14 Repairs UTILITIES + TELEPHONE	14	3,500
15 Bad debts (see instructions)	15	
16 Rents	16	6,000
17 Taxes SOC. SEC.	17	2,045
18 Interest	18	
19 Contributions (see instructions for 10% limitation)	19	
20 Depreciation (attach Form 4562) · · · · 20	1,000	
21 Less depreciation claimed in Schedule A and elsewhere on return · 21a	0	21b	1,000
22 Depletion	22	
23 Advertising	23	
24 Pension, profit-sharing, etc., plans	24	10,000
25 Employee benefit programs MEDICAL	25	6,000
26 Other deductions (attach schedule)	26	4,500
27 TOTAL deductions—Add lines 12 through 26 and enter here ▶	27	73,045
28 Taxable income before net operating loss deduction and special deductions (line 11 less line 27) ·	28	36,955
29 Less: a Net operating loss deduction (see instructions) · · · 29a		
b Special deductions (Schedule C) · · · 29b	8,000	29c	8,000
30 Taxable income (line 28 less line 29c) · · · ·	30	28,955
31 TOTAL TAX (Schedule J)	31	4,403

Tax and Payments

32 Payments: a 1986 overpayment credited to 1987		
b 1987 estimated tax payments · · · · 4,400		
c Less 1987 refund applied for on Form 4466 · ( )		
d Tax deposited with Form 7004 · · · ·		
e Credit from regulated investment companies (attach Form 2439) ·		
f Credit for Federal tax on gasoline and special fuels (attach Form 4136) ·	32	4,400
33 Enter any PENALTY for underpayment of estimated tax—check ▶ ☐ if Form 2220 is attached ·	33	
34 TAX DUE—If the total of lines 31 and 33 is larger than line 32, enter AMOUNT OWED · · · ·	34	3
35 OVERPAYMENT—If line 32 is larger than the total of lines 31 and 33, enter AMOUNT OVERPAID · ·	35	
36 Enter amount of line 35 you want: Credited to 1988 estimated tax ▶ _____ Refunded ▶	36	

Please Sign Here

Under penalties of perjury, I declare that I have examined this return, including accompanying schedules and statements, and to the best of my knowledge and belief, it is true, correct, and complete. Declaration of preparer (other than taxpayer) is based on all information of which preparer has any knowledge.

Signature of officer | Date: 3/15/88 | Title: PRESIDENT

Paid Preparer's Use Only

Preparer's signature ▶ | Date | Check if self-employed ☐ | Preparer's social security number

Firm's name (or yours, if self-employed) and address ▶ | E.I. No. ▶ | ZIP code ▶

149

Schedule A   Cost of Goods Sold and/or Operations (See instructions for line 2, page 1.)

1 Inventory at beginning of year	1	
2 Purchases	2	
3 Cost of labor	3	
4a Additional section 263A costs (see instructions)	4a	
b Other costs (attach schedule)	4b	
5 Total—Add lines 1 through 4b	5	
6 Inventory at end of year	6	
7 Cost of goods sold and/or operations—Line 5 less line 6. Enter here and on line 2, page 1	7	

8a Check all methods used for valuing closing inventory:

   (i) ☐ Cost   (ii) ☐ Lower of cost or market as described in Regulations section 1.471-4 (see instructions)

   (iii) ☐ Writedown of "subnormal" goods as described in Regulations section 1.471-2(c) (see instructions)

   (iv) ☐ Other (Specify method used and attach explanation.) ▶ -

  b Check if the LIFO inventory method was adopted this tax year for any goods (if checked, attach Form 970) . . . . . . ☐

  c If the LIFO inventory method was used for this tax year, enter percentage (or amounts) of

    closing inventory computed under LIFO . . . . | 8c | |

  d Do the rules of section 263A (with respect to property produced or acquired for resale) apply to the corporation? . . ☐ Yes ☐ No

  e Was there any change (other than for section 263A purposes) in determining quantities, cost, or valuations between

    opening and closing inventory? If "Yes," attach explanation . . . . ☐ Yes ☐ No

Schedule C   Dividends and Special Deductions (See Schedule C instructions.)

	(a) Dividends received	(b) %	(c) Special deductions: multiply (a) × (b)
1 Domestic corporations subject to section 243(a) deduction (other than debt-financed stock)	10,000	see instructions	8,000
2 Debt-financed stock of domestic and foreign corporations (section 246A)		see instructions	
3 Certain preferred stock of public utilities		see instructions	
4 Foreign corporations and certain FSCs subject to section 245 deduction		see instructions	
5 Wholly owned foreign subsidiaries and FSCs subject to 100% deduction (sections 245(b) and (c))		100	
6 Total—Add lines 1 through 5. See instructions for limitation			8,000
7 Affiliated groups subject to the 100% deduction (section 243(a)(3))		100	
8 Other dividends from foreign corporations not included in lines 4 and 5			
9 Income from controlled foreign corporations under subpart F (attach Forms 5471)			
10 Foreign dividend gross-up (section 78)			
11 IC–DISC or former DISC dividends not included in lines 1 and/or 2 (section 246(d))			
12 Other dividends			
13 Deduction for dividends paid on certain preferred stock of public utilities (see instructions)			
14 Total dividends—Add lines 1 through 12. Enter here and on line 4, page 1 ▶	10,000		
15 Total deductions—Add lines 6, 7, and 13. Enter here and on line 29b, page 1 ▶			8,000

Schedule E   Compensation of Officers (See instructions for line 12, page 1.)

Complete Schedule E only if total receipts (line 1a, plus lines 4 through 10, of page 1, Form 1120) are $150,000 or more.

(a) Name of officer	(b) Social security number	(c) Percent of time devoted to business	Percent of corporation stock owned (d) Common	(e) Preferred	(f) Amount of compensation
		%	%	%	
		%	%	%	
		%	%	%	
		%	%	%	
		%	%	%	
		%	%	%	
		%	%	%	

Total compensation of officers—Enter here and on line 12, page 1 . . . .

Form 1120 (1987)

Page **3**

Schedule J Tax Computation (See instructions.)

1 Check if you are a member of a controlled group (see sections 1561 and 1563) . . . . ▶ ☐

2 If line 1 is checked, see instructions. If your tax year includes June 30, 1987, complete both a and b below. Otherwise, complete only b.

a (i) $ .... (ii) $ .... (iii) $ .... (iv) $ ....

b (i) $ .... (ii) $ ....

3 Income tax (see instructions to figure the tax; enter this tax or alternative tax from Schedule D, whichever is less). Check if from Schedule D ▶ ☐ . . . . | **3** | 2,305

4a Foreign tax credit (attach Form 1118)	4a	
b Possessions tax credit (attach Form 5735)	b	
c Orphan drug credit (attach Form 6765)	c	
d Credit for fuel produced from a nonconventional source (see instructions)	d	
e General business credit. Enter here and check which forms are attached ☐ Form 3800 ☐ Form 3468 ☐ Form 5884 ☐ Form 6478 ☐ Form 6765 ☐ Form 8586	e	

5 Total—Add lines 4a through 4e . . . . | **5** | 0
6 Line 3 less line 5 . . . . | **6** | 2,305
7 Personal holding company tax (attach Schedule PH (Form 1120)) . . . | **7** | 0
8 Tax from recomputing prior-year investment credit (attach Form 4255) . . | **8** | 0
9a Alternative minimum tax (see instructions—attach Form 4626) . . . | **9a** | 0
b Environmental tax (see instructions—attach Form 4626) . . . . | **9b** | 0
10 Total tax—Add lines 6 through 9b. Enter here and on line 31, page 1 . . | **10** | 2,305

Additional Information (See instruction F.)

H Did the corporation claim a deduction for expenses connected with: **Yes No**

(1) An entertainment facility (boat, resort, ranch, etc.)? No
(2) Living accommodations (except employees on business)? No
(3) Employees attending conventions or meetings outside the North American area? (See section 274(h).) No
(4) Employees' families at conventions or meetings? No
If "Yes," were any of these conventions or meetings outside the North American area? (See section 274(h).) Yes
(5) Employee or family vacations not reported on Form W-2? No

I (1) Did the corporation at the end of the tax year own, directly or indirectly, 50% or more of the voting stock of a domestic corporation? (For rules of attribution, see section 267(c).) No
If "Yes," attach a schedule showing: (a) name, address, and identifying number; (b) percentage owned; (c) taxable income or (loss) before NOL and special deductions of such corporation for the tax year ending with or within your tax year; (d) highest amount owed by the corporation to such corporation during the year; and (e) highest amount owed to the corporation by such corporation during the year.

(2) Did any individual, partnership, corporation, estate, or trust at the end of the tax year own, directly or indirectly, 50% or more of the corporation's voting stock? (For rules of attribution, see section 267(c).) If "Yes," complete (a) through (d) . . . Yes

(a) Attach a schedule showing name, address, and identifying number. Enter percentage owned ▶ TIFFANY FIELD, 745 FIFTH AVE NYC/100% 100%

(b) Was the owner of such voting stock a person other than a U.S. person? (See instructions.) **Note:** If "Yes," the corporation may have to file Form 5472. No
If "Yes," enter owner's country ▶ ....

(c) Enter highest amount owed by the corporation to such owner during the year ▶ ....

(d) Enter highest amount owed to the corporation by such owner during the year ▶ ....

Note: For purposes of I(1) and I(2), "highest amount owed" includes loans and accounts receivable/payable.

J Refer to the list in the instructions and state the principal: **Yes No**

Business activity ▶ ....
Product or service ▶ ....

K Was the corporation a U.S. shareholder of any controlled foreign corporation? (See sections 951 and 957.) . . . No
If "Yes," attach Form 5471 for each such corporation.

L At any time during the tax year, did the corporation have an interest in or a signature or other authority over a financial account in a foreign country (such as a bank account, securities account, or other financial account)? . . . . . . No
(See instruction F and filing requirements for form TD F 90-22.1.)
If "Yes," enter name of foreign country ▶ ....

M Was the corporation the grantor of, or transferor to, a foreign trust which existed during the current tax year, whether or not the corporation has any beneficial interest in it? . . . No
If "Yes," the corporation may have to file Forms 3520, 3520-A, or 926.

N During this tax year, did the corporation pay dividends (other than stock dividends and distributions in exchange for stock) in excess of the corporation's current and accumulated earnings and profits? (See sections 301 and 316.). . . . . . . No
If "Yes," file Form 5452. If this is a consolidated return, answer here for parent corporation and on Form 851, Affiliations Schedule, for each subsidiary.

O During this tax year did the corporation maintain any part of its accounting/tax records on a computerized system? . . . .

P Check method of accounting:
(1) ☐ Cash (2) ☐ Accrual
(3) ☐ Other (specify) ▶ ....

Q Check this box if the corporation issued publicly offered debt instruments with original issue discount . . . . . ☐
If so, the corporation may have to file Form 8281.

R Enter the amount of tax-exempt interest received or accrued during the tax year ▶ ....

S If you are a member of a controlled group, enter the amount of taxable income for the entire group ▶ ....

151

Schedule L **Balance Sheets**	Beginning of tax year		End of tax year	
Assets	(a)	(b)	(c)	(d)
1 Cash				27,219
2 Trade notes and accounts receivable				
a Less allowance for bad debts				
3 Inventories				
4 Federal and state government obligations		INCORPORATED		
5 Other current assets (attach schedule)		1/1/87		
6 Loans to stockholders				
7 Mortgage and real estate loans				
8 Other investments (attach schedule)				80,000
9 Buildings and other depreciable assets			3,333	
a Less accumulated depreciation			1,000	2,333
10 Depletable assets				
a Less accumulated depletion				
11 Land (net of any amortization)				
12 Intangible assets (amortizable only)				
a Less accumulated amortization				
13 Other assets (attach schedule)				
14 Total assets				109,552
Liabilities and Stockholders' Equity				
15 Accounts payable				
16 Mortgages, notes, bonds payable in less than 1 year				
17 Other current liabilities (attach schedule)		INITIAL		2,000
18 Loans from stockholders		RETURN		
19 Mortgages, notes, bonds payable in 1 year or more				
20 Other liabilities (attach schedule)				
21 Capital stock: a preferred stock				
b common stock			10,000	10,000
22 Paid-in or capital surplus				65,000
23 Retained earnings—Appropriated (attach schedule)				
24 Retained earnings—Unappropriated				
25 Less cost of treasury stock		( )		(32,552)
26 Total liabilities and stockholders' equity				109,552

Schedule M-1 **Reconciliation of Income per Books With Income per Return** You are not required to complete this schedule if the total assets on line 14, column (d), of Schedule L are less than $25,000.

1 Net income per books	32,552	7 Income recorded on books this year not included in this return (itemize)	
2 Federal income tax	4,403		
3 Excess of capital losses over capital gains		a Tax-exempt interest $	
4 Income subject to tax not recorded on books this year (itemize)			
		8 Deductions in this tax return not charged against book income this year (itemize)	
5 Expenses recorded on books this year not deducted in this return (itemize)		a Depreciation $	
a Depreciation $		b Contributions carryover $	
b Contributions carryover $			
		9 Total of lines 7 and 8	
6 Total of lines 1 through 5	36,955	10 Income (line 28, page 1)—line 6 less line 9	36,955

Schedule M-2 **Analysis of Unappropriated Retained Earnings per Books (line 24, Schedule L)** You are not required to complete this schedule if the total assets on line 14, column (d), of Schedule L are less than $25,000.

1 Balance at beginning of year	—	5 Distributions: a Cash	
2 Net income per books	32,552	b Stock	
3 Other increases (itemize)		c Property	
		6 Other decreases (itemize)	
		7 Total of lines 5 and 6	
4 Total of lines 1, 2, and 3	32,552	8 Balance at end of year (line 4 less line 7)	32,552

Form **1040** Department of the Treasury—Internal Revenue Service **1987**
U.S. Individual Income Tax Return

For the year Jan.–Dec. 31, 1987, or other tax year beginning , 1987, ending , 19 | OMB No. 1545-0074

Label

Use IRS label.
Otherwise,
please print or
type.

Your first name and initial (if joint return, also give spouse's name and initial) TIFFANY | Last name FIELD
Present home address (number and street or rural route). (If you have a P.O. Box, see page 6 of Instructions.) 795 FIFTH AVENUE
City, town or post office, state, and ZIP code NEW YORK NY 10021

Your social security number 000 00 0000
Spouse's social security number

For Privacy Act and Paperwork Reduction Act Notice, see Instructions.

Presidential Election Campaign ▶ Do you want $1 to go to this fund? . . . . . | Yes | No ✓
If joint return, does your spouse want $1 to go to this fund? . . | Yes | No

Note: Checking "Yes" will not change your tax or reduce your refund.

Filing Status

Check only
one box.

1 ✓ Single
2 Married filing joint return (even if only one had income)
3 Married filing separate return. Enter spouse's social security no. above and full name here. ___
4 Head of household (with qualifying person). (See page 7 of Instructions.) If the qualifying person is your child but not your dependent, enter child's name here. ___
5 Qualifying widow(er) with dependent child (year spouse died ▶ 19). (See page 7 of Instructions.)

Exemptions

(See
Instructions
on page 7.)

If more than 7
dependents, see
Instructions on
page 7.

Caution: If you can be claimed as a dependent on another person's tax return (such as your parents' return), do not check box 6a. But be sure to check the box on line 32b on page 2.

6a ✓ Yourself   6b Spouse

No. of boxes checked on 6a and 6b ▶ 1

c Dependents
(1) Name (first, initial and last name) | (2) Check if under age 5 | (3) If age 5 or over, dependent's social security number | (4) Relationship | (5) No. of months lived in your home in 1987

No. of children on 6c who lived with you ▶
No. of children on 6c who didn't live with you due to divorce or separation ▶
No. of parents listed on 6c ▶
No. of other dependents listed on 6c ▶

d If your child didn't live with you but is claimed as your dependent under a pre-1985 agreement, check here . ▶ ☐
e Total number of exemptions claimed (also complete line 35) . . . .

Add numbers entered in boxes above ▶ 1

Income

Please attach
Copy B of your
Forms W-2, W-2G,
and W-2P here.

If you do not have
a W-2, see
page 6 of
Instructions.

Please
attach check
or money
order here.

7 Wages, salaries, tips, etc. (attach Form(s) W-2) . . . . | 7 | 40,000
8 Taxable interest income (also attach Schedule B if over $400) . . . | 8 |
9 Tax-exempt interest income (see page 10). DON'T include on line 8 | 9 |
10 Dividend income (also attach Schedule B if over $400) . . . . . . | 10 |
11 Taxable refunds of state and local income taxes, if any, from worksheet on page 11 of Instructions . | 11 |
12 Alimony received . . . . | 12 |
13 Business income or (loss) (attach Schedule C) . . . . | 13 |
14 Capital gain or (loss) (attach Schedule D) . . . . | 14 |
15 Other gains or (losses) (attach Form 4797) . . . . | 15 |
16a Pensions, IRA distributions, annuities, and rollovers. Total received | 16a |
b Taxable amount (see page 11) . . . . | 16b |
17 Rents, royalties, partnerships, estates, trusts, etc. (attach Schedule E) . | 17 |
18 Farm income or (loss) (attach Schedule F) . . . . | 18 |
19 Unemployment compensation (insurance) (see page 11) . . . . . | 19 |
20a Social security benefits (see page 12) . . . . . | 20a |
b Taxable amount, if any, from the worksheet on page 12 . . . . . | 20b |
21 Other income (list type and amount—see page 12) . . . . | 21 |
22 Add the amounts shown in the far right column for lines 7, 8, and 10–21. This is your **total income** ▶ | 22 | 40,000

Adjustments to Income

(See
Instructions
on page 12.)

23 Reimbursed employee business expenses from Form 2106 . . . | 23 |
24a Your IRA deduction, from applicable worksheet on page 13 or 14 | 24a |
b Spouse's IRA deduction, from applicable worksheet on page 13 or 14 | 24b |
25 Self-employed health insurance deduction, from worksheet on page 14 . | 25 |
26 Keogh retirement plan and self-employed SEP deduction . . . | 26 |
27 Penalty on early withdrawal of savings . . . . | 27 |
28 Alimony paid (recipient's last name ___ and social security no. ___) . | 28 |
29 Add lines 23 through 28. These are your **total adjustments** . . . . . ▶ | 29 | 0

Adjusted Gross Income

30 Subtract line 29 from line 22. This is your **adjusted gross income**. If this line is less than $15,432 and a child lived with you, see "Earned Income Credit" (line 56) on page 18 of the Instructions. If you want IRS to figure your tax, see page 15 of the Instructions . . . ▶ | 30 | 40,000

153

Tax Compu- tation	**31**	Amount from line 30 (adjusted gross income)	**31**	40,000
	32a	Check if: ☐ **You** were 65 or over ☐ Blind; ☐ **Spouse** was 65 or over ☐ Blind.		
		Add the number of boxes checked and enter the total here . . . . . . ▶	**32a**	
	b	If you can be claimed as a dependent on another person's return, check here . . ▶	**32b** ☐	
	c	If you are married filing a separate return and your spouse itemizes deductions, or you are a dual-status alien, see page 15 and check here . . . . ▶	**32c** ☐	
	33a	**Itemized deductions.** See page 15 to see if you should itemize. If you don't itemize, enter zero. If you do itemize, attach Schedule A, enter the amount from Schedule A, line 26, **AND** skip line 33b .	**33a**	0
Caution: ◀ If you checked any box on line 32a, b, or c **and** you don't itemize, see page 16 for the amount to enter on line 33b.	**b**	**Standard deduction.** Read Caution to left. If it applies, see page 16 for the amount to enter. If **Caution** doesn't apply and your filing status from page 1 is: {Single or Head of household, enter $2,540 / Married filing jointly or Qualifying widow(er), enter $3,760 / Married filing separately, enter $1,880}	**33b**	2,540
	34	Subtract line 33a or 33b, whichever applies, from line 31. Enter the result here	**34**	37,460
	35	Multiply $1,900 by the total number of exemptions claimed on line 6e or see chart on page 16 . .	**35**	1,900
	36	**Taxable income.** Subtract line 35 from line 34. Enter the result (but not less than zero) . .	**36**	35,560
		Caution: If under age 14 and you have more than $1,000 of investment income, check here ▶☐ and see page 16 to see if you have to use Form 8615 to figure your tax.		
	37	Enter tax. Check if from ☑ Tax Table, ☐ Tax Rate Schedules, ☐ Schedule D, or ☐ Form 8615	**37**	8,305
	38	Additional taxes (see page 16). Check if from ☐ Form 4970 or ☐ Form 4972	**38**	0
	39	Add lines 37 and 38. Enter the total . . . . ▶	**39**	8,305
Credits (See Instructions on page 17.)	**40**	Credit for child and dependent care expenses (attach Form 2441) **40**		
	41	Credit for the elderly or for the permanently and totally disabled (attach Schedule R) **41**		
	42	Add lines 40 and 41. Enter the total	**42**	
	43	Subtract line 42 from line 39. Enter the result (but not less than zero)	**43**	
	44	Foreign tax credit (attach Form 1116) **44**		
	45	General business credit. Check if from ☐ Form 3800, ☐ Form 3468, ☐ Form 5884, ☐ Form 6478, ☐ Form 6765, or ☐ Form 8586 **45**		
	46	Add lines 44 and 45. Enter the total	**46**	
	47	Subtract line 46 from line 43. Enter the result (but not less than zero) . . . . ▶	**47**	8,305
Other Taxes (Including Advance EIC Payments)	**48**	Self-employment tax (attach Schedule SE)	**48**	
	49	Alternative minimum tax (attach Form 6251)	**49**	
	50	Tax from recapture of investment credit (attach Form 4255)	**50**	
	51	Social security tax on tip income not reported to employer (attach Form 4137)	**51**	
	52	Tax on an IRA or a qualified retirement plan (attach Form 5329) . . .	**52**	
	53	Add lines 47 through 52. This is your **total tax** . . . . ▶	**53**	8,305
Payments Attach Forms W-2, W-2G, and W-2P to front.	**54**	Federal income tax withheld (including tax shown on Form(s) 1099) **54** 8,000		
	55	1987 estimated tax payments and amount applied from 1986 return **55**		
	56	Earned income credit (see page 18) **56**		
	57	Amount paid with Form 4868 (extension request) . . . **57**		
	58	Excess social security tax and RRTA tax withheld (see page 19) **58**		
	59	Credit for Federal tax on gasoline and special fuels (attach Form 4136) **59**		
	60	Regulated investment company credit (attach Form 2439) . . . **60**		
	61	Add lines 54 through 60. These are your **total payments** . . . . . ▶	**61**	8,000
Refund or Amount You Owe	**62**	If line 61 is larger than line 53, enter amount **OVERPAID** . . . . . ▶	**62**	
	63	Amount of line 62 to be **REFUNDED TO YOU** . . . . ▶	**63**	
	64	Amount of line 62 to be applied to your 1988 estimated tax . . ▶ **64**		
	65	If line 53 is larger than line 61, enter **AMOUNT YOU OWE.** Attach check or money order for full amount payable to "Internal Revenue Service." Write your social security number, daytime phone number, and "1987 Form 1040" on it . . . . ▶	**65**	305
		Check ▶ ☐ if Form 2210 (2210F) is attached. See page 20. **Penalty: $**		

Please Sign Here	Under penalties of perjury, I declare that I have examined this return and accompanying schedules and statements, and to the best of my knowledge and belief, they are true, correct, and complete. Declaration of preparer (other than taxpayer) is based on all information of which preparer has any knowledge.

Your signature	Date	Your occupation	
	4/15/88	DESIGNER	
Spouse's signature (if joint return, BOTH must sign)	Date	Spouse's occupation	

Paid Preparer's Use Only	Preparer's signature ▶	Date	Check if self-employed ☐ Preparer's social security no.
	Firm's name (or yours if self-employed) and address ▶		E.I. No. ZIP code

Form **1040** Department of the Treasury—Internal Revenue Service **1987**
U.S. Individual Income Tax Return

For the year Jan.–Dec. 31, 1987, or other tax year beginning _____ , 1987, ending _____ , 19 ____ | OMB No 1545-0074

Label

Use IRS label.
Otherwise,
please print or
type.

Your first name and initial (if joint return, also give spouse's name and initial) | Last name
TIFFANY | FIELD

Your social security number
000 00 0000

Present home address (number and street or rural route). (If you have a P.O. Box, see page 6 of Instructions.)
795 FIFTH AVENUE

Spouse's social security number

City, town or post office, state, and ZIP code
NEW YORK, NY 10021

For Privacy Act and Paperwork Reduction Act Notice, see Instructions.

Presidential Election Campaign ▶ Do you want $1 to go to this fund? | Yes ▨ | No ✓ | Note: Checking "Yes" will not change your tax or reduce your refund.
If joint return, does your spouse want $1 to go to this fund?. | Yes | No

Filing Status

Check only one box.

1 ✓ Single
2 ☐ Married filing joint return (even if only one had income)
3 ☐ Married filing separate return. Enter spouse's social security no. above and full name here. _____
4 ☐ Head of household (with qualifying person). (See page 7 of Instructions.) If the qualifying person is your child but not your dependent, enter child's name here. _____
5 ☐ Qualifying widow(er) with dependent child (year spouse died ▶ 19 ____). (See page 7 of Instructions.)

Exemptions

(See Instructions on page 7.)

Caution: If you can be claimed as a dependent on another person's tax return (such as your parents' return), do not check box 6a. But be sure to check the box on line 32b on page 2.

6a ✓ Yourself   6b ☐ Spouse

No. of boxes checked on 6a and 6b ▶ 1

c Dependents (1) Name (first, initial, and last name)	(2) Check if under age 5	(3) If age 5 or over, dependent's social security number	(4) Relationship	(5) No. of months lived in your home in 1987

No. of children on 6c who lived with you ▶
No. of children on 6c who didn't live with you due to divorce or separation ▶
No. of parents listed on 6c ▶
No. of other dependents listed on 6c ▶

If more than 7 dependents, see Instructions on page 7.

d If your child didn't live with you but is claimed as your dependent under a pre-1985 agreement, check here . ▶ ☐
e Total number of exemptions claimed (also complete line 35) . . . .

Add numbers entered in boxes above ▶ 1

Income

Please attach Copy B of your Forms W-2, W-2G, and W-2P here.

If you do not have a W-2, see page 6 of Instructions.

7 Wages, salaries, tips, etc. *(attach Form(s) W-2)* . . . . | 7 |
8 Taxable interest income *(also attach Schedule B if over $400)* . . . | 8 |
9 Tax-exempt interest income (see page 10). DON'T include on line 8 | 9 | |
10 Dividend income *(also attach Schedule B if over $400)* . . . . . | 10 | 10,000
11 Taxable refunds of state and local income taxes, if any, from worksheet on page 11 of Instructions . | 11 |
12 Alimony received . . . . | 12 |
13 Business income or (loss) *(attach Schedule C)* . . . . | 13 | 74,800
14 Capital gain or (loss) *(attach Schedule D)* . . . . | 14 |
15 Other gains or (losses) *(attach Form 4797)* . . . . | 15 |
16a Pensions, IRA distributions, annuities, and rollovers. Total received | 16a | |
b Taxable amount (see page 11) . . . . | 16b |
17 Rents, royalties, partnerships, estates, trusts, etc. *(attach Schedule E)* | 17 |
18 Farm income or (loss) *(attach Schedule F)* . . . . | 18 |
19 Unemployment compensation (insurance) (see page 11) . . . . | 19 |

Please attach check or money order here.

20a Social security benefits (see page 12) . . . . . . | 20a | |
b Taxable amount, if any, from the worksheet on page 12 . . . . | 20b |
21 Other income (list type and amount—see page 12) . . . . . . | 21 |
22 Add the amounts shown in the far right column for lines 7, 8, and 10–21. This is your **total income** ▶ | 22 | 84,800

Adjustments to Income

(See Instructions on page 12.)

23 Reimbursed employee business expenses from Form 2106 . | 23 | |
24a Your IRA deduction, from applicable worksheet on page 13 or 14 | 24a | |
b Spouse's IRA deduction, from applicable worksheet on page 13 or 14 | 24b | |
25 Self-employed health insurance deduction, from worksheet on page 14 . | 25 | |
26 Keogh retirement plan and self-employed SEP deduction . . | 26 | |
27 Penalty on early withdrawal of savings . . . . | 27 | |
28 Alimony paid (recipient's last name _____ and social security no. _____) . | 28 | |
29 Add lines 23 through 28. These are your **total adjustments** . . . . . . ▶ | 29 |

Adjusted Gross Income

30 Subtract line 29 from line 22. This is your **adjusted gross income**. If this line is less than $15,432 and a child lived with you, see "Earned Income Credit" (line 56) on page 18 of the Instructions. If you want IRS to figure your tax, see page 15 of the Instructions . . . ▶ | 30 | 84,800

Tax Compu-tation	31	Amount from line 30 (adjusted gross income)	**31** 84,800
	32a	Check if: ☐ **You** were 65 or over ☐ Blind; ☐ **Spouse** was 65 or over ☐ Blind. Add the number of boxes checked and enter the total here . . . . . . ▶	32a
	b	If you can be claimed as a dependent on another person's return, check here . . ▶	32b ☐
	c	If you are married filing a separate return and your spouse itemizes deductions, or you are a dual-status alien, see page 15 and check here . . . . ▶	32c ☐
	33a	**Itemized deductions.** See page 15 to see if you should itemize. If you don't itemize, enter zero. If you do itemize, attach Schedule A, enter the amount from Schedule A, line 26, **AND** skip line 33b .	**33a** 0
Caution: ◀— If you checked any box on line 32a, b, or c **and** you don't itemize, see page 16 for the amount to enter on line 33b.	b	**Standard deduction.** Read Caution to left. If it applies, see page 16 for the amount to enter. If **Caution** doesn't apply and your filing status from page 1 is: { Single or Head of household, enter $2,540 / Married filing jointly or Qualifying widow(er), enter $3,760 / Married filing separately, enter $1,880 }	**33b** 2,540
	34	Subtract line 33a or 33b, whichever applies, from line 31. Enter the result here	**34** 82,260
	35	Multiply $1,900 by the total number of exemptions claimed on line 6e or see chart on page 16 .	**35** 1,900
	36	**Taxable income.** Subtract line 35 from line 34. Enter the result (but not less than zero) .	**36** 80,360
		Caution: If under age 14 and you have more than $1,000 of investment income, check here ▶☐ and see page 16 to see if you have to use Form 8615 to figure your tax.	
	37	Enter tax. Check if from ☐ Tax Table, ☑ Tax Rate Schedules, ☐ Schedule D, or ☐ Form 8615	**37** 24,903
	38	Additional taxes (see page 16). Check if from ☐ Form 4970 or ☐ Form 4972	**38** 0
	39	Add lines 37 and 38. Enter the total . . . . ▶	**39** 24,903
Credits (See Instructions on page 17.)	40	Credit for child and dependent care expenses *(attach Form 2441)*	**40**	
	41	Credit for the elderly or for the permanently and totally disabled *(attach Schedule R)*	**41**	
	42	Add lines 40 and 41. Enter the total	**42**
	43	Subtract line 42 from line 39. Enter the result (but not less than zero) . . .	**43**
	44	Foreign tax credit *(attach Form 1116)*	**44**	
	45	General business credit. Check if from ☐ Form 3800, ☐ Form 3468, ☐ Form 5884, ☐ Form 6478, ☐ Form 6765, or ☐ Form 8586	**45**	
	46	Add lines 44 and 45. Enter the total	**46**
	47	Subtract line 46 from line 43. Enter the result (but not less than zero) . . . . . . ▶	**47** 24,903
Other Taxes (Including Advance EIC Payments)	48	Self-employment tax *(attach Schedule SE)*	**48** 5,387
	49	Alternative minimum tax *(attach Form 6251)*	**49**
	50	Tax from recapture of investment credit *(attach Form 4255)*	**50**
	51	Social security tax on tip income not reported to employer *(attach Form 4137)* .	**51**
	52	Tax on an IRA or a qualified retirement plan *(attach Form 5329)*	**52**
	53	Add lines 47 through 52. This is your **total tax** . . . . ▶	**53** 30,290
Payments Attach Forms W-2, W-2G, and W-2P to front.	54	Federal income tax withheld (including tax shown on Form(s) 1099)	**54**	
	55	1987 estimated tax payments and amount applied from 1986 return	**55** 30,000
	56	Earned income credit (see page 18)	**56**	
	57	Amount paid with Form 4868 (extension request)	**57**	
	58	Excess social security tax and RRTA tax withheld (see page 19) . .	**58**	
	59	Credit for Federal tax on gasoline and special fuels *(attach Form 4136)*	**59**	
	60	Regulated investment company credit *(attach Form 2439)* . . .	**60**	
	61	Add lines 54 through 60. These are your **total payments** . . . . ▶	**61** 30,000
Refund or Amount You Owe	62	If line 61 is larger than line 53, enter amount **OVERPAID** . . . . ▶	**62**
	63	Amount of line 62 to be **REFUNDED TO YOU** . . . . ▶	**63**
	64	Amount of line 62 to be applied to your 1988 estimated tax . . . ▶	64
	65	If line 53 is larger than line 61, enter **AMOUNT YOU OWE.** Attach check or money order for full amount payable to "Internal Revenue Service." Write your social security number, daytime phone number, and "1987 Form 1040" on it	**65** 290
		Check ▶ ☐ if Form 2210 (2210F) is attached. See page 20. **Penalty: $**	

Please Sign Here

Under penalties of perjury, I declare that I have examined this return and accompanying schedules and statements, and to the best of my knowledge and belief, they are true, correct, and complete. Declaration of preparer (other than taxpayer) is based on all information of which preparer has any knowledge.

Your signature	Date 4/15/88	Your occupation DESIGNER
Spouse's signature (if joint return, BOTH must sign)	Date	Spouse's occupation

Paid Preparer's Use Only

Preparer's signature ▶	Date	Check if self-employed ☐	Preparer's social security no.
Firm's name (or yours if self-employed) and address ▶		E.I. No.	
		ZIP code	

SCHEDULE C
(Form 1040)

Department of the Treasury
Internal Revenue Service

Profit or (Loss) From Business or Profession
(Sole Proprietorship)
Partnerships, Joint Ventures, etc., Must File Form 1065.
▶ Attach to Form 1040, Form 1041, or Form 1041S. ▶ See Instructions for Schedule C (Form 1040).

OMB No. 1545-0074

1987

Attachment
Sequence No. 09

Name of proprietor	Social security number (SSN)
TIFFANY FIELD	000 00 0000

A Principal business or profession, including product or service (see Instructions)
DESIGNER

B Principal business code
(from Part IV) ▶ 7 8 8 0

C Business name and address ▶ TIFFANY FIELD
795 FIFTH AVENUE, New YoRK, NY 10021

D Employer ID number (Not SSN)

E Method(s) used to value closing inventory:
(1) ☐ Cost   (2) ☐ Lower of cost or market   (3) ☐ Other (attach explanation)

		Yes	No
F Accounting method: (1) ☑ Cash (2) ☐ Accrual (3) ☐ Other (specify) ▶			
G Was there any change in determining quantities, costs, or valuations between opening and closing inventory? (If "Yes," attach explanation.)			✓
H Are you deducting expenses for an office in your home?			✓
I Did you file **Form 941** for this business for any quarter in 1987?			✓
J Did you "materially participate" in the operation of this business during 1987? (If "No," see Instructions for limitations on losses.)		✓	
K Was this business in operation at the end of 1987?		✓	
L How many months was this business in operation during 1987? ▶ 12			

M If this schedule includes a loss, credit, deduction, income, or other tax benefit relating to a tax shelter required to be registered, check here. ▶ ☐
If you check this box, you **MUST** attach **Form 8271**

Part I Income

1a Gross receipts or sales	1a		
b Less: Returns and allowances	1b		
c Subtract line 1b from line 1a and enter the balance here	1c		
2 Cost of goods sold and/or operations (from Part III, line 8)	2		
3 Subtract line 2 from line 1c and enter the **gross profit** here	3	100,000	
4 Other income (including windfall profit tax credit or refund received in 1987)	4	0	
5 Add lines 3 and 4. This is the **gross income** ▶	5	100,000	

Part II Deductions

6 Advertising		**23** Repairs		
7 Bad debts from sales or services (see Instructions.)		**24** Supplies (not included in Part III)		
8 Bank service charges		**25** Taxes		
9 Car and truck expenses		**26** Travel, meals, and entertainment:		
10 Commissions		**a** Travel		1,000
11 Depletion		**b** Total meals and entertainment		
12 Depreciation and section 179 deduction from Form 4562 (not included in Part III)	1,000	**c** Enter 20% of line 26b subject to limitations (see Instructions)		
13 Dues and publications	1,500	**d** Subtract line 26c from 26b		
14 Employee benefit programs Med. Ins.	200	**27** Utilities and telephone		3,500
15 Freight (not included in Part III)		**28a** Wages		
16 Insurance		**b** Jobs credit		
17 Interest:		**c** Subtract line 28b from 28a		
a Mortgage (paid to financial institutions)		**29** Other expenses (list type and amount):		
b Other		Postage + Xeroxing		1,000
18 Laundry and cleaning		....		
19 Legal and professional services		....		
20 Office expense	1,000	....		
21 Pension and profit-sharing plans	10,000	....		
22 Rent on business property	6,000			

30 Add amounts in columns for lines 6 through 29. These are the **total deductions** ▶	30	23,200	

31 Net profit or (loss). Subtract line 30 from line 5. If a profit, enter here and on Form 1040, line 13, and on Schedule SE, line 2 (or line 5 of Form 1041 or Form 1041S). If a loss, you **MUST** go on to line 32

31	74,800

32 If you have a loss, you **MUST** answer this question: "Do you have amounts for which you are not at risk in this business?" (See Instructions.) ☐ Yes ☐ No
If "Yes," you **MUST** attach **Form 6198.** If "No," enter the loss on Form 1040, line 13, and on Schedule SE, line 2 (or line 5 of Form 1041 or Form 1041S).

For Paperwork Reduction Act Notice, see Form 1040 Instructions.

Schedule C (Form 1040) 1987

SCHEDULE SE
(Form 1040)

Department of the Treasury
Internal Revenue Service

Computation of Social Security Self-Employment Tax

▶ See Instructions for Schedule SE (Form 1040).

▶ Attach to Form 1040.

OMB No. 1545-0074

1987

Attachment
Sequence No **18**

Name of person with **self-employment** income (as shown on social security card)

TIFFANY FIELD

Social security number of person
with **self-employment** income ▶   000 ∶ 00 ∶ 0000

A If your only self-employment income was from earnings as a minister, member of a religious order, or Christian Science practitioner, AND you filed Form 4361, then DO NOT file Schedule SE. Instead, write "Exempt-Form 4361" on Form 1040, line 48. However, if you filed Form 4361, but have $400 or more of other earnings subject to self-employment tax, continue with Part I and check here ▶ ☐

B If you filed Form 4029 and have received IRS approval, DO NOT file Schedule SE. Write "Exempt-Form 4029" on Form 1040, line 48.

C If your only earnings subject to self-employment tax are wages from an electing church or church-controlled organization that is exempt from employer social security taxes and you are not a minister or a member of a religious order, skip lines 1–8. Enter zero on line 9. Continue with line 11a.

	Part I	**Regular Computation of Net Earnings From Self-Employment**		
1		Net farm profit (or loss) from Schedule F (Form 1040), line 37, and farm partnerships, Schedule K-1 (Form 1065), line 14a	**1**	
2		Net profit (or loss) from Schedule C (Form 1040), line 31, and Schedule K-1 (Form 1065), line 14a (other than farming). (See Instructions for other income to report.) Employees of an electing church or church-controlled organization DO NOT enter your Form W-2 wages on line 2. See the Instructions	**2**	74,800

	Part II	**Optional Computation of Net Earnings From Self-Employment** (See "Who Can Use Schedule SE" in the Instructions.)

See Instructions for limitations: Generally, this part may be used **only** if you meet any of the following tests:

A Your **gross** farm income[1] was not more than $2,400; **or**

B Your **gross** farm income[1] was more than $2,400 and your **net** farm profits[2] were **less** than $1,600; **or**

C Your **net** nonfarm profits[3] were less than $1,600 and your **net** nonfarm profits[3] were also **less** than two-thirds (⅔) of your **gross** nonfarm income.[4]

Note: If line 2 above is two-thirds (⅔) or more of your gross nonfarm income,[4] or, if line 2 is $1,600 or more, you may **not** use the optional method.

[1]From Schedule F (Form 1040), line 12, and Schedule K-1 (Form 1065), line 14b.   [3]From Schedule C (Form 1040), line 31, and Schedule K-1 (Form 1065), line 14a.

[2]From Schedule F (Form 1040), line 37, and Schedule K-1 (Form 1065), line 14a.   [4]From Schedule C (Form 1040), line 5, and Schedule K-1 (Form 1065), line 14c.

3	Maximum income for optional methods	**3**	$1,600 00
4	Farm Optional Method—If you meet test A or B above, enter the **smaller of:** two-thirds (⅔) of gross farm income from Schedule F (Form 1040), line 12, and farm partnerships, Schedule K-1 (Form 1065), line 14b; **or** $1,600	**4**	
5	Subtract line 4 from line 3	**5**	
6	Nonfarm Optional Method—If you meet test C above, enter the **smallest of:** two-thirds (⅔) of gross nonfarm income from Schedule C (Form 1040), line 5, and Schedule K-1 (Form 1065), line 14c (other than farming); **or** $1,600; **or**, if you elected the farm optional method, the amount on line 5	**6**	

	Part III	**Computation of Social Security Self-Employment Tax**		
7		Enter the amount from Part I, line 1, **or,** if you elected the farm optional method, Part II, line 4 . . .	**7**	
8		Enter the amount from Part I, line 2, **or,** if you elected the nonfarm optional method, Part II, line 6	**8**	74,800
9		Add lines 7 and 8. If less than $400, do not file this schedule. (Exception: If you are an employee of an electing church or church-controlled organization and the total of lines 7 and 8 is less than $400, enter zero and complete the rest of this schedule.)	**9**	74,800
10		The largest amount of combined wages and self-employment earnings subject to social security or railroad retirement tax (tier 1) for 1987 is	**10**	$43,800 00

11a	Total social security wages and tips from Forms W-2 and railroad retirement compensation (tier 1). **Note:** Medicare qualified government employees whose wages are only subject to the 1.45% medicare (hospital insurance benefits) tax and employees of certain church or church-controlled organizations should **not** include those wages on this line. (See Instructions.)	**11a**			
b	Unreported tips subject to social security tax from Form 4137, line 9, or to railroad retirement tax (tier 1)	**11b**			
c	Add lines 11a and 11b		**11c**	0	
12a	Subtract line 11c from line 10. (If zero or less, enter zero.)		**12a**	43,800	
b	Enter your medicare qualified government wages if you are required to use the worksheet in Part III of the Instructions . . . **12b**				
c	Enter your Form W-2 wages of $100 or more from an electing church or church-controlled organization **12c**				
d	Add lines 9 and 12c		**12d**	74,800	
13	Enter the smaller of line 12a or line 12d		**13**	43,800	
	If line 13 is $43,800, enter $5,387.40 on line 14. Otherwise, multiply line 13 by .123 and enter the result on line 14			× .123	
14	Self-employment tax. Enter this amount on Form 1040, line 48		**14**	5,387	

For Paperwork Reduction Act Notice, see Form 1040 Instructions.

Schedule SE (Form 1040) 1987

Form **4562**

Department of the Treasury
Internal Revenue Service

Depreciation and Amortization

▶ See separate instructions.
▶ Attach this form to your return.

OMB No 1545-0172

1987

Attachment
Sequence No 67

Name(s) as shown on return

TIFFANY FIELD

Business or activity to which this form relates

DESIGNER

Identifying number

000-00-0000

Part I **Depreciation** (Do not use this part for automobiles, certain other vehicles, computers, and property used for entertainment, recreation, or amusement. Instead, use Part III.)

Section A.—Election To Expense Depreciable Assets Placed in Service During This Tax Year (Section 179)

(a) Description of property	(b) Date placed in service	(c) Cost	(d) Expense deduction
1			

2 Listed property—Enter total from Part III, Section A, column (h)·
3 Total (add lines 1 and 2, but do not enter more than $10,000)
4 Enter the amount, if any, by which the cost of all section 179 property placed in service during this tax year is more than $200,000
5 Subtract line 4 from line 3. If result is less than zero, enter zero. (See instructions for other limitations)

Section B.—Depreciation

(a) Class of property	(b) Date placed in service	(c) Basis for depreciation (Business use only—see instructions)	(d) Recovery period	(e) Method of figuring depreciation	(f) Deduction
6 Accelerated Cost Recovery System (ACRS) (see instructions): For assets placed in service ONLY during tax year beginning in 1987					
a 3-year property					
b 5-year property					
c 7-year property					
d 10-year property					
e 15-year property					
f 20-year property					
g Residential rental property					
h Nonresidential real property					

7 Listed property—Enter total from Part III, Section A, column (g)·
8 ACRS deduction for assets placed in service prior to 1987 (see instructions) ... 1,000

Section C.—Other Depreciation

9 Property subject to section 168(f)(1) election (see instructions)
10 Other depreciation (see instructions)

Section D.—Summary

11 Total (add deductions on lines 5 through 10). Enter here and on the Depreciation line of your return (Partnerships and S corporations—Do NOT include any amounts entered on line 5.)
12 For assets above placed in service during the current year, enter the portion of the basis attributable to additional section 263A costs. (See instructions for who must use.)

Part II **Amortization**

(a) Description of property	(b) Date acquired	(c) Cost or other basis	(d) Code section	(e) Amortization period or percentage	(f) Amortization for this year
1 Amortization for property placed in service only during tax year beginning in 1987					
2 Amortization for property placed in service prior to 1987 .					
3 Total. Enter here and on Other Deductions or Other Expenses line of your return .					

See Paperwork Reduction Act Notice on page 1 of the separate instructions.

Form **4562** (1987)

159

In fact, the tax savings on dividend income are so enormous that they deserve their own tables:

AS INDIVIDUAL

Name	Dividends	Other Net Income	Total	Marginal Tax Bracket for Dividends	Tax on Dividends
Gordon	$6,000	$35,809	$41,809	35%	$2,100
Fourmyle	6,000	33,421	39,421	35	2,100
Field	10,000	74,800	84,800	38.5	3,850

AS CORPORATION

Name	Dividends	Less Exclusion	Net Dividends	Marginal Tax Bracket for Dividends	Tax on Dividends
Gordon	$6,000	$4,800	$1,200	15%	$180
Fourmyle	6,000	4,800	1,200	15	180
Field	10,000	8,000	2,000	16.5*	330

*The 16.5 percent is a blended rate for 1987; for 1988 the rate dropped to 15 percent.

SUMMARY

	Gordon & Fourmyle		Field	
	As Individual	As Corporation	As Individual	As Corporation
Dividends escaping tax	$ 0	$4,800	$ 0	$8,000
Dividends taxed	6,000	1,200	10,000	2,000
Tax rate	35%	15%	38.5%	16.5%
Tax on dividends	2,100	180	3,850	330
Amount saved		1,920		3,520
Percent saved		91%		91%

Just for fun, why don't you pull out last year's tax return and pencil your numbers in on one of the sample returns. If your figures show savings of several thousand dollars a year, it might be a good idea for you to incorporate.

15

Retire with the Biggest
Tax Break Possible

When you retire, you will be liquidating your corporation, which has served you well all these years, and distributing all the assets and liabilities to the stockholders in exchange for all the stock. The excess of the value of the assets over the liabilities and investment in the stock is treated as a capital gain. Although the Tax Reform Act of 1986 destroyed favorable capital-gains treatment by repealing the capital-gains deduction, as of early 1988 there was congressional support for reinstating some form of favorable capital-gains treatment. As it will be some years before you liquidate your corporation, to the extent to which you haven't declared corporate dividends, which would be taxed to you at ordinary income-tax rates, you may be able to turn those dividends into capital gains if you can wait until you liquidate your corporation.

You don't necessarily have to sell the stock in your corporate portfolio, either. You can distribute in cash or in kind: you give your stock back to the corporation, and the corporation gives you its assets—its stock portfolio and anything else it owns.

In this case, you'd have to send the corporation's stock to the transfer agent so that it can be reissued in your name alone.

You would also have to notify the IRS thirty days after adopting your plan of liquidation. You would have to have a meeting of the board of directors, which, as you know by now, can be just you, while you're watching "M*A*S*H" reruns.

Liquidation of your corporation is treated by the IRS as a sale because essentially it's a sale of your stock. Liquidation rules have changed with virtually every edition of *Inc. Yourself,* and they are likely to change again before you are ready to liquidate your corporation. At present, you can choose from two forms of liquidation: the lump-sum method (§331) or the installment method. To understand how these differ, let's take the same corporation through both liquidation options.

Example: The XYZ Corporation liquidates on June 30, 1989. It has fixed assets valued at $10,000, receivables of $30,000, and inventory of $10,000. The stockholder's basis in his stock is $20,000.

§331—LUMP-SUM METHOD

The lump-sum method is a complete liquidation. There is no time requirement. With this method, each asset takes a basis to its value at the date of liquidation:

Total assets	$50,000
Less basis in stock	−20,000
Capital gain	$30,000

The stockholder pays tax on a capital gain of $30,000.

Whether the corporation pays taxes depends upon *its* basis. For example, if its fixed assets had been depreciated to $5,000, it would have a basis of $45,000 and a taxable capital gain of $5,000.

To elect the lump-sum method of liquidation, your corporation would file IRS Form 966.

§333—ONE-MONTH LIQUIDATION METHOD

The one-month liquidation method was repealed under the Tax Reform Act of 1986.

INSTALLMENT METHOD

§453 liquidation, mentioned in earlier editions of *Inc. Yourself,* was killed by the Tax Equity and Fiscal Responsibility Act, but there is still a way to get installment treatment when you liquidate your corporation. This method is suitable only for sales of real estate, plant and equipment, or other major tangible assets worth at least $50,000.

Essentially, the corporation makes the sale at the corporate level at liquidation and passes the mortgage notes on to the shareholder, who is taxed as payment is received, as though he himself had made the installment sale.

Let's return to XYZ Corporation to see how the installment method works.

First, the gross profit percentage is calculated by dividing the gross profit (total assets less the stockholder's basis) by the contract price (total assets):

$$\$30,000 \div \$50,000 = 60\%$$

Thus, the gross profit percentage is 60 percent. Therefore, only 60 percent of each annual installment is taxed at capital-gains rates; the remaining 40 percent is treated as a return of capital and is therefore not taxed.

If your stockholder takes 30 percent in 1989—the year of the sale—as his first installment, the calculations look like this:

$15,000	Installment payment
−6,000	Return of capital
$ 9,000	Gain—taxed at capital-gains rates

In the remaining seven years—from 1990 through 1996—if 10 percent is paid out each year, the calculations for each year look like this:

$5,000	Installment payment
−2,000	Return of capital
$3,000	Gain—taxed at capital-gains rates

This method of liquidation is complicated and requires professional tax advice. Again, it's important to note that you must make sure that your corporation is in liquidation status during this entire time. Of course, you could close down the corporation and still work in semiretirement as a sole proprietor; many people do.

To elect the installment method of liquidation, your corporation would file IRS Form 966.

YOUR PENSION

But liquidating your corporation is only half the story; the other half is drawing your pension. Like corporate assets, retirement-fund assets can be either converted to cash or distributed in kind. If the shareholder elects lump-sum distribution (the entire balance of the retirement fund within one taxable year), which has several favorable tax advantages, the occasion must be either (1) separation from the employer; (2) reaching the age of 59½; or (3) disability. Lump-sum distributions cannot be taken because the plan has been terminated.

Workaholics will be delighted to know that there is no maximum age for retirement.

If the shareholder/employee is less than 59½ years old, there is an unresolved problem: what comes first as the triggering event in a one-person corporation—separation from the employer or termination of the plan, since it is a one-person corporation? These events cannot be simultaneous.

There is a fairly easy way to resolve this problem. The shareholder/employee can make his separation from service a little earlier than the termination of his plan by going on a one-month terminal leave and then liquidating the corporation.

When you liquidate your pension plan, your gain is calculated as the value of its assets in excess of any amounts you may have contributed to it yourself. (This is the 10 percent Voluntary Contribution mentioned in Chapter 10, "All About ERISA.") Similar to an installment method of liquidation, your pension gain is subject to a special 5-year averaging computation, so that taxes are minimized.

In order to perform the calculation, reduce the gain by the minimum distribution allowance. The minimum distribution allowance is equal to the lesser of $10,000 or ½ the distribution − (⅕ the distributions in excess of $20,000).

Let's look at some examples:

If your pension is $25,000 and your contribution is $0, your gain is $25,000. The minimum distribution allowance is equal to

$10,000-\frac{1}{5} (\$25,000-\$20,000)$
$10,000-\frac{1}{5} (\$5,000)$
$10,000-\$1,000 = \$9,000$

Thus, your minimum distribution allowance is $9,000, and the net value of your pension is $16,000.

As you can see, the smaller the distribution is, the higher the minimum distribution allowance will be. On pensions smaller than $20,000, the minimum distribution allowance is the full $10,000; the benefits of the minimum distribution allowance are completely phased out when the distribution is $70,000 or more:

$10,000-\frac{1}{5} (\$70,000-\$20,000)$
$10,000-\frac{1}{5} (\$50,000)$
$10,000-\$10,000 = \$0$

Although the $25,000 in the first example (taxed as $16,000) or the $70,000 in the second example (taxed as $70,000) is received as a lump sum, the distribution is taxed as though it was received over a period of 5 years. The tax is paid all in one year, but the tax rate is the low income-averaging rate. In a sense, this lump-sum pension distribution is analogous to the lump-sum liquidation of the corporation's assets under §331.

There is also a pension-distribution plan analogous to the installment-method liquidation of the corporation. In this case, the pension distribution is taken down as an annuity and would be taxed under the annuity rules, which are the same as the installment rules.

Thus, you are left with two choices: taking your pension as a lump sum or as an annuity. Since both the lump-sum and the annuity options are treated similarly by the IRS, which should you take? Essentially, it's a question of life-style. Some people are happier with a lump sum; some people need that lump sum; some people need to have their money doled out to them because they're spendthrifts. But since taxes in the aggregate are higher with the annuity option, it may be wisest for even the spendthrifts to take the lump sum, pay the taxes on it, and then buy a mutual fund that will send them a check every month or every quarter.

16

If You Should Die First— Planning for Your Heirs

If you should die before liquidating your corporation, using the example of XYZ Corporation in the preceding chapter, your heirs can use your stock's value on the date of your death as the adjusted cost. Thus, instead of your basis of $20,000, your heirs can use the new stepped-up figure of $50,000. Then, when they liquidated the corporation at $50,000, they would not have to pay any capital-gains taxes, since under the law there was no gain ($50,000 − $50,000 = $0).

Your heirs will be able to choose the same liquidation options— §331 or the installment method—as you would have had.

If the distribution (either pension or the liquidation of the corporation) is taken as a lump sum by your beneficiaries, it is included in your estate. However, if the distribution is taken as an annuity, it will bypass the estate and not be subject to estate taxes. Therefore, the shortest length of annuity that will satisfy the IRS would seem to be an ideal way to save paying estate taxes.

Incorporation permits another estate-planning feature: deferred compensation, which is not available to sole proprietors. Deferred compensation defers current income to the individual and provides future benefit. A deferred-compensation agreement can even designate your choice of beneficiary.

But deferred compensation is a good idea for you, as well as in planning for your heirs. A deferred-compensation agreement can fund your retirement and provide security for the future. The key difference between this form of deferred compensation and the deferred compensation in a 401(k) plan (see pages 105–106) is that there is no limit to the amount of salary you can defer, while the 401(k)'s limit for 1988 is just over $7,300.

If you defer some of your salary, you are not subject to current taxes because you have not received this income. The corporation is the stakeholder: the deferred compensation is an asset of the corporation and becomes a benefit to the corporation because it can be carried as an asset, as a balance-sheet item.

Deferred-compensation plans offer an advantage to the corporation. If the corporation puts $200,000 into your deferred-compensation plan, it has an expense of $200,000. But if the $200,000 grows to $300,000, depending on the terms of the deferred-compensation agreement, the corporation can either pay out the $300,000 and write off an expense of $300,000 or pay out the $200,000, write off $200,000, and keep $100,000 as an asset.

However, there is a disadvantage to deferred-compensation plans: if the corporation goes bankrupt, the assets of the plan can be attached by creditors.

Deferred-compensation plans are not for the average employee because he or she needs current income. Plans could be set up for $50 a month, and many state and city employees and employees of large corporations participate in such plans. But deferred compensation really becomes very advantageous to the higher-paid employee who doesn't need all that current income. Instead of taking $60,000 a year, the employee may take a salary of $40,000 and defer $20,000.

In order to do this, a deferred-compensation agreement must be drawn up by a lawyer, setting up the amount or percentage of salary to be deferred, the number of years the funds will be deferred, and the terms of the payout. The agreement can be drawn flexibly enough so that the employee agrees to defer his bonus, which, in a one-person corporation, he controls completely. The cost of drawing up a deferred-compensation agreement varies; if you find a lawyer who's done many of these and is familiar with them, the bill should be for no more than two or three hours of his or her time.

The deferred-compensation agreement must be a valid plan, in writing. It must impose reasonable obligations on the corporation to pay the deferred compensation, and it must anticipate that at the end of the time period, the money will be paid to the employee. The deferred-compensation agreement can't be a sham, where at the end of 10 years the corporation throws the money away and can't pay. The corporation must intend to repay the funds.

Now: what happens to the deferred-compensation funds? The corporation carries them as an asset. There is no current write-off to the corporation, but there is no income to the employee, either.

Because deferred-compensation plans are not qualified under Section 401 of the Internal Revenue Code, the corporation can make use of these assets, borrow against them, use them as collateral, etc. The corporation can fund the plan any way it wants to. It doesn't even have to fund the plan: it can just pay the employee the agreed-upon sum at the end of the time period. The deferred-compensation plan permits the corporation to accumulate money in a special fund— without regard to the $150,000/$250,000 limitation—because it's for a valid business purpose and therefore not subject to the accumulated earnings tax discussed in Chapter 1, "So You Want to Be a Corporation."

Deferred compensation is not only a way for an individual to avoid paying taxes on a salary he does not need, it's also a way for his corporation to accumulate funds in excess of $150,000/$250,000 without being subjected to the accumulated earnings tax.

Deferred compensation can also work for smaller amounts of money. It can work for amounts as small as $5,000 or $10,000 a year or for a one-shot lump sum, as in the case of a prizefighter or an author who signs a contract for a large advance. In these cases, a deferred-compensation plan could be drawn up along with the contract.

Deferred compensation isn't for everyone, but if you think it may be for you, consult your lawyer and your accountant.

There you have the basic tax-planning options: for your heirs' liquidation of your corporation, for their being paid your pension benefits, and for your own deferred compensation. Hopefully, the first two won't be needed, and you can enjoy the third for many, many years.

APPENDIX A

State Requirements
for General Business and
Professional Corporations

State	Professions Covered by P. C. Act	Title and No. of P. C. Act
Alabama	All licensed professions	Professional Corp. Act No. 260
Alaska	All licensed professions	Alaska Statute 10.45
Arizona	Accountants, doctors, lawyers	Arizona Revised Statute 10–908
Arkansas	All licensed professions	Act 155 of 1963
California	Accountants, chiropractors, clinical social workers, dentists, doctors, lawyers, marriage, family & child counselors, optometrists, osteopaths, physical therapists, podiatrists, psychologists, shorthand reporters, speech pathologists	Part 4, Division 3, Title 1, California Corps. Code
Colorado	Accountants, architects, chiropractors, dentists, doctors, lawyers, optometrists, veterinarians	Title 12
Connecticut	All licensed professions	Professional Service Corps. Chap. 594a

Min. No. of Shareholders*	Title of Form to Be Filed	Address and Telephone No.	Filing Fee
1	Charter	Judge of Probate of County where corporate office will be located	$60
1	Duplicate Originals of Articles of Incorporation	Dept. of Commerce & Economic Development Pouch D Juneau, AK 99811 (907) 465-2530	$135 min.
1	Articles of Incorporation	Sec'y of State 2222 W. Encanto Blvd. Phoenix, AZ 85009 (602) 255-3026	$50
1	Articles of Incorporation	Sec'y of State Corporation Dept. State Capitol Bldg. Little Rock, AR 72201 (501) 652-5151	$50
1	Articles of Incorporation.**	Sec'y of State—Corporate Filings 1230 J St. Sacramento, CA 95814 (916) 445-7205	$370
Not given	Articles of Incorporation	Sec'y of State 1575 Sherman Denver, CO 80203 (303) 894-2251	$22
1	Certificate of Incorporation	Sec'y of State P. O. Box 846 30 Trinity St. Hartford, CT 06106 (203) 566-8570	$110 min.

*In nearly all states, the minimum number of incorporators and directors is also one.
**After incorporation, application is made to the proper licensing board of the profession for a Certificate of Authority, which, when granted, legally permits the corporation to practice the profession.

State	Professions Covered by P. C. Act	Title and No. of P. C. Act
Delaware	Accountants, architects, chiropodists, chiropractors, dentists, doctors, engineers, lawyers, optometrists, osteopaths, veterinarians	Chapter 6, General Corp. Law
Florida	Accountants, architects, chiropodists, chiropractors, dentists, doctors, lawyers, life insurance agents, osteopaths, podiatrists, veterinarians	Professional Corp. Act Chap. 621
Georgia	Accountants, architects, chiropractors, dentists, doctors, engineers, land surveyors, lawyers, optometrists, osteopaths, podiatrists, psychologists (applied), veterinarians	Georgia Professional Corp. Act. No. 943
Hawaii	Accountants, chiropractors, dentists, doctors, lawyers and district court practitioners, naturopaths, opticians, optometrists, osteopaths, pharmacists, veterinarians	Part VIII of Chap. 416, Hawaii Revised Statutes
Idaho	All licensed professions	Title 30, Chap. 13
Illinois	All licensed professions	Professional Service Corp. Act
Indiana	All licensed professions	Professional Corp. Acts IC 23
Iowa	Accountants, architects, chiropractors, dentists, doctors, engineers, land surveyors, lawyers, optometrists, osteopaths, podiatrists, veterinarians	Professional Corp. Act 496C

Min. No. of Shareholders*	Title of Form to Be Filed	Address and Telephone No.	Filing Fee
1	Certificate of Incorporation**	Sec'y of State Division of Corporations P. O. Box 898 Dover, DE 19903 (302) 736-3073	$50 min.
1	Articles of Incorporation	Charter Section Sec'y of State Tallahassee, FL 32304 (904) 487-6052	$70
1	Articles of Incorporation	Sec'y of State Business Services & Regulations Suite 315, West Tower 2 Martin Luther King Jr. Dr., SE Atlanta, GA 30334 (404) 656-2817	$100 + county fee, which varies
1	Articles of Incorporation and Affidavits of Officers	Dept. of Commerce & Consumer Affairs Business Registration Division P. O. Box 40 Honolulu, HI 96810 (808) 548-6111	$50 min. + optional $40 expediting fee***
1	None	Division of Corporations Boise, ID 83720 (208) 334-2300	$60
1	Articles of Incorporation	Sec'y of State Corporation Division Springfield, IL 62756 (217) 782-7880	$100.50 min.
1	Articles of Incorporation	Corporations Division 155 State House Indianapolis, IN 46204 (317) 232-6576	$90
1	Articles of Incorporation	Sec'y of State Corporation Division Des Moines, IA 50319 (515) 281-5204	$50

*In nearly all states, the minimum number of incorporators and directors is also one.
**Corporation must have registered office with registered agent in state.
***Paying this fee guarantees three-day service; without it, incorporators may have to wait two to three months.

State	Professions Covered by P. C. Act	Title and No. of P. C. Act
Kansas	All licensed professions	Professional Corp. Law of Kansas Chap. 17
Kentucky	All licensed professions	Professional Service Corps., Kentucky Revised Statutes Chap. 274
Louisiana	Accountants, chiropractors, dentists, doctors, lawyers	Louisiana Revised Statutes 12:8, 9, 11, 12, 14
Maine	Accountants, architects, chiropodists, chiropractors, dentists, doctors, lawyers, life insurance agents, osteopaths, podiatrists	Professional Service Corp. Act Chap. 22
Maryland	Accountants, doctors, lawyers, veterinarians. Architects and engineers can choose P. C.s or general business corporations.	Title 5, Maryland Code
Massachusetts	Accountants, chiropractors, dentists, doctors, electrologists, engineers, lawyers, optometrists, physical therapists, podiatrists, psychologists, veterinarians	Professional Corps., Chap. 156A
Michigan	All licensed professions	Act 192, P. A. of 1962, as amended
Minnesota	Accountants, chiropractors, dentists, doctors, lawyers, optometrists, osteopaths, podiatrists, psychologists, veterinarians	Minnesota Professional Corps. Act, Minn. Stat. 319A

174

Min. No. of Shareholders*	Title of Form to Be Filed	Address and Telephone No.	Filing Fee
1	Articles of Incorporation	Sec'y of State Corporation Division Topeka, KS 66612 (913) 296-4564	$75
1	No standard form for public use	Sec'y of State State Capitol Bldg. Frankfort, KY 40601 (502) 564-2848	$35 min.
1	No forms available. Notarized affidavit of registered agent must accompany filing	Sec'y of State Corporations Division P. O. Box 94125 Baton Rouge, LA 70804–9125 (504) 925-4704	$60
1	Articles of Incorporation	Sec'y of State Corporation & UCC Division Augusta, ME 04333 (207) 289-4195	$85 min.
1	Form No. 1 Form No. 25 (every year)	State Dept. of Assessments & Taxation 301 W. Preston St. Baltimore, MD 21201 (301) 225-1340	$40 min.
1	Articles of Organization	Sec'y of the Commonwealth Corporation Division One Ashburton Pl. Boston, MA 02133 (617) 727-2850	$150 min.
1	Articles of Incorporation Form C&S 101	Michigan Dept. of Commerce Corporation & Securities Bureau Box 30054 Lansing, MI 48909 (517) 334-6304	$35 min.
1	Articles of Incorporation	Sec'y of State Corporation Division 180 State Office Bldg. St. Paul, MN 55155 (612) 296-2803	$125

*In nearly all states, the minimum number of incorporators and directors is also one.

State	Professions Covered by P. C. Act	Title and No. of P. C. Act
Mississippi	All licensed professions	Mississippi Professional Corp. Law
Missouri	Accountants, architects, chiropodists, chiropractors, dentists, doctors, engineers, lawyers, optometrists, osteopaths, podiatrists, veterinarians	Title XXIII, Chap. 356 Revised Statutes of Missouri 1969, as amended
Montana	Accountants, architects, chiropodists, chiropractors, dentists, doctors, engineers, lawyers, nurses, optometrists, osteopaths, pharmacists, physical therapists, veterinarians	Professional Service Corp. Act, Chap. 21, Title 15, Revised Codes of Montana
Nebraska	All registered professions	Nebraska Professional Corp. Act, Chap. 21, Article 22
Nevada	All licensed professions	Professional Corps. and Associations Act
New Hampshire	Accountants, architects, chiropractors, dentists, doctors, engineers, nurses, optometrists, pharmacists, psychologists, veterinarians	Revised Statutes Annotated—Chap. 294-A, Professional Assns.
New Jersey	All licensed professions	Professional Service Corp. Act NJSA 14A:17-1 et seq.
New Mexico	All licensed professions	Professional Corp. Act Sections 51-22-1 to 51-22-13 NMSA 1953 Compilation

Min. No. of Shareholders*	Title of Form to Be Filed	Address and Telephone No.	Filing Fee
1	Articles of Incorporation	Sec'y of State P. O. Box 136 Jackson, MS 39205 (601) 359-1350	$50 min.
1	Articles of Incorporation Corp. Form #41	Sec'y of State Jefferson City, MO 65101 (314) 751-2359	$53 min.
1	Forms not prescribed or furnished by state	Sec'y of State Capitol Helena, MT 59601 (406) 444-3665	$70 min.
1	Articles of Incorporation	Sec'y of State Corporation Division 2304 State Capitol Bldg. Lincoln, NE 68509 (402) 471-4079	$40 min. + $3 per page recording fee
1	Articles of Incorporation	Sec'y of State Corporation Division Carson City, NV 89710 (702) 885-5203	$75 min.
1	Record of Organization	Sec'y of State Corporation Division 204 State House Concord, NH 03301 (603) 271-3244	$85 min.
1	Certificate of Incorporation	New Jersey Department of State Commercial Recording Bureau Corporate Filing Section CN-308 Trenton, NJ 08625 (609) 530-6400	$75
1	Articles of Incorporation	State Corporation Commission Corporation & Franchise Tax Depts. P. O. Drawer 1269 Santa Fe, NM 87501 (505) 827-4504	$50

*In nearly all states, the minimum number of incorporators and directors is also one.

State	Professions Covered by P. C. Act	Title and No. of P. C. Act
New York	All licensed professions	Business Corp. Law Article 15
North Carolina	Accountants, architects, chiropractors, dentists, doctors, engineers, landscape architects, lawyers, optometrists, osteopaths, podiatrists, psychologists, surveyors, veterinarians	Professional Corp. Act Chap. 55B
North Dakota	All licensed professions	Professional Corp. Act Chap. 10–13
Ohio	All licensed professions	Chap. 1785, Ohio Revised Code
Oklahoma	Accountants, architects, chiropodists, chiropractors, dentists, doctors, nurses, optometrists, osteopaths, physical therapists, podiatrists, psychologists, veterinarians	Professional Corp. Act Title 18
Oregon	All licensed professions	Chap. 58, Professional Corps.

Min. No. of Shareholders*	Title of Form to Be Filed	Address and Telephone No.	Filing Fee
1	Certificate of Incorporation	New York State Division of Corporations 162 Washington Ave. Albany, NY 12231 (518) 474-6200	$110
1	Articles of Incorporation; Certification of Eligibility to Practice from licensing board	Sec'y of State Corporations Division 300 N. Salisbury St. Raleigh, NC 27611 (919) 733-4201	$90 min.
1	Duplicate Originals of Articles of Incorporation	Sec'y of State Division of Corporations Bismarck, ND 58505 (701) 224-2905	$90 min.
1	Articles of Incorporation	Sec'y of State Division of Corporations State Office Tower, 14th Fl. 30 E. Broad St. Columbus, OH 43266–0418 (614) 466-3910	$75 min.
1	Duplicate Originals of Articles of Incorporation	Sec'y of State Rm. 101 Oklahoma State Capitol Bldg. Oklahoma City, OK 73105 (405) 521-3911	$50 min.
1	Duplicate Originals of Professional Corp. Articles of Incorporation 11–P	Corporation Commissioner Commerce Bldg. Salem, OR 97310 (503) 378-4166	$40

*In nearly all states, the minimum number of incorporators and directors is also one.

State	Professions Covered by P. C. Act	Title and No. of P. C. Act
Pennsylvania	Accountants, architects, auctioneers, chiropractors, dentists, doctors, engineers, funeral directors, landscape architects, lawyers, nurses, optometrists, osteopaths, pharmacists, podiatrists, psychologists, veterinarians	Pennsylvania Corp. Law—Act 160 of 1970
Rhode Island	Accountants, architects, chiropodists, chiropractors, dentists, doctors, engineers, nurses, optometrists, veterinarians	Title 7, Chap. 5.1 Professional Service Corps.
South Carolina	All licensed professions	South Carolina Professional Association Act
South Dakota	Accountants, chiropractors, dentists, doctors, lawyers, optometrists, veterinarians	SDCL Chapter 47–11 through 47–138–18
Tennessee	All licensed professions	Title 48, Chap. 20, Tennessee Code Annotated (Tennessee Professional Corp. Act)
Texas	Accountants, dentists, doctors, nurses, optometrists, osteopaths, podiatrists, psychologists, surveyors, veterinarians	Texas Professional Corp. Act
Utah	All licensed professions	Title 16, Chap. 11, Professional Corp. Act

Min. No. of Shareholders*	Title of Form to Be Filed	Address and Telephone No.	Filing Fee
1	Articles of Incorporation— Domestic Professional Corp.	Commonwealth of Pennsylvania Corporation Bureau Harrisburg, PA 17120 (717) 787-1057	$75
1	Duplicate Originals of Articles of Incorporation	Sec'y of State 270 Westminster Mall Providence, RI 02903 (401) 277-3040	$110
1	Articles of Association	Filed at courthouse in county where professional corporation is located	$45 min.
1	Articles of Incorporation	Sec'y of State State Capitol Pierre, SD 57501 (605) 773-4845	$40 min.
1	Corporation Charter	Sec'y of State Corporation Division Nashville, TN 37219 (615) 741-2286	$50
1	Articles of Incorporation	Sec'y of State Corporation Division Sam Houston State Office Bldg. Austin, TX 78711 (512) 463-5555	$300, $310 to expedite in 24–48 hrs.
1	Application for a Certificate of Authority; Articles of Incorporation	Business Regulation Office Corporation Division 160 East 300 South P. O. Box 45801 Salt Lake City, UT 84145–0801 (801) 530-6016	$50 min.

*In nearly all states, the minimum number of incorporators and directors is also one.

State	Professions Covered by P. C. Act	Title and No. of P. C. Act
Vermont	Architects, doctors, lawyers	Title 11
Virginia	All licensed professions	Chap. 7, Professional Corps.
Washington	All licensed professions	RCW 18.100
West Virginia	All licensed professions	Under general corporation laws
Wisconsin	All licensed professions	Service Corp. Law, Wisconsin Statute 180.99
Wyoming	Not specifically covered by statute	Sections 17–49.1 and 17.49–2 Wyoming Statutes 1957

Min. No. of Shareholders*	Title of Form to Be Filed	Address and Telephone No.	Filing Fee
2	DCI Articles of Association with proof of profession attached	Sec'y of State Corporations Division Montpelier, VT 05602–2710 (802) 828-2386	$35 min.
1	Articles of Incorporation	Clerk of the Commission State Corporation Commissioner Box 1197 Richmond, VA 23209 (804) 786-6704	$45 min.
1	Forms not supplied	Corporations Division Republic Bldg., 2nd Fl. 505 E. Union Olympia, WA 98504 (206) 753-7115	$175 min.
1	Form 101, Articles of Incorporation	Sec'y of State Corporation Division Charleston, WV 25305 (304) 342-8000	$30 min.
1	Articles of Incorporation, Form 2	Sec'y of State Corporation Division State Capitol Bldg. Madison, WI 53702 (608) 266-3590	$70 min. + $10 min. recording fee
No provision for minimum	No forms are furnished	Sec'y of State Division of Corporations Cheyenne, WY 82002 (307) 777-7311	$50 min.

*In nearly all states, the minimum number of incorporators and directors is also one.

State	Title and No. of General Business Corp. Act	Min. No. of Shareholders*	Title of Form to Be Filed	Address and Telephone No.	Filing Fee
Alabama	Title 10, 1958 Recompiled Code	1	Charter	Judge of Probate of County where corporate office will be located	$60
Alaska	Alaska Statute 10.05	1	Duplicate Originals of Articles of Incorporation	Dept. of Commerce and Economic Development Pouch D Juneau, AK 99811 (907) 465-2530	$135 min.
Arizona	Arizona Revised Statutes 10–050—10–149	1	Articles of Incorporation	Sec'y of State 2222 W. Encanto Blvd. Phoenix, AZ 85009 (602) 255-3026	$50
Arkansas	Act 576 of 1965	1	Articles of Incorporation	Sec'y of State Corporation Dept. State Capitol Bldg. Little Rock, AR 72201 (501) 652-5151	$50
California	Title 1, Division 1, Calif. Corps. Code	1	Articles of Incorporation	Sec'y of State—Corporate Filings 1230 J St. Sacramento, CA 95814 (916) 445-7205	$370
Colorado	Title 7, Volume 3	1	Articles of Incorporation	Sec'y of State 1575 Sherman Denver, CO 80203 (303) 894-2251	$22

*In nearly all states, the minimum number of incorporators and directors is also one.

184

State	Title and No. of General Business Corp. Act	Min. No. of Shareholders*	Title of Form to Be Filed	Address and Telephone No.	Filing Fee
Connecticut	Stock Corporation Act Chap. 599	1	Certificate of Incorporation	Sec'y of State P. O. Box 846 30 Trinity St. Hartford, CT 06106 (203) 566-8570	$110 min.
Delaware	Title 8, General Corp. Law	1	Certificate of Incorporation**	Sec'y of State Division of Corporations P. O. Box 898 Dover, DE 19903 (302) 736-3073	$50 min.
Florida	General Corp. Act Chap. 607	1	Articles of Incorporation	Charter Section Sec'y of State Tallahassee, FL 32304 (904) 487-6052	$70
Georgia	Georgia Title 22—Corporations	1	Articles of Incorporation	Sec'y of State Business Services & Regulations Suite 315, West Tower 2 Martin Luther King Jr. Dr., SE Atlanta, GA 30334 (404) 656-2817	$100 + county fee, which varies

*In nearly all states, the minimum number of incorporators and directors is also one.
**Corporation must have registered office with registered agent in state.

185

State	Title and No. of General Business Corp. Act	Min. No. of Shareholders*	Title of Form to Be Filed	Address and Telephone No.	Filing Fee
Hawaii	Chap. 416, Hawaii Revised Statutes	1	Articles of Incorporation and Affidavits of Officers	Dept. of Commerce & Consumer Affairs Business Registration Division P. O. Box 40 Honolulu, HI 96810 (808) 548-6111	$50 min. + optional $40 expediting fee**
Idaho	Title 30, Chap. 1	1	None	Division of Corporations Boise, ID 83720 (208) 334-2300	$60 min.
Illinois	Business Corp. Act	1	Articles of Incorporation	Sec'y of State Corporation Division Springfield, IL 62756 (217) 782-7880	$100.50 min.
Indiana	Indiana General Corp. Act IC 23	1	Articles of Incorporation	Corporations Division 155 State House Indianapolis, IN 46204 (317) 232-6576	$90
Iowa	Iowa Business Corp. Act Chap. 496A	1	Articles of Incorporation	Sec'y of State Corporation Division Des Moines, IA 50319 (515) 281-5204	$50

*In nearly all states, the minimum number of incorporators and directors is also one.
**Paying this fee guarantees three-day service; without it, incorporators may have to wait two to three months.

186

State	Title and No. of General Business Corp. Act	Min. No. of Shareholders*	Title of Form to Be Filed	Address and Telephone No.	Filing Fee
Kansas	Kansas General Corp. Code Chap. 17	1	Articles of Incorporation	Sec'y of State Corporation Division Topeka, KS 66612 (913) 296-4564	$75
Kentucky	Kentucky Business Corp. Act, Kentucky Revised Statutes Chap. 271A	1	No standard form for public use	Sec'y of State State Capitol Bldg. Frankfort, KY 40601 (502) 564-2848	$35 min.
Louisiana	Louisiana Revised Statutes 12:1, 2, 3	1	No standard Notarized affidavit of registered agent must accompany filing	Sec'y of State Corporations Division P. O. Box 94125 Baton Rouge, LA 70804–9125 (504) 925-4704	$60
Maine	Maine Business Corp. Act Title 13–A	1	Articles of Incorporation	Sec'y of State Corporation & UCC Division Augusta, ME 04333 (207) 289-4195	$85 min.
Maryland	Corps. and Assns. Article of Annotated Code of Maryland	1	Form 1 Form No. 25 (every year)	State Dept. of Assessments & Taxation 301 W. Preston St. Baltimore, MD 21201 (301) 225-1340	$40 min.

*In nearly all states, the minimum number of incorporators and directors is also one.

187

State	Title and No. of General Business Corp. Act	Min. No. of Shareholders*	Title of Form to Be Filed	Address and Telephone No.	Filing Fee
Massachusetts	Business Corps. Chap. 156B	1	Articles of Organization	Sec'y of the Commonwealth Corporation Division One Ashburton Pl. Boston, MA 02133 (617) 727-2850	$150 min.
Michigan	Act 284, P. A. of 1972, as amended	1	Articles of Incorporation Form C&S 101	Michigan Dept. of Commerce Corporation & Securities Bureau Box 30054 Lansing, MI 48909 (517) 334-6304	$35 min.
Minnesota	Minn. Stat. 301	1	Articles of Incorporation	Sec'y of State Corporation Division 180 State Office Bldg. St. Paul, MN 55155 (612) 296-2803	$125
Mississippi	Mississippi Business Corp. Law	1	Articles of Incorporation	Sec'y of State P. O. Box 136 Jackson, MS 39205 (601) 359-1350	$50 min.
Missouri	Title XXIII, Chap. 351 Revised Statutes of Missouri 1969, as amended	1	Articles of Incorporation Corp. Form #41	Sec'y of State Jefferson City, MO 65101 (314) 751-2359	$53 min.

*In nearly all states, the minimum number of incorporators and directors is also one.

188

State	Title and No. of General Business Corp. Act	Min. No. of Shareholders*	Title of Form to Be Filed	Address and Telephone No.	Filing Fee
Montana	Montana Business Corp. Act, Chap. 22, Title 15, Revised Code of Montana	1	Forms not prescribed or furnished by state	Sec'y of State Capitol Helena, MT 59601 (406) 444-3665	$70 min.
Nebraska	Nebraska Business Corp. Act, Chap. 21, Article 20	1	Articles of Incorporation	Sec'y of State Corporation Division 2304 State Capitol Bldg. Lincoln, NE 68509 (402) 471-4079	$40 min. + $3 per page recording fee
Nevada	Private Corps. Chap. 78	1	Articles of Incorporation	Sec'y of State Corporation Division Carson City, NV 89710 (702) 885-5203	$75 min.
New Hampshire	Revised Statutes Annotated (1955) Chap. 294, Business Corps.	1	Record of Organization	Sec'y of State Corporation Division 204 State House Concord, NH 03301 (603) 271-3244	$85 min.
New Jersey	New Jersey Business Corp. Act NJSA 14:A 1-1 et seq.	1	Certificate of Incorporation	New Jersey Department of State Commercial Recording Bureau Corporate Filing Section CN-308 Trenton, NJ 08625 (609) 530-6400	$75

*In nearly all states, the minimum number of incorporators and directors is also one.

189

State	Title and No. of General Business Corp. Act	Min. No. of Shareholders*	Title of Form to Be Filed	Address and Telephone No.	Filing Fee
New Mexico	Business Corp. Act Sections 51-24-1—51-31-11, NMSA 1953 Compilation	1	Articles of Incorporation	State Corporation Commission Corporation & Franchise Tax Depts. P. O. Drawer 1269 Santa Fe, NM 87501 (505) 827-4504	$50
New York	Business Corp. Law	1	Certificate of Incorporation	New York State Division of Corporations 162 Washington Ave. Albany, NY 12231 (518) 474-6200	$110
North Carolina	Business Corp. Act Chap. 55	1	Articles of Incorporation	Sec'y of State Corporations Division 300 N. Salisbury St. Raleigh, NC 27611 (919) 733-4201	$90 min.
North Dakota	North Dakota Business Act	1	Duplicate Originals of Articles of Incorporation	Sec'y of State Division of Corporations Bismarck, ND 58505 (701) 224-2905	$90 min.

*In nearly all states, the minimum number of incorporators and directors is also one.

190

State	Title and No. of General Business Corp. Act	Min. No. of Shareholders*	Title of Form to Be Filed	Address and Telephone No.	Filing Fee
Ohio	Chap. 1701, Ohio Revised Code	1	Articles of Incorporation	Sec'y of State Division of Corporations State Office Tower, 14th Fl. 30 E. Broad St. Columbus, OH 43266-0418 (614) 466-3910	$75 min.
Oklahoma	General Business Corp. Act Title 18	1	Duplicate Originals of Articles of Incorporation	Sec'y of State Rm. 101 Oklahoma State Capitol Bldg. Oklahoma City, OK 73105 (405) 521-3911	$50 min.
Oregon	Chap. 57, Private Corporations	1	Duplicate Originals of Articles of Incorporation 11–B	Corporation Commissioner Commerce Bldg. Salem, OR 97310 (503) 378-4166	$40
Pennsylvania	P. L. 364	1	Articles of Incorporation— Domestic Business Corp.; Registry Statement (triplicate)	Commonwealth of Pennsylvania Corporation Bureau Harrisburg, PA 17120 (717) 787-1057	$75

*In nearly all states, the minimum number of incorporators and directors is also one.

191

State	Title and No. of General Business Corp. Act	Min. No. of Shareholders*	Title of Form to Be Filed	Address and Telephone No.	Filing Fee
Rhode Island	Title 7, Corporations, Associations and Partnerships	1	Duplicate Originals of Articles of Incorporation	Sec'y of State 270 Westminster Mall Providence, RI 02903 (401) 277-3040	$110
South Carolina	Chap. 1 of 1962 Code—Vol. 3	1	Articles of Incorporation	Sec'y of State Box 11350 Columbia, SC 29201 (803) 758-2744	$45 min.
South Dakota	SDCL 47-1—47-31	1	Articles of Incorporation	Sec'y of State State Capitol Pierre, SD 57501 (605) 773-4845	$40 min.
Tennessee	Title 48, Tennessee Code Annotated (Tennessee General Corp. Act)	1	Corporation Charter	Sec'y of State Corporation Division Nashville, TN 37219 (615) 741-2286	$50
Texas	Texas Business Corp. Act	1	Articles of Incorporation	Sec'y of State Corporation Division Sam Houston State Office Bldg. Austin, TX 78711 (512) 463-5555	$300, $310 to expedite in 24–48 hrs.

*In nearly all states, the minimum number of incorporators and directors is also one.

State	Title and No. of General Business Corp. Act	Min. No. of Shareholders*	Title of Form to Be Filed	Address and Telephone No.	Filing Fee
Utah	Title 16, Chap. 10	1	Application for Certificate of Authority; Articles of Incorporation	Business Regulation Office Corporation Division 160 East 300 South P. O. Box 45801 Salt Lake City, UT 84145–0801 (801) 530-6016	$50 min.
Vermont	Title 11	1	DCI—Articles of Association	Sec'y of State Corporations Division Montpelier, VT 05602–2710 (802) 828-2386	$35 min.
Virginia	Virginia Stock Corp. Act	1	Articles of Incorporation	Clerk of the Commission State Corporation Commission Box 1197 Richmond, VA 23209 (804) 786-6704	$45 min.
Washington	RCW 23A	1	Forms not supplied	Corporations Division Republic Bldg., 2nd Fl. 505 E. Union Olympia, WA 98504 (206) 753-7115	$175 min.
West Virginia	Chap. 31 Article 1	1	Articles of Incorporation	Sec'y of State Corporation Division Charleston, WV 25305 (304) 348-0262	$30 min.

*In nearly all states, the minimum number of incorporators and directors is also one.

193

State	Title and No. of General Business Corp. Act	Min. No. of Shareholders*	Title of Form to Be Filed	Address and Telephone No.	Filing Fee
Wisconsin	Wisconsin Business Corp. Law, Chap. 180	1	Articles of Incorporation, Form 2	Sec'y of State Corporation Division State Capitol Bldg. Madison, WI 53702 (608) 266-3590	$70 min. + $10 min. recording fee
Wyoming	Section 17–36.1—Section 17–36.128 Wyoming Statutes 1957	No provision for minimum	No forms are furnished	Sec'y of State Division of Corporations Cheyenne, WY 82002 (307) 777-7311	$50 min.

*In nearly all states, the minimum number of incorporators and directors is also one.

APPENDIX B

Sample Minutes and Bylaws
for a Small Corporation

(FOR USE IF THERE IS ONE INCORPORATOR)

MINUTES OF ORGANIZATION MEETING OF
(NAME OF YOUR CORPORATION)

The undersigned, being the sole incorporator of this corporation, held an organization meeting at the date and place set forth below, at which meeting the following action was taken:

It was resolved that a copy of the Certificate of Incorporation together with the receipt issued by the Department of State showing payment of the statutory organization tax and the date and payment of the fee for filing the original Certificate of Incorporation be appended to these minutes.

Bylaws regulating the conduct of the business and affairs of the corporation, as prepared by ＿＿＿ ＿＿＿, counsel for the corporation, were adopted and ordered appended hereto.

The persons whose names appear below were named as directors.

The board of directors was authorized to issue all of the unsubscribed shares of the corporation at such time and in such amounts as determined by the board and to accept in payment money or other property, tangible or intangible, actually received or labor or services actually performed for the corporation or for its benefit or in its formation.

The principal office of the corporation was fixed at

Dated at
this   day of   19   _____

                                           Sole Incorporator

The undersigned accept their nomination as directors:

_____   _____

         Type director's name   Signature

_____   _____

_____   _____

The following are appended to the minutes of this meeting:

     Copy of Certificate of Incorporation, filed on ____(date)____
     Receipt of Department of State
     Bylaws

(FOR USE IF THERE IS MORE THAN ONE
INCORPORATOR)

MINUTES OF ORGANIZATION MEETING OF
(NAME OF YOUR CORPORATION)

The organization meeting of the incorporators was held at
_____ on the _____ day of _____ , 19 , at _____ o'clock M.
The following were present:

being a quorum and all of the incorporators.

One of the incorporators called the meeting to order. Upon motion
duly made, seconded, and carried, _____ was duly elected chairman
of the meeting and _____ duly elected secretary thereof. They accepted their respective offices and proceeded with the discharge of
their duties.

A written Waiver of Notice of this meeting signed by all the
incorporators was submitted, read by the secretary, and ordered appended to these minutes.

The secretary then presented and read to the meeting a copy of
the Certificate of Incorporation of the corporation and reported that
on the _____ day of _____ , 19 , the original thereof was duly filed
by the Department of State.

Upon motion duly made, seconded, and carried, said report was
adopted and the secretary was directed to append to these minutes a
copy of the Certificate of Incorporation, together with the original
receipt issued by the Department of State, showing payment of the
statutory organization tax, the filing fee, and the date of filing of the
certificate.

The chairman stated that the election of directors was then in
order.

The following were nominated as directors:

Upon motion duly made, seconded, and carried, it was unanimously

RESOLVED, that each of the abovenamed nominees be and hereby is elected a director of the corporation.

Upon motion duly made, seconded, and carried, and by the affirmative vote of all present, it was

RESOLVED, that the board of directors be and it is hereby authorized to issue all of the unsubscribed shares of the corporation at such time and in such amounts as determined by the board, and to accept in payment money or other property, tangible or intangible, actually received or labor or other services actually performed for the corporation or for its benefit or in its formation.

The chairman presented and read, article by article, the proposed bylaws for the conduct and regulation of the business and affairs of the corporation as prepared by _____ _____, counsel for the corporation.

Upon motion duly made, seconded, and carried, they were adopted and in all respects ratified, confirmed, and approved, as and for the bylaws of this corporation.

The secretary was directed to cause them to be inserted in the minute book immediately following the receipt of the Department of State.

Upon motion duly made, seconded, and carried, the principal office of the corporation was fixed at _____, County of _____, State of New York.

Upon motion duly made, seconded, and carried, and by the affirmative vote of all present, it was

RESOLVED, that the signing of these minutes shall constitute full ratification thereof and Waiver of Notice of the Meeting by the signatories.

There being no further business before the meeting, the same was, on motion, duly adjourned.

Dated this   day of   , 19   .

_____

Secretary of meeting

_____   _____

_____   Chairman of meeting

_____

_____

The following are appended to the minutes of this meeting:

Waiver of Notice of organization meeting
Copy of Certificate of Incorporation, filed on _____(date)_____
Receipt of Department of State
Bylaws

WAIVER OF NOTICE OF ORGANIZATION MEETING
OF
(NAME OF YOUR CORPORATION)

We, the undersigned, being all the incorporators named in the Certificate of Incorporation of the above corporation, hereby agree and consent that the organization meeting thereof be held on the date and at the time and place stated below and hereby waive all notice of such meeting and of any adjournment thereof.

Place of meeting:
Date of meeting:
Time of meeting:

_____
Incorporator

_____
Incorporator

_____
Incorporator

Dated:

BYLAWS
OF
(NAME OF YOUR CORPORATION)

ARTICLE I Offices

The principal office of the corporation shall be in the
of   , County of   , State of New York. The corporation may
also have offices at such other places within or without the State of
New York as the board may from time to time determine or the
business of the corporation may require.

ARTICLE II Shareholders

1. *Place of Meetings.* Meetings of shareholders shall be held at
the principal office of the corporation or at such place within or
without the State of New York as the board shall authorize.

2. *Annual Meeting.* The annual meeting of the shareholders shall
be held on the   day of   at   M. in each year if not a
legal holiday, and, if a legal holiday, then on the next business day
following at the same hour, when the shareholders shall elect a board
and transact such other business as may properly come before the
meeting.

3. *Special Meetings.* Special meetings of the shareholders may be
called by the board or by the president and shall be called by the
president or the secretary at the request in writing of a majority of the
board or at the request in writing by shareholders owning a majority
in amount of the shares issued and outstanding. Such request shall
state the purpose or purposes of the proposed meeting. Business trans-
acted at a special meeting shall be confined to the purposes stated in
the notice.

4. *Fixing Record Date.* For the purpose of determining the shareholders entitled to notice of or to vote at any meeting of shareholders
or any adjournment thereof, or to express consent to or dissent from
any proposal without a meeting, or for the purpose of determining
shareholders entitled to receive payment of any dividend or the allot-
ment of any rights, or for the purpose of any other action, the board
shall fix, in advance, a date as the record date for any such determination of shareholders. Such date shall not be more than fifty nor less
than ten days before the date of such meeting, nor more than fifty days

prior to any other action. If no record date is fixed, it shall be determined in accordance with the provisions of law.

5. *Notice of Meetings of Shareholders.* Written notice of each meeting of shareholders shall state the purpose or purposes for which the meeting is called, the place, date, and hour of the meeting, and unless it is the annual meeting, shall indicate that it is being issued by or at the direction of the person or persons calling the meeting. Notice shall be given either personally or by mail to each shareholder entitled to vote at such meeting, not less than ten nor more than fifty days before the date of the meeting. If action is proposed to be taken that might entitle shareholders to payment for their shares, the notice shall include a statement of that purpose and to that effect. If mailed, the notice is given when deposited in the United States mail, with postage thereon prepaid, directed to the shareholder at his or her address as it appears on the record of shareholders, or, if he or she shall have filed with the secretary a written request that notices to him or her be mailed to some other address, then directed to him or her at such other address.

6. *Waivers.* Notice of meeting need not be given to any shareholder who signs a waiver of notice, in person or by proxy, whether before or after the meeting. The attendance of any shareholder at a meeting, in person or by proxy, without protesting prior to the conclusion of the meeting the lack of notice of such meeting, shall constitute a waiver of notice by him.

7. *Quorum of Shareholders.* Unless the Certificate of Incorporation provides otherwise, the holders of (a majority) (your own determination of a quorum, expressed either as a fraction or a percentage) of the shares entitled to vote thereat shall constitute a quorum at a meeting of shareholders for the transaction of any business, provided that when a specified item of business is required to be voted on by a class or classes, the holders of (a majority) (your own determination of a quorum, expressed either as a fraction or a percentage) of the shares of such class or classes shall constitute a quorum for the transaction of such specified item of business.

When a quorum is once present to organize a meeting, it is not broken by the subsequent withdrawal of any shareholders.

The shareholders present may adjourn the meeting despite the absence of a quorum.

8. *Proxies.* Every shareholder entitled to vote at a meeting of

shareholders or to express consent or dissent without a meeting may authorize another person or persons to act for him or her by proxy.

Every proxy must be signed by the shareholder or his or her attorney-in-fact. No proxy shall be valid after expiration of eleven months from the date thereof unless otherwise provided in the proxy. Every proxy shall be revocable at the pleasure of the shareholder executing it, except as otherwise provided by law.

9. *Qualification of Voters.* Every shareholder of record shall be entitled at every meeting of shareholders to one vote for every share standing in his or her name on the record of shareholders, unless otherwise provided in the Certificate of Incorporation.

10. *Vote of Shareholders.* Except as otherwise required by statute or by the Certificate of Incorporation:

(Create your own election requirements, or use the following:)

(a) directors shall be elected by a plurality of the votes cast at a meeting of shareholders by the holders of shares entitled to vote in the election;

(b) all other corporate action shall be authorized by a majority of the votes cast.

11. *Written Consent of Shareholders.* Any action that may be taken by vote may be taken without a meeting on written consent, setting forth the action so taken, signed by the holders of all the outstanding shares entitled to vote thereon or signed by such lesser number of holders as may be provided for in the Certificate of Incorporation.

ARTICLE III   Directors

1. *Board of Directors.* Subject to any provision in the Certificate of Incorporation, the business of the corporation shall be managed by its board of directors, each of whom shall be at least 18 years of age and (choose the number) be shareholders.

2. *Number of Directors.* The number of directors shall be _____. When all of the shares are owned by less than three shareholders, the number of directors may be less than three but not less than the number of shareholders.

3. *Election and Term of Directors.* At each annual meeting of shareholders, the shareholders shall elect directors to hold office until the next annual meeting. Each director shall hold office until the expiration of the term for which he or she is elected and until his or

her successor has been elected and qualified, or until his or her prior resignation or removal.

4. *Newly Created Directorships and Vacancies.* Newly created directorships resulting from an increase in the number of directors and vacancies occurring in the board for any reason except the removal of directors without cause may be filled by a vote of a majority of the directors then in office, although less than a quorum exists, unless otherwise provided in the Certificate of Incorporation. Vacancies occurring by reason of the removal of directors without cause shall be filled by vote of the shareholders unless otherwise provided in the Certificate of Incorporation. A director elected to fill a vacancy caused by resignation, death, or removal shall be elected to hold office for the unexpired term of his or her predecessor.

5. *Removal of Directors.* Any or all of the directors may be removed for cause by vote of the shareholders or by action of the board. Directors may be removed without cause only by vote of the shareholders.

6. *Resignation.* A director may resign at any time by giving written notice to the board, the president, or the secretary of the corporation. Unless otherwise specified in the notice, the resignation shall take effect upon receipt thereof by the board or such officer, and the acceptance of the resignation shall not be necessary to make it effective.

7. *Quorum of Directors.* Unless otherwise provided in the Certificate of Incorporation, (a majority) (your own determination of a quorum, expressed either as a fraction or a percentage) of the entire board shall constitute a quorum for the transaction of business or of any specified item of business.

8. *Action of the Board.* Unless otherwise required by law, the vote of (a majority) (your own determination of a quorum, expressed either as a fraction or a percentage) of directors present at the time of the vote, if a quorum is present at such time, shall be the act of the board. Each director present shall have one vote regardless of the number of shares, if any, which he or she may hold.

9. *Place and Time of Board Meetings.* The board may hold its meetings at the office of the corporation or at such other places, either within or without the State of New York, as it may from time to time determine.

10. *Regular Annual Meeting.* A regular annual meeting of the board shall be held immediately following the annual meeting of shareholders at the place of such annual meeting of shareholders.

11. *Notice of Meetings of the Board, Adjournment.*

a. Regular meetings of the board may be held without notice at such time and place as it shall from time to time determine. Special meetings of the board shall be held upon notice to the directors and may be called by the president upon three days' notice to each director either personally or by mail or by wire; special meetings shall be called by the president or by the secretary in a like manner on written request of two directors. Notice of a meeting need not be given to any director who submits a Waiver of Notice whether before or after the meeting or who attends the meeting without protesting prior thereto or at its commencement, the lack of notice to him or her.

b. A majority of the directors present, whether or not a quorum is present, may adjourn any meeting to another time and place. Notice of the adjournment shall be given all directors who were absent at the time of the adjournment and, unless such time and place are announced at the meeting, to the other directors.

12. *Chairman.* The president, or, in his or her absence, a chairman chosen by the board, shall preside at all meetings of the board.

13. *Executive and Other Committees.* By resolution adopted by a majority of the entire board, the board may designate from among its members an executive committee and other committees, each consisting of three or more directors. Each such committee shall serve at the pleasure of the board.

14. *Compensation.* No compensation, as such, shall be paid to directors for their services, but by resolution of the board, a fixed sum and expenses for actual attendance at each regular or special meeting of the board may be authorized. Nothing herein contained shall be construed to preclude any director from serving the corporation in any other capacity and receiving compensation therefor.

ARTICLE IV   Officers

1. *Offices, Election, Term.*

a. Unless otherwise provided for in the Certificate of Incorporation, the board may elect or appoint a president, one or more vice-presidents, a secretary, and a treasurer, and such other officers as it may determine, who shall have such duties, powers, and functions as hereinafter provided.

b. All officers shall be elected or appointed to hold office until the meeting of the board following the annual meeting of shareholders.

c. Each officer shall hold office for the term for which he or she is elected or appointed and until his or her successor has been elected or appointed and qualified.

2. *Removal, Resignation, Salary, Etc.*

a. Any officer elected or appointed by the board may be removed by the board with or without cause.

b. In the event of the death, resignation, or removal of an officer, the board in its discretion may elect or appoint a successor to fill the unexpired term.

c. Unless there is only one shareholder, any two or more offices may be held by the same person, except the offices of president and secretary. If there is only one shareholder, all offices may be held by the same person.

d. The salaries of all officers shall be fixed by the board.

e. The directors may require any officer to give security for the faithful performance of his or her duties.

3. *President.* The president shall be the chief executive officer of the corporation; he or she shall preside at all meetings of the shareholders and of the board; he or she shall have the management of the business of the corporation and shall see that all orders and resolutions of the board are effected.

4. *Vice-presidents.* During the absence or disability of the president, the vice-president, or, if there are more than one, the executive vice-president, shall have all the powers and functions of the president. Each vice-president shall perform such other duties as the board shall prescribe.

5. *Secretary.* The secretary shall:

a. attend all meetings of the board and of the shareholders;

b. record all votes and minutes of all proceedings in a book to be kept for that purpose;

c. give or cause to be given notice of all meetings of shareholders and of special meetings of the board;

d. keep in safe custody the seal of the corporation and affix it to any instrument when authorized by the board;

e. when required, prepare or cause to be prepared and available at each meeting of shareholders a certified list in alphabetical order of the names of shareholders entitled to vote thereat, indicating the number of shares of each respective class held by each;

f. keep all the documents and records of the corporation as required by law or otherwise in a proper and safe manner;

g. perform such other duties as may be prescribed by the board.

6. *Assistant Secretaries.* During the absence or disability of the secretary, the assistant secretary, or, if there are more than one, the one so designated by the secretary or by the board, shall have all the powers and functions of the secretary.

7. *Treasurer.* The treasurer shall:

a. have the custody of the corporate funds and securities;

b. keep full and accurate accounts of receipts and disbursements in the corporate books;

c. deposit all money and other valuables in the name and to the credit of the corporation in such depositories as may be designated by the board;

d. disburse the funds of the corporation as may be ordered or authorized by the board and preserve proper vouchers for such disbursements;

e. render to the president and the board at the regular meetings of the board, or whenever they require it, an account of all his or her transactions as treasurer and of the financial condition of the corporation;

f. render a full financial report at the annual meeting of the shareholders if so requested;

g. be furnished by all corporate officers and agents, at his or her request, with such reports and statements as he or she may require as to all financial transactions of the corporation;

h. perform such other duties as are given to him or her by these bylaws or as from time to time are assigned to him or her by the board or the president.

8. *Assistant Treasurer.* During the absence or disability of the treasurer, the assistant treasurer, or, if there are more than one, the one so designated by the secretary or by the board, shall have all the powers and functions of the treasurer.

9. *Sureties and Bonds.* In case the board shall so require, any officer or agent of the corporation shall execute to the corporation a bond in such sum and with such surety or sureties as the board may direct, conditioned upon the faithful performance of his or her duties to the corporation and including responsibility for negligence and for the accounting for all property, funds, or securities of the corporation which may come into his or her hands.

ARTICLE V Certificates for Shares

1. *Certificates.* The shares of the corporation shall be represented by certificates. They shall be numbered and entered in the books of the corporation as they are issued. They shall exhibit the holder's name and the number of shares and shall be signed by the president or a vice-president and the treasurer or the secretary and shall bear the corporate seal.

2. *Lost or Destroyed Certificates.* The board may direct a new certificate or certificates to be issued in place of any certificate or certificates theretofore issued by the corporation, alleged to have been lost or destroyed, upon the making of an affidavit of that fact by the person claiming the certificate to be lost or destroyed. When authorizing such issue of a new certificate or certificates, the board may, in its discretion and as a condition precedent to the issuance thereof, require the owner of such lost or destroyed certificate or certificates, or his or her legal representative, to advertise the same in such manner as it shall require and/or to give the corporation a bond in such sum and with such surety or sureties as it may direct as indemnity against any claim that may be made against the corporation with respect to the certificate alleged to have been lost or destroyed.

3. *Transfers of Shares.*

    a. Upon surrender to the corporation or the transfer agent of the corporation of a certificate for shares duly endorsed or accompanied by proper evidence of succession, assignment, or authority to transfer, it shall be the duty of the corporation to issue a new certificate to the person entitled thereto and to cancel the old certificate; every such transfer shall be entered in the transfer book of the corporation, which shall be kept at its principal office. No transfer shall be made within ten days next preceding the annual meeting of shareholders.

    b. The corporation shall be entitled to treat the holder of record of any share as the holder in fact thereof and, accordingly, shall not be bound to recognize any equitable or other claim to or interest in such share on the part of any other person whether or not it shall have express or other notice thereof, except as expressly provided by the laws of the State of New York.

4. *Closing Transfer Books.* The board shall have the power to close the share transfer books of the corporation for a period of not more than ten days during the thirty-day period immediately preceding (1) any shareholders' meeting, or (2) any date upon which shareholders shall be called upon to or have a right to take action without a meeting, or (3) any date fixed for the payment of a dividend or any other form of distribution, and only those shareholders of record at the time the transfer books are closed, shall be recognized as such for the purpose of (1) receiving notice of or voting at such meeting, or (2) allowing them to take appropriate action, or (3) entitling them to receive any dividend or other form of distribution.

ARTICLE VI Dividends

Subject to the provisions of the Certificate of Incorporation and to applicable law, dividends on the outstanding shares of the corporation may be declared in such amounts and at such time or times as the board may determine. Before payment of any dividend, there may be set aside out of the net profits of the corporation available for dividends such sum or sums as the board from time to time in its absolute discretion deems proper as a reserve fund to meet contingencies, or for equalizing dividends, or for repairing or maintaining any property of the corporation, or for such other purpose as the board shall think conducive to the interests of the corporation, and the board may modify or abolish any such reserve.

ARTICLE VII Corporate Seal

The seal of the corporation shall be circular in form and bear the name of the corporation, the year of its organization, and the words "Corporate Seal, New York." The seal may be used by causing it to be impressed directly on the instrument or writing to be sealed, or upon adhesive substance affixed thereto. The seal on the certificates for shares or on any corporate obligation for the payment of money may be a facsimile, engraved or printed.

ARTICLE VIII   Execution of Instruments

All corporate instruments and documents shall be signed or countersigned, executed, verified, or acknowledged by such officer or officers or other person or persons as the board may from time to time designate.

ARTICLE IX   Fiscal Year

This fiscal year shall begin the first day of (month) in each year.

ARTICLE X   References to Certificate of Incorporation

References to the Certificate of Incorporation in these bylaws shall include all amendments thereto or changes thereof unless specifically excepted.

ARTICLE XI   Bylaw Changes

Amendment, Repeal, Adoption, Election of Directors

a. Except as otherwise provided in the Certificate of Incorporation, the bylaws may be amended, repealed, or adopted by vote of the holders of the shares at the time entitled to vote in the election of any directors. Bylaws may also be amended, repealed, or adopted by the board, but any bylaw adopted by the board may be amended by the shareholders entitled to vote thereon as hereinabove provided.

b. If any bylaw regulating an impending election of directors is adopted, amended, or repealed by the board, there shall be set forth in the notice of the next meeting of shareholders for the election of directors the bylaw so adopted, amended, or repealed, together with a concise statement of the changes made.

MINUTES OF FIRST MEETING OF BOARD OF DIRECTORS
OF
(NAME OF YOUR CORPORATION)

The first meeting of the board was held at   on the
day of   , 19 , at   o'clock   M.
The following were present:

being a quorum and all of the directors of the corporation.
_____ was nominated and elected temporary chairman
and acted as such until relieved by the president.
_____ was nominated and elected temporary secretary,
and acted as such until relieved by the permanent secretary.

The secretary then presented and read to the meeting a Waiver
of Notice of Meeting, subscribed by all the directors of the corporation, and it was ordered that it be appended to the minutes of this
meeting.

The following were duly nominated and, a vote having been taken,
were unanimously elected officers of the corporation to serve for one
year and until their successors are elected and qualified:

President:
Vice-President:
Secretary:
Treasurer:

The president and secretary thereupon assumed their respective
offices in place and stead of the temporary chairman and the temporary secretary.

Upon motion duly made, seconded, and carried, it was

RESOLVED, that the seal now presented
at this meeting, an impression of which is directed to be made in the margin of the minute
book, be and the same is hereby adopted as the
seal of this corporation, and further

RESOLVED, that the president and treasurer be and they hereby are authorized to

issue certificates for shares in the form as submitted to this meeting, and further

RESOLVED, that the share and transfer book now presented at this meeting be and the same hereby is adopted as the share and transfer book of the corporation. Upon motion duly made, seconded, and carried, it was

RESOLVED, that the treasurer be and hereby is authorized to open a bank account in behalf of the corporation with (name of bank) located at (address) and a resolution for that purpose on the printed form of said bank was adopted and was ordered appended to the minutes of this meeting. Upon motion duly made, seconded, and carried, it was

RESOLVED, that the corporation proceed to carry on the business for which it was incorporated.

(The following is the appropriate form to be included here if a proposal or offer for the sale, transfer, or exchange of property has been made to the corporation:)

The secretary then presented to the meeting a written proposal from _____ _____ to the corporation.

Upon motion duly made, seconded, and carried, the said proposal was ordered filed with the secretary, and he or she was requested to spread the same at length upon the minutes, said proposal being as follows:

(Insert proposal here.)

The proposal was taken up for consideration, and, on motion, the following resolution was unanimously adopted:

WHEREAS, a written proposal has been made to this corporation in the form as set forth above in these minutes, and

WHEREAS, in the judgment of this board the assets proposed to be transferred to the corporation are reasonably worth the amount of the consideration demanded therefor, and that it is in the best interests of this corporation to accept the said offer as set forth in said proposal,

NOW, THEREFORE, IT IS RESOLVED, that said offer, as set forth in said proposal, be and the same hereby is approved and accepted, and that in accordance with the terms thereof, this corporation shall, as full payment for said property, issue to said offeror(s) or nominee(s) (number of shares) fully paid and nonassessable shares of this corporation, and it is

FURTHER RESOLVED, that upon the delivery to this corporation of said assets and the execution and delivery of such proper instruments as may be necessary to transfer and convey the same to this corporation, the officers of this corporation are authorized and directed to execute and deliver the certificate or certificates for such shares as are required to be issued and delivered on acceptance of said offer in accordance with the foregoing.

The chairman presented to the meeting a form of certificate required under Tax Law Section 275A to be filed in the office of the tax commission.

Upon motion duly made, seconded, and carried, it was

RESOLVED, that the proper officers of this corporation are hereby authorized and directed to execute and file such certificate forthwith. On motion duly made, seconded, and carried, it was

RESOLVED, that all of the acts taken and decisions made at the organization meeting be and they hereby are ratified, and it was

FURTHER RESOLVED, that the signing of these minutes shall constitute full ratification thereof and Waiver of Notice of the Meeting by the signatories.

There being no further business before the meeting, on motion duly made, seconded, and carried, the meeting was adjourned. Dated this   day of   , 19   .

_____   _____
                                                              Secretary

_____   _____
                                                              Chairman

_____

_____

A true copy of each of the following documents referred to in the foregoing minutes is appended hereto.

Waiver of Notice of Meeting

Specimen certificate for shares

Resolution designating depository of funds

WAIVER OF NOTICE OF FIRST MEETING OF BOARD
OF
(NAME OF YOUR CORPORATION)

We, the undersigned, being all the directors of the above corporation, hereby agree and consent that the first meeting of the board be held on the date and at the time and place stated below for the purpose of electing officers and the transaction thereat of all such other business as may lawfully come before said meeting and hereby waive all notice of the meeting and of any adjournment thereof.

Place of meeting:
Date of meeting:
Time of meeting:

_____
Director

_____
Director

_____
Director

Dated:

MINUTES OF FIRST MEETING OF SHAREHOLDERS
OF
(NAME OF YOUR CORPORATION)

The first meeting of the shareholders was held at   on the   day of   , 19   , at   o'clock   M.

The meeting was duly called to order by the president, who stated the object of the meeting.

The secretary then read the roll of the shareholders as they appear in the share record book of the corporation and reported that a quorum of the shareholders was present.

The secretary then read a Waiver of Notice of Meeting signed by all the shareholders and on motion duly made, seconded, and carried, it was ordered that the said waiver be appended to the minutes of this meeting.

The president then asked the secretary to read the minutes of the organization meeting and the minutes of the first meeting of the board.

On motion duly made, seconded, and unanimously carried, the following resolution was adopted:

WHEREAS, the minutes of the organization meeting and the minutes of the first meeting of the board have been read to this meeting, and

WHEREAS, at the organization meeting the bylaws of the corporation were adopted, it is

RESOLVED, that this meeting hereby approves, ratifies, and adopts the said bylaws as the bylaws of the corporation, and it is

FURTHER RESOLVED, that all of the acts taken and the decisions made at the organization meeting and at the first meeting of the board hereby are approved and ratified, and it is

FURTHER RESOLVED, that the signing of these minutes shall constitute full ratification thereof and Waiver of Notice of the Meeting by the signatories.

There being no further business, the meeting was adjourned. Dated this   day of   , 19   .

_____   **Secretary**
_____

_____

The following is appended hereto:
Waiver of Notice of Meeting

WAIVER OF NOTICE OF FIRST MEETING OF
SHAREHOLDERS
OF
(NAME OF YOUR CORPORATION)

We, the undersigned, being all of the shareholders of the above corporation, hereby agree and consent that the first meeting of the shareholders be held on the date and at the time and place stated below for the purpose of electing officers and the transaction thereat of all such other business as may lawfully come before said meeting and hereby waive all notice of the meeting and of any adjournment thereof.

Place of meeting:
Date of meeting:
Time of meeting:

_____

_____

_____

Dated:

MINUTES OF A SPECIAL MEETING OF SHAREHOLDERS
OF
(NAME OF YOUR CORPORATION)

MINUTES of a special meeting of shareholders held at   , in the State of   , on the   day of   , 19   , at   o'clock in the

The meeting was duly called to order by the president, who stated the object of the meeting.

On motion duly made, seconded, and unanimously carried, the following resolution was adopted:

WHEREAS, the corporation's clients are delaying payments for work performed earlier and are now paying in the month of January, rather than in December, it is

RESOLVED, that a feasibility study be made as to shifting from a calendar year to a January fiscal year so that income more appropriately matches the work done, and it is

FURTHER RESOLVED, that if such a study indicates that a January fiscal-year election is appropriate, that such an election be made.

There being no further business, the meeting was adjourned. Dated the   day of   , 19   .

_____
Secretary

_____
President

APPENDIX C

Model Profit-Sharing Plan

(Under Section 401(a) of the
Internal Revenue Code)

(NAME OF YOUR CORPORATION)
PROFIT-SHARING PLAN

ARTICLE I   Purpose

The _____ (hereafter referred to as "Employer") establishes this Plan to provide for the participation of its Employees in the Profits, to provide funds for their retirement, and to provide funds for their Beneficiaries in the event of death. The benefits provided in this Plan shall be paid from the Trust established by the Employer.

The Plan and the Trust forming a part hereof are established and shall be maintained for the exclusive benefit of eligible Employees and their Beneficiaries. Except as provided in Article XI, no part of the Trust funds shall revert to the Employer, or be used for or diverted to purposes other than the exclusive benefit of Employees or their Beneficiaries.

ARTICLE II   Definitions

As used in this Plan, the following words and phrases shall have the meanings set forth below, unless the context clearly indicates otherwise:

2.1 *Allocation Date.* The last day of each Plan Year.

2.2 *Beneficiary.* The person or persons designated in writing by the Participant or if (i) no such person is designated, (ii) all such persons predecease the Participant, or (iii) the Plan Administrator is unable to locate the designated beneficiary, the spouse followed by the Participant's descendants per stirpes (including adopted children), and lastly, the Participant's estate.

2.3 *Compensation.* A Participant's wages, salaries, and other amounts received for personal services rendered to the Employer as an Employee which are actually paid during the Limitation Year. This term shall not include deferred compensation, stock options, and other distributions which receive special Federal income tax benefit.

2.4 *Disability.* A physical or mental impairment which in the opinion of the Plan Administrator is of such permanence and degree that a Participant is unable because of such impairment to perform any gainful activity for which he/she is suited by virtue of his/her experience, training, or education. The permanence and degree of such impairment shall be supported by medical evidence.

2.5 *Effective Date.* The first day of the Plan Year for which the Employer adopts the Plan.

2.6 *Employee.* An individual who is employed by the Employer.

2.7 *Employer.* The person named in Article I.

2.8 *Employer Contribution Account.* A separate account maintained for a Participant consisting of his/her allocable share of Employer contributions and earnings of the Trust, Plan forfeitures, and realized and unrealized gains and losses allocable to such account, less any amounts distributed to the Participant or his/her Beneficiary from such account.

2.9 *Investment Adjustment.* The fair market value of Trust assets determined as of the current Allocation Date, less all contributions made during the Plan Year, plus distributions made during the Plan Year, less the fair market value of the Trust assets as of the preceding Allocation Date. For purposes of this Section, the fair market value of assets as of an Allocation Date and contributions made during a Plan Year do not include amounts contributed for a Plan Year which are made after such Plan Year.

2.10 *Limitation Year.* A calendar year—unless any other twelve-consecutive-month period is designated pursuant to a written resolution adopted by the Employer.

2.11 *Nonforfeitable Interest.* The unconditional and legally enforceable right to which the Participant or his/her Beneficiary (whichever is applicable) is entitled in the Participant's entire Voluntary Contribution Account balance and in that percentage of his/her Employer Contribution Account balance which has vested pursuant to Article VI.

2.12 *Normal Retirement Date.* The Participant's sixty-fifth (65th) birthday.

2.13 *One-Year Break in Service.* A twelve (12)-consecutive-month Period of Severance.

2.14 *Period of Separation.* A period of time commencing with the date an Employee separates from service and ending with the date such Employee resumes employment with the Employer.

2.15 *Period of Service.* For purposes of determining an Employee's initial or continued eligibility to participate in the Plan or his/her vested interest in his/her Employer Contribution Account, an Employee shall be credited for the time period commencing with his/her employment commencement date and ending on the date a Period of Severance begins. A Period of Service for these purposes includes a Period of Separation of less than twelve (12) consecutive months. In the case of an Employee who separates from service and later resumes employment with the Employer, the Period of Service prior to his/her resumption of employment shall be aggregated only if such Employee is a Reemployed Individual.

2.16 *Period of Severance.* A period of time commencing with the earlier of:

a. the date an Employee separates from service by reason of quitting, retirement, death, or discharge, or

b. the date twelve (12) months after the date an Employee separates from service,

and ending, in the case of an Employee who separates from service by reason other than death, with the date such Employee resumes employment with the Employer.

2.17 *Participant.* An Employee who satisfies the eligibility requirements of Article III.

2.18 *Plan.* This document, the provisions of the Trust Agreement, and any amendments to either.

2.19 *Plan Administrator.* The Employer or the person or persons designated by the Employer in Section 12.2(a) to administer the Plan in accordance with its provisions.

2.20 *Plan Year.* A twelve (12)-consecutive-month period coinciding with the Limitation Year, including any such period completed before the Effective Date of the Plan.

2.21 *Profits.* Current and accumulated profits determined in accordance with generally accepted accounting principles.

2.22 *Qualified Public Accountant.* (i) A person who is a certified public accountant, certified by a regulatory authority of a state; (ii) a person who is a licensed public accountant, licensed by a regulatory authority of a state; or (iii) a person certified by the Secretary of Labor as a qualified public accountant.

2.23 *Reemployed Individual.* A person who, after having separated from service, resumes employment:

> a. with any Nonforfeitable Interest in his/her Employer Contribution Account, or

> b. with no such Nonforfeitable Interest, and who resumes such employment either (i) before a One-Year Break in Service, or (ii) after a One-Year Break in Service but before his/her latest Period of Severance equals or exceeds his/her Period of Service.

2.24 *Suspense Account.* An account established pursuant to Section 4.3.

2.25 *Trust Agreement.* The agreement between the Trustee and the Employer entered into for the purpose of holding, managing, and administering all property held by the Trustee for the exclusive benefit of the Participants and their Beneficiaries.

2.26 *Trustee.* The person designated by the Employer pursuant to Section 12.2 in accordance with the Trust Agreement and any successor who is appointed pursuant to the terms of that Section.

2.27 *Voluntary Contribution Account.* A separate account maintained for each Participant consisting of all Employee voluntary contributions and earnings of the Trust and adjustments for withdrawals, and realized and unrealized gains and losses attributable thereto.

ARTICLE III   Participation

3.1 *Age and Service.* Except as provided in Section 3.2, an Employee who has attained age twenty-one (21) and has completed one year of employment will participate on the first day of the first Plan Year after such age and service requirements are satisfied.

3.2 *Reemployed Individuals.* A Reemployed Individual shall participate in the Plan on the later of the date he/she is reemployed by the Employer or the date described in Section 3.1.

ARTICLE IV Contributions and Allocations

4.1 *Employer Contributions.*

a. The Employer shall contribute to the Trust for each Limitation Year that ends with or within the Employer's taxable year an amount determined annually by the Employer out of Profits. The contribution shall be made to the Trust at or shortly before the close of the Limitation Year or within a period of two and one-half (2½) months after the close of the Limitation Year. If the contribution is on account of he Employer's preceding taxable year, the contribution shall be accompanied by the Employer's signed statement to the Trustee that payment is on account of such taxable year. The amount of the contribution shall not be:

(i) in excess of the sum of the amounts described in Section 4.5 for all Participants,

(ii) reduced by forfeitures arising under Section 4.3.

b. In the case of the reinstatement of any amounts forfeited prior to a One-Year Break in Service under Section 6.6, the Employer shall contribute, within a reasonable time after the repayment described in Section 6.6, an amount sufficient when added to forfeitures to reinstate such amounts. Such contributions shall be made without regard to Profits.

4.2 *Voluntary Contributions.* At any time after an initial allocation is made on his/her behalf in accordance with Section 4.4(a), an Employee who has satisfied the requirements of Section 3.1 and who is currently employed by the Employer may contribute to the Trust in respect of each Limitation Year an amount not to exceed six (6) percent of Compensation paid to him/her by the Employer during such Limitation Year. Voluntary Contributions under this Plan shall be credited to each Participant's Voluntary Contribution Account as of the date of receipt by the Trustee.

4.3 *Forfeitures.* Except as provided in Sections 7.2 and 7.3, a forfeiture with respect to a Participant who separates from service shall arise as of:

a. the date such Participant received a distribution in the case of a Participant who received a distribution of any portion of his/her Employer Contribution Account pursuant to Section 9.3, or

b. in the case of a Participant who elects to defer his/her

benefit pursuant to Section 9.3, the date such Participant has completed a One-Year Break in Service.

Such forfeitures shall be credited to a Suspense Account to be utilized in a manner prescribed in Section 4.4(a).

4.4 *Allocation of Contributions and Forfeitures.*

a. The aggregate limitation prescribed by Section 4.5 shall be determined for all Active Participants described in Subsection (d) as of each Allocation Date. If forfeitures that have arisen under Section 4.3 exceed the total amount so determined, then such total amount so determined shall be withdrawn from the Suspense Account and allocated in accordance with Sections 4.4(b) and (c). The amount by which such forfeitures exceed such total amount shall remain in the Suspense Account until the next succeeding Allocation Date as of which time any balance in the Suspense Account shall be treated as forfeitures arising under Section 4.3.

b. Next, Employer contributions and forfeitures shall be allocated to the Employer Contribution Accounts of all Employees or Beneficiaries entitled to the reinstatement of any amounts forfeited prior to a One-Year Break in Service under Section 6.6, if the Participant has repaid the amount distributed to him/her on such separation from service as provided in Section 6.6. This amount shall be allocated in the proportion that the amount required for each entitled Employee or Beneficiary bears to the amount required for all entitled Employees and Beneficiaries until all such amounts are fully allocated.

c. Finally, any remaining Employer contributions and forfeitures shall be allocated to the Employer Contribution Account of each Participant employed on the Allocation Date in the proportion that each Participant's Compensation for the Limitation Year in which the Allocation Date falls bears to the Compensation of all Participants employed on the Allocation Date for such Limitation Year. The allocation for any Participant shall not exceed the amount prescribed by Section 4.5. If, after the first such allocation, any Employer contributions and forfeitures remain, the remainder shall be allocated and reallocated in the following manner until exhausted. In each subsequent allocation, any remainder shall be allocated to the Employee Contribution Accounts of all Participants employed on the Allocation Date for whom the total allocation is then less than the amount prescribed in Section 4.5 in the proportion that each such Participant's Compensation bears to the Compensation of all such Participants employed on the Allocation Date for such Limitation Year. The total allocation for any such Participant shall not exceed the amount prescribed in Section 4.5.

    d. Any Participant employed during the Limitation Year shall be entitled to an allocation of Employer contributions and forfeitures, if any, if he/she is employed on the Plan's Allocation Date, pursuant to Subsection (c).

    e. For purposes of this Section, Compensation earned before an Employee commences participation in accordance with Section 3.1 shall be disregarded.

4.5 *Limitation on Allocation of Employer Contributions and Forfeitures.*

    a. In no case shall the amount allocated to a Participant's Employer Contribution Account for the Limitation Year exceed the lesser of:

        i. the amount specified in Section 415(c)(1)(A) of the Internal Revenue Code as adjusted annually for increases in the cost of living in accordance with Section 415(d) of the Code, as in effect on the last day of the Limitation Year, or

        ii. twenty-five (25) percent of the Participant's Compensation for such Limitation Year.

    b. Amounts contributed pursuant to Section 4.1(b) shall not be taken into account for purposes of Section 4.5(a).

ARTICLE V Valuation of Accounts

As of each Allocation Date, all Plan assets held in the Trust shall be valued at fair market value and the Investment Adjustment shall be determined. Such Investment Adjustment shall be allocated among all account balances as of the current Allocation Date (after reduction for any forfeitures arising under Section 4.3) in the proportion each such account balance as of the immediately preceding Allocation Date bears to the total of all such account balances as of such immediately preceding Allocation Date, including any contributions made for the prior year which were made after such immediately preceding Allocation Date but allocated as of such date. For purposes of this Article, all account balances include (i) the account balances of all Participants and Beneficiaries who have account balances as of the current Allocation Date (including Beneficiaries who have acquired account balances since the immediately preceding Allocation Date) and (ii) the Suspense Account (prior to allocations to or from such account for the Limitation Year).

ARTICLE VI Vesting

6.1 *Normal Retirement.* Notwithstanding Section 6.4, a Participant shall have a Nonforfeitable Interest in his/her entire Employer Contribution Account if he/she is employed on or after his/her Normal Retirement Date. No forfeiture shall thereafter arise under Section 4.3.

6.2 *Voluntary Contribution Account.* A Participant shall have a Nonforfeitable Interest in his/her Voluntary Contribution Account at all times.

6.3 *Termination, Partial Termination, or Complete Discontinuance of Employer Contributions.* Notwithstanding any other provision of this Plan, in the event of a termination or partial termination of the Plan, or a complete discontinuance of Employer contributions under the Plan, all affected Participants shall have a Nonforfeitable Interest in their Employer Contribution Accounts determined as of the date of such event. The value of these accounts and their Voluntary Contribution Accounts shall be determined as of the date of such event. The value of these accounts and their Voluntary Contribution Accounts as of such date shall be determined in accordance with the method described in Article V as if such date were the Allocation Date for the Limitation Year in which the termination or complete discontinuance occurs.

6.4 *Vesting of Employer Contributions.* A Participant shall have a Nonforfeitable Interest in the percentage of his/her Employer Contribution Account determined pursuant to the following schedule:

Period of Service	Nonforfeitable Percentage
Less than 2 years	0
2	20
3	40
4	60
5	80
6 or more	100

Except as provided in Section 6.5, credit shall be given for the Period of Service described in Section 2.15 completed after the Participant commences employment with the Employer, including service before any One-Year Break in Service. In the event of a forfeiture, the percentage of a Participant's Employer Contribution Account which has not become nonforfeitable under this Section shall be forfeited in accordance with Section 4.3.

6.5 *Vesting after a One-Year Break in Service.* No Period of Service after a One-Year Break in Service shall be taken into account in determining the nonforfeitable percentage in a Participant's Employer Contribution Account accrued up to any such One-Year Break in Service.

6.6 *Vesting after a Distribution without a One-Year Break in Service.* A Participant who separates from service of the Employer and receives a distribution of his/her Nonforfeitable Interest (of less than one hundred [100] percent) in his/her Employer Contribution Account in accordance with Section 7.4 shall forfeit amounts that are not nonforfeitable as of the Allocation Date following the distribution if he/she is not employed on such Allocation Date. However, if the Participant returns to the employment of the Employer before incurring a One-Year Break in Service, any amounts so forfeited shall be reinstated to the Participant's Employer Contribution Account within a reasonable time after repayment by the Participant of the amount of the distribution. Such repayment must be made before the earlier of:

a. the date two years after the date of resumption of employment, or

b. the conclusion of a One-Year Break in Service after such resumption of employment.

ARTICLE VII Benefits

7.1 *Normal Retirement.* Upon separation from service on or after his/her Normal Retirement Date, other than by reason of death, a Participant shall be entitled to a benefit based on the combined balance of his/her Employer and Voluntary Contribution Accounts distributed in a manner provided in Article X.

7.2 *Disability.* In the event that a Participant incurs a Disability before his/her Normal Retirement Date, either before or after he/she separates from service of the Employer, he/she shall be entitled to a Disability benefit based on the combined balance of his/her Employer and Voluntary Contribution Accounts distributed in the manner provided in Section 10.2.

7.3 *Death.* In the event of the death of a Participant prior to the commencement of a benefit described in Sections 7.1, 7.2, and 7.4, the Beneficiary shall be paid the combined balance in the Participant's Employer Contribution and Voluntary Contribution Accounts distributed in the manner provided in Section 10.2.

7.4 *Termination of Service.* In the event that a Participant separates from the service of the Employer prior to his/her Normal Retirement Date for any reason other than death or Disability, his/her Nonforfeitable Interest in his/her Employer Contribution Account determined pursuant to Article VI and the balance of his/her Voluntary Contribution Account shall be distributable to him/her in accordance with the election procedure provided in Section 9.3.

7.5 *Valuation Date to Be Used for Computation of Benefits.* If a Participant or Beneficiary becomes entitled to a benefit pursuant to Section 7.1, 7.2, 7.3, or 7.4, the value of the account balances to be distributed shall be determined as of the Allocation Date immediately preceding or coinciding with the event giving rise to the distribution plus voluntary contributions made after such date less withdrawals made after such date. For purposes of Section 7.1, the event occasioning the benefit shall be the Participant's separation from service on or after his/her Normal Retirement Date other than by reason of death.

For purposes of Section 7.2, the event occasioning the benefit shall be the Employee's separation from service of the Employer on account of Disability. For purposes of Section 7.3, the event occasioning the benefit shall be the death of the Participant prior to the commencement of a benefit described in Section 7.1, 7.2, or 7.4. For purposes of Section 7.4, if a Participant does not make the election described in Section 9.3 to defer the distribution of benefits, the event occasioning the benefit shall be the date he/she separates from service.

However, if a Participant does make the election described in Section 9.3 and payment is deferred, the event occasioning the benefit shall be the earlier of the Participant's death, Disability, or his/her attaining Normal Retirement Date.

ARTICLE VIII   Withdrawal of Voluntary Employee Contributions

At any time, upon written request to the Plan Administrator, an Employee may withdraw from his/her Voluntary Contribution Account an amount not to exceed the lesser of (i) his/her net voluntary contributions or (ii) his/her Voluntary Contribution Account balance. His/her net voluntary contributions shall equal the total amount of his/her voluntary contributions, less withdrawals.

ARTICLE IX   Commencement of Benefits

9.1 *Benefits after Normal Retirement Date.* Payments shall be made or commence within one hundred twenty (120) days after the Participant separates from service of the Employer (including separation by reason of death or Disability) on or after attaining his/her Normal Retirement Date.

9.2 *Certain Benefits before Normal Retirement Date.* Except as provided in Section 9.1, upon death, payment shall be made not later than one hundred twenty (120) days after receipt by the Plan Administrator of proof of death. Except as provided in Section 9.1, upon Disability, payment shall be made no earlier than the first day the Participant is absent from work on account of Disability and no later than the later of (i) one hundred twenty (120) days after the determination by the Plan Administrator that Disability exists or (ii) the first day the Participant is absent from work on account of Disability.

9.3 *Termination of Service before Normal Retirement Date.* Upon separation from service before Normal Retirement Date other than by reason of death or Disability, any benefit to which a Participant is entitled under Section 7.4 shall be paid or commence not later than one hundred twenty (120) days after his/her separation from service unless he/she has previously irrevocably elected to defer such benefit until the earlier of his/her death or attainment of his/her Normal Retirement Date, such benefit to be paid within the time prescribed in Sections 9.1 or 9.2 (whichever is applicable) in the form prescribed in Section 10.2. A Participant may irrevocably elect by written notice to the Plan Administrator no later than thirty (30) days before his/her separation from service to defer payment of such benefit.

9.4 *Commencement of Benefits.* Notwithstanding anything in Sections 9.1, 9.2, and 9.3, payments of benefits shall be made or commence no more than sixty (60) days after the close of the Plan Year in which the Participant separates from service on or after his/her Normal Retirement Date.

ARTICLE X   Modes of Distribution of Benefits

10.1 *Period Certain.*

a. Unless a Participant elects otherwise, as specified in Section 10.2, the Plan benefit to be distributed on account of separation from service other than by reason of death or Disability shall be paid in monthly installments over a period certain designated by the Participant not greater than 120 months. In the event that the Participant fails to designate a period certain, the benefit shall be paid in monthly installments over a period certain equal to 120 months. The amount to be distributed from the Trust each month shall be determined as follows:

b. For the Plan Year in which benefits commence, the Participant's account(s) shall be valued in accordance with Section 7.5. The monthly benefit payable shall be an amount equal to the quotient obtained by dividing the amount determined under the preceding sentence by the number of months determined in Section 10.1(a). Such benefits shall continue to be paid until the Participant's account balances have been adjusted in accordance with Article V.

c. As of each Allocation Date, the monthly benefit payable shall be adjusted by dividing the Participant's or Beneficiary's entire interest in the Trust by the number of months determined in Section 10.1(a) less the number of months for which benefits have been paid as of such Allocation Date. If the monthly benefits paid since such Allocation Date differ from the amount determined in the preceding sentence, the accumulated underpayment (or overpayment) since such Allocation Date shall be divided by the number of months for which benefits have yet to be paid before the next Allocation Date, and the amount so determined shall be added to (or subtracted from) subsequent monthly benefit payments until a subsequent adjustment is made in accordance with this Subsection.

d. Should the death of the last annuitant entitled to a benefit under this Section occur prior to the expiration of the period certain, any remaining balance in the Participant's Employer and Voluntary Contribution Accounts determined as of the Allocation Date immediately preceding death, reduced by any payments made since such Allocation Date, shall be paid in a lump sum to the Beneficiary in accordance with Section 9.2.

10.2 *Lump Sum.* The payment of a benefit occasioned by death or Disability shall be paid in a single lump sum. A Participant who is entitled to a benefit on account of separation from service who does not elect to defer the payment of such benefit in the manner prescribed in Section 9.3 shall receive a single lump-sum payment. In addition, a Participant who is entitled to a benefit on account of separation from service after his/her Normal Retirement Date, including benefits deferred under Section 9.3, may, not later than thirty (30) days after his/her separation from service, elect by written notice to the Plan Administrator to receive a single lump-sum payment.

ARTICLE XI   Plan Amendment and Termination

The Employer reserves the right to amend the Plan at any time and to terminate the Plan or discontinue contributions hereunder. However, in the event of such amendment, termination, or discontinuance of contributions, no part of the funds held in the Trust shall be used for or diverted to any purpose other than for the exclusive benefit of the Participants or their Beneficiaries, except as provided in this Article.

All amendments, including one to terminate the Plan, shall be adopted in writing by the Employer's board of directors. Any material modification of the Plan by amendment or termination shall be communicated to all interested parties and the Secretaries of Labor and the Treasury in the time and manner prescribed by law.

Upon Plan termination or discontinuance of Employer contributions under the Plan, all account balances shall be valued in accordance with Section 6.3. The Suspense Account shall be allocated and reallocated to the Employer Contribution Accounts of all Participants in the manner prescribed in Section 4.4(c) up to the limits of Section 4.5 determined without regard to compensation paid after the date of plan termination or discontinuance of Employer contributions. The Trustee shall then, as soon as administratively feasible, pay each Participant and Beneficiary his/her entire interest in the Trust in a lump sum and shall pay any remaining amount to the Employer. In the case of any Participant whose whereabouts is unknown, the Plan Administrator shall notify such Participant at his/her last known address by certified mail with return receipt requested advising him/her of his/her right to a pending distribution. Except as provided in the following sentence, if the Participant cannot be located in this manner, the Trustee shall establish a custodial account for such Participant's benefit in a federally insured bank, savings and loan association, or credit union in which the Participant account balance(s) shall be deposited. However, if proof of death of the Participant satisfactory to the Plan Administrator is received by the Plan Administrator, he/she shall pay the balance to the Participant's Beneficiary.

ARTICLE XII   Administration

12.1 *Named Fiduciary.* The named fiduciaries shall be:

a. the Plan Administrator, and

b. any person designated by the Employer as a named fiduciary in the manner prescribed in Section 12.2(a).

12.2 *Appointment of Plan Administrator, Other Designated Named Fiduciary, and Trustee.*

a. The Employer shall designate the Plan Administrator (if the Employer is not to be the Plan Administrator), the Trustee, and any person described in Section 12.1(b), in a written statement filed with the Employer's board of directors. No appointment of a Plan Administrator or a person described in Section 12.1(b) shall become effective until the party designated accepts those powers and duties bestowed upon him/her in accordance with the terms of the Plan in writing filed with the board. The appointment of the Trustee shall become effective at such time as the Trustee and the Employer execute a valid written trust which definitely and affirmatively precludes prohibited diversion. The details of any appointment described in this Subsection shall be recorded in the minutes of the board, and notice of any appointment shall be communicated at those locations customarily used by the Employer for notices to Employees with regard to labor-management matters at work sites of the Employer.

b. The resignation of a Plan Administrator, a person described in Section 12.1(b), or a Trustee shall be made in writing, submitted to the Employer, and recorded in the minutes of the board. The discharge of any person described in the preceding sentence shall be effectuated in writing by the Employer and delivered to such person with the details thereof recorded in the minutes of the Employer's board of directors. Appointment of a successor shall be carried out in the manner prescribed in Subsection (a).

12.3 *Administrative Expenses.* Except for commissions on acquisition or disposition of securities, the Employer shall pay the administrative expenses of the Plan and Trust, including the reasonable compensation of the Trustee and Plan Administrator and reimbursement for their reasonable expenses.

12.4 *Plan Administrator's Powers and Duties.* The Plan Administrator shall have the following powers and duties:

a. To construe and interpret the provisions of the Plan;

b. To decide all questions of eligibility for Plan participation and for the payment of benefits;

c. To provide appropriate parties, including government agencies, with such returns, reports, schedules, descriptions, and individual statements as are required by law within the times prescribed by law; and to furnish to the Employer, upon request, copies of any or all such materials, and further, to make copies of such instruments, reports, and descriptions as are required by law available for examination by Participants and such of their Beneficiaries who are or may be entitled to benefits under the Plan in such places and in such manner as required by law;

d. To obtain from the Employer, the Employees, and the Trustee such information as shall be necessary for the proper administration of the Plan;

e. To determine the amount, manner, and time of payment of benefits hereunder;

f. Subject to the approval of the Employer only as to any additional expense, to appoint and retain such agents, counsel, and accountants for the purpose of properly administering the Plan and, when required to do so by law, to engage an independent Qualified Public Accountant to annually prepare the audited financial statement of the Plan's operations;

g. To take all actions and to communicate to the Trustee in writing all necessary information to carry out the terms of the Plan and Trust Agreement;

h. To notify the Trustee in writing of the termination of

the Plan or the complete discontinuance of Employer contributions;

     i. To direct the Trustee to distribute assets of the Trust to each Participant and Beneficiary in accordance with Article X of the Plan; and

     j. To do such other acts reasonably required to administer the Plan in accordance with its provisions or as may be provided for or required by law.

12.5 *Designated Named Fiduciary's Powers and Duties.* A designated named fiduciary described in Section 12.1(b) who is appointed pursuant to Section 12.2(a) may, subject to the approval of the Employer only as to additional expense, appoint and retain an investment manager to manage any assets of the Trust (including the power to acquire and dispose of such assets). The investment manager shall be the person designated by the designated named fiduciary in a writing filed with the Employer's board of directors, and details of the appointment shall be recorded in the minutes of the board. No appointment shall become effective until the investment manager enters into a signed agreement with the designated named fiduciary which sets out such enumerated powers and duties. In the event that an investment manager is appointed pursuant to this Section, it shall be his/her responsibility to establish and/or maintain a funding policy for the Plan in accordance with Section 12.6.

It shall be the responsibility of a designated named fiduciary to afford any Participant or Beneficiary whose claim for benefits has been denied by the Plan Administrator a reasonable opportunity for a full and fair review of that decision.

If no designated named fiduciary is appointed pursuant to Section 12.2(a), the powers and duties described in this Section shall reside with the Plan Administrator.

12.6 *Trustee's Powers and Duties.* The powers and duties of the Trustee shall be to manage and control the funds of the Trust in accordance with the terms of the Trust Agreement forming a part hereof. Unless an investment manager has been appointed pursuant to Section 12.5, upon acceptance of the Trust, it shall be the duty of the Trustee, at a meeting duly called for such purpose, to establish a funding policy and method to carry out the objectives of the Plan. Thereafter, following the close of each Plan Year, the Trustee (or the investment manager, if one has been appointed) shall convene a similar meeting to review and, if necessary, revise such funding policy and method. If an investment manager has been appointed pursuant to Section 12.5, it shall be the duty of the named fiduciary who has chosen such investment manager to establish a funding policy and method to carry out the objectives of the Plan and to thereafter review and, if necessary, revise such funding policy and method. All actions taken with respect to such funding policy and method and the reasons therefor shall be recorded in the minutes of the Trustee's (named fiduciary's) meetings and shall be communicated to the Employer. The general objective of the funding policy of this Plan shall be at all times to maintain a balance between safety in capital investment and investment return. All of the Trustee's other powers and duties shall be governed by the Trust Agreement forming a part thereof.

12.7 *Allocation of Functions.* Any person or group of persons may serve in more than one fiduciary capacity with respect to the Plan (including service both as Trustee and Plan Administrator). Where more than one person serves as Plan Administrator, such persons may agree in writing to allocate among themselves the various powers and duties prescribed in Section 12.4 provided all such persons sign such agreement. A copy of any such agreement shall be promptly relayed to the Employer.

ARTICLE XIII Miscellaneous

13.1 *Mergers, Consolidations, and Transfers of Assets.* This Plan shall not be merged into or consolidated with any other plan, nor shall any of its assets or liabilities be transferred to any other plan.

13.2 *Assignment and Alienation of Benefits.* Benefits provided under this Plan shall not be subject to assignment or alienation.

13.3 *Communication to Employees.* The Plan Administrator shall furnish to each Participant and each Beneficiary receiving benefits under the Plan a copy of a summary plan description and a summary of any material modifications thereof at the time and in the manner prescribed by law.

13.4 *Number.* Whenever words are used in this document in the singular form, they shall, where appropriate, be construed to include the plural.

13.5 *Construction.* The terms of the Plan shall be construed under the laws of the State of the situs of the Trust except to the extent that such laws are preempted by Federal law.

_____   _____
      (Date of Adoption)   (Employer)

                          By: _____
                                          (Officer)

APPENDIX D

Trust Agreement for Investing Contributions under a Variable Prototype Retirement Plan

(NAME OF YOUR CORPORATION)

UNDER THE TRUSTEESHIP OF THE TRUSTEE NAMED BELOW AND IN THE APPLICATION

SECTION 1 Introduction

The _____ (hereafter referred to as "Employer") has established a Retirement Plan (attached hereto as Exhibit A [this is Appendix C]) for the benefit of the participants therein (the "Participants") pursuant to the Internal Revenue Code of 1954 as amended. As part of the Plan, the "Trustee" shall establish a Trust Account for the investment of contributions under the Plan in regulated Investment Company Shares and any other investments considered prudent at the discretion of the Trustee, upon the terms and conditions set forth in this Agreement.

The Employer shall ascertain that the Participant has received a copy of the then-current Prospectus for the Investment Company Shares to be acquired whenever the same are to be so acquired, whether by reason of a contribution thereto (either by the Employer or by the Participant) or otherwise. By remitting such a contribution, or otherwise instructing the Trustee regarding the acquisition of such shares, the Employer shall be deemed to warrant to the Trustee that the Participant has received such a Prospectus.

SECTION 2   Receipt of Contributions

The Trustee shall accept and hold in the Trust such contributions of money on behalf of the Employer and Participants as it may receive from time to time from the Employer other than those which it may be instructed to remit to the Insurance Company in payment of premiums in accordance with the Plan, if the insurance option is selected.

The Trustee may accept assets transferred to it from a trust serving any other qualified retirement plan which is maintained by the Employer, for the benefit of any of the Participants, provided that the Employer represents that said other plan satisfies the applicable requirements of Section 401 of the Internal Revenue Code of 1954, as amended, and provided that the Trustee has received a description of the assets and such other information as it may reasonably require. The Trustee will not accept assets which are not either in a medium properly designated by the Employer for investment hereunder or in cash, unless it is determined that their prompt liquidation is feasible. In that event, it will promptly effect liquidation of such other assets, and then shall make appropriate credits to the accounts of the Participants for whose benefits assets have been transferred, all in accordance with the instructions of the Employer. Amounts shall be credited as contributions previously made under the Plan of the Employer either by the Employer or by such Participants, as the case may be.

SECTION 3   Investment of Receipts

3.1 Contributions shall be applied to the purchase of Investment Company Shares at the price and in the manner in which such shares are being publicly offered, or to any investments considered prudent, at the discretion of the Trustee.

3.2 If the insurance option is selected, the Employer may remit to the Trustee insurance premiums which constitute contributions under the Plan or, for purposes of administrative convenience, the Employer may forward premiums directly to the insurer. The Trustee shall accept and hold in the Trust Account, or pay out as premiums on insurance, all contributions under the Plan which it may receive from the Employer. Each contribution shall be accompanied by written instructions of the Employer which direct how the contribution is to be held, allocated to Participants' Accounts, or paid out as premiums on insurance. The Trustee need not accept or need not invest a contribution which is not accompanied by adequate instructions. All contributions, except those allocated to payment of insurance premiums, shall be applied to the purchase of Investment Company Shares or to any investments considered prudent at the discretion of the Trustee, and shall be credited to each Participant's Account in such proportions as is designated by the Employer.

3.3 If the Trustee is instructed to allocate a part of a contribution for the payment of insurance premiums, its sole responsibility to the Employer or any Participant shall be to pay the premiums to the insurance company in accordance with the instructions, and its liability for a mistake or omission shall be limited to the amount of the premium involved. In all respects involving insurance premiums, the Trustee shall be deemed to be the agent of the Insurance Company. The Trustee shall have no liability with respect to money transferred to an insurance company pursuant to such instructions, and the Trustee shall not be responsible for remitting to the Insurance Company any premium or for taking any other action before the end of the seventh (7th) full business day following its receipt of the contribution, authorization, direction, or information which enables it to make such payment or take such action.

3.4. The Trustee shall not be obligated to receive a contribution, instruction, or request from a Participant unless the same is forwarded by the Employer, but it may do so in its discretion.

3.5. The Trustee shall have no responsibility to verify the accuracy of any information supplied by the Insurance Company, and the Trustee shall not incur any liability for its distribution of any inaccurate information supplied by the Insurance Company.

3.6. Whenever feasible, all dividends received on common stock shall be reinvested in such stock.

3.7. All dividends and capital-gain distributions received on Investment Company Shares shall be reinvested in such Shares.

3.8. Whenever feasible, if any distribution on such common stock may be received at the election of the shareholder in additional shares of stock or in cash or other property, the Trustee shall elect to receive it in additional shares.

3.9. If any distribution on such Investment Company Shares may be received at the election of the shareholder in additional Investment Company Shares or in cash or other property, the Trustee shall elect to receive it in additional shares.

3.10. All investments acquired by the Trustee shall be registered in the name of the Trustee or of its nominee.

SECTION 4 Distributions

Distributions from the Trust shall be made by the Trustee in accordance with written directions of the Employer or the Plan Manager who shall have the sole responsibility for determining that directions given conform to provisions of the Plan. Depending on the Employer's directions, the Trustee shall either (1) transfer the appropriate amount of cash and number of shares of stock, Investment Company Shares, and/or other Trust investments into the name of such Participant, his estate, or his or her designated beneficiary; or (2) redeem the appropriate number of shares of stock, Investment Company Shares, and/or other Trust investments and distribute them in accordance with the Payment of Benefits provision of the Plan.

SECTION 5 Voting and Other Action

The Trustee shall deliver to the Employer all notices, prospectuses, financial statements, proxies, and proxy-soliciting material relating to the shares of stock and Investment Company Shares held in the Trust. The Trustee shall not vote any of the shares of stock or Investment Company Shares except in accordance with the written instructions of the Employer.

SECTION 6 Administration and Reports

6.1. The Trustee shall adopt rules for the conduct of its administration which it considers reasonable and which do not conflict with the substance of the Plan.

6.2. The Trustee may construe and interpret the Trust Agreement, correct defects, supply omissions, or reconcile inconsistencies to the extent necessary to carry out the purposes of the Plan.

6.3. The Trustee shall disburse from the Trust Account to such persons, in such manner, in such amounts, and for such purposes as the Plan provides.

6.4. The Trustee shall keep a record of all its proceedings and acts and shall keep such books of accounts, records, and other data as may be necessary for proper administration. The record shall include accurate and detailed accounts of investments, receipts, disbursements, and other transactions. Such records shall be open to inspection and audit by persons designated by the Employer, and Participants may examine records pertaining directly to them at a convenient time and place.

6.5. The Trustee may authorize any agent to act on its behalf and may employ actuarial, legal, investment advisory, clerical, accounting, or other services to carry out the Plan, the cost for which shall be borne by the Trust Fund.

6.6. Within ninety (90) days after each Plan Year or following its removal or resignation, the Trustee shall file with the Employer an account of its administration of the fund during such year or from the end of the preceding Plan Year to the date of removal or resignation. Neither the Employer nor any other persons shall be entitled to any further accounting by the Trustee.

SECTION 7   Trustee's Fee and Expenses

Any income taxes or other taxes of any kind whatsoever that may be levied or assessed upon or in respect of the Trust Account shall be paid from the assets of the Account and shall, unless allocable to the Accounts of specific Participants, be charged proportionately to their respective Accounts. Any transfer taxes incurred in connection with the investment and reinvestment of the assets of the Trust Account, all other administrative expenses incurred by the Trustee in the performance of its duties including fees for legal services rendered to the Trustee, and such compensation to the Trustee as may be agreed upon in writing from time to time between the Trustee and the Employer shall be paid by the Employer, but until paid shall constitute a charge upon the assets of the Trust Account.

However, if the Employer so directs, such expenses may be charged in whole or in part against the Trust assets, and shall, unless allocable to the Accounts of specific Participants, be charged proportionately to their respective Accounts. The Trustee may designate an administrative agent who may be a corporation or individual(s) to perform any of the duties or functions of the Trustee. Fees charged by such agent or other expenses incurred by the Trustee shall be paid in whatever time and manner required by the Payee.

On termination of the Trust, transfer of the Trust, transfer of Trust assets under Section 4, or on resignation or removal of the Trustee, the Trustee may reserve in connection with any payment or distribution an amount adequate to assure it of its fees and expenses, or other liabilities, properly incurred or to be incurred.

SECTION 8 The Trustee

8.1. The Trustee shall carry out the instructions of the Plan Manager which are in accordance with the provisions of the Plan and Trust Agreement. The Trustee, acting in a uniform and nondiscriminatory manner, may adopt forms, including requests for selection of an investment medium or designations of beneficiary, or whatever is feasible to permit effective administration. The Trustee shall be entitled to rely upon written orders or instructions from the Plan Manager.

In case of the death of a Participant, the Trustee may require the submission of appropriate certificates, tax waivers, and other documents or evidence in preparation for distribution.

The Trustee must, within the area of its responsibilities, act with the same care that a prudent man familiar with such matters would exercise on acting in a like capacity in a similar enterprise having similar purposes. The Trustee shall, under the direction of the Plan Manager, make available to the Participants the opportunity to diversify investments within their Accounts in order to minimize the risk of large losses.

8.2. In addition to such powers as the Trustee has by law and under other provisions of the Plan and Trust Agreement, the Trustee will have the following powers, subject to the limitations set forth in Sections 2, 3, 4, and 12 hereof: (a) to deal with any part or all of the Trust Fund; (b) to retain uninvested such cash as it may deem necessary or advisable, for reasonable periods of time, without liability for interest thereon; (c) to enforce by suit or otherwise, or to waive, its rights on behalf of the Trust, and to defend claims asserted against the Trustee or the Trust, provided that the Trustee is indemnified to its satisfaction against liability and expenses; (d) to compromise, adjust, and settle any and all claims against or in favor of it or the Trust; (e) subject to the provisions of this Plan, to vote, or give proxies to vote, any stock or other security, and to waive notice of meetings; (f) to vote or otherwise oppose, or participate in and consent to the reorganization of any company, to pay assessments and expenses in connection therewith, and to deposit securities under deposit agreements; (g) to retain securities in unregistered form, or to register in the name of nominees; (h) to make, execute, and deliver any instruments necessary or appropriate to fulfill the powers described herein; (i) to exercise any other incidental powers necessary to apply the duties and authorities of an owner respecting all or any part of the Trust Fund.

8.3. The Employer and the personal representative or successors of the Employer shall have the sole authority to enforce this Agreement on behalf of any and all persons having or claiming any interest in the Trust by virtue of the Plan or Trust Agreement.

SECTION 9 Amendment

This Trust Agreement may be amended at any time, in whole or in part, by either the Sponsor of the Investment Company Shares or by written agreement between the Employer and the Trustee. A copy of any amendment made by the Sponsor shall be mailed to the Employer and the Trustee, who shall be deemed to have consented to the Amendment unless within thirty (30) days after the date of its mailing, the Employer and the Trustee agree to continue under the original Trust Agreement, or take such other action negating such implied consent. However, the Employer cannot proceed under the procedures respecting prototype plans if the Trust Agreement is other than that offered by the Sponsor.

SECTION 10 Resignation or Removal of Trustee

10.1 a. The Trustee may resign upon thirty (30) days' written notice to the Employer and may be removed by the Employer upon thirty (30) days' written notice to the Trustee.

b. If a group of Employers have adopted the Plan, the Trustee may resign upon written notice to the Sponsor, and it may be removed by the Sponsor upon written notice to the Trustee.

10.2. The Employer (if resignation or removal of the Trustee is made under Section 10.1a) or the Sponsor (if resignation or removal of the Trustee is made under Section 10.1b) shall appoint a qualified successor Trustee who shall notify the resigning or removed Trustee in writing of its acceptance of appointment.

10.3. As soon as reasonably convenient after receipt of notice under Section 10.2, the then-Trustee shall transfer to the successor Trustee the assets of the Trust Account or Accounts affected by the appointment and all records pertaining thereto.

10.4. If the Trustee resigns or is removed by the Sponsor as to the entire group of Employers under the foregoing Section 10.1(b), the Trustee (in case of resignation) or the Sponsor (in case of removal) shall notify each Employer of the fact of removal or resignation and of the fact of appointment of a successor Trustee notification shall be given in writing to each Employer in accordance with the records of the Trustee, within ten (10) days after acceptance of appointment by the qualified successor Trustee. Failure to notify any Employer shall not affect the designation of the successor Trustee as to that Employer.

Section 11 Distribution upon Termination

The Trustee may elect to terminate the Trust Account if within thirty (30) days after its resignation or removal pursuant to Section 10, a qualified successor Trustee has not been appointed which has accepted such appointment. The Trustee shall terminate the Account upon termination of the Plan pursuant to its terms. The Trustee shall terminate the Account if the Trustee terminates the Plan for reason of abandonment as provided in Article XI of the Plan. Termination of the Trust Account shall be effected by distributing the assets thereof as provided in Article XI of the Plan. Upon completion of such distribution, the Trustee shall be relieved from all liability with respect to all amounts so paid.

Section 12 Prohibited Transactions

At no time shall it be possible for the Trustee to engage, directly or indirectly, in any of the following transactions with the Employer or any other party in interest, except for exemptions authorized by appropriate authorities, including Employees, advisers, consultants, or any person controlling or controlled by the Employer, or an Employee organization having members included as Participants of the Plan and its employees, officers and directors and affiliates, and relatives, partners, or joint venturers of any of the persons heretofore enumerated:

a. Lend any part of the corpus or income of the Trust except for applying insurance or annuity values for premium payment.

b. Pay any compensation for personal services rendered to the Trust. The Trustee may contract or make reasonable arrangements with a party in interest for office space, or legal, accounting, or other services necessary for the establishment or operation of the Plan, if no more than reasonable compensation is paid therefor.

c. Make services available on a preferential basis.

d. Acquire for the Trust any property from or sell any property to.

SECTION 13   Miscellaneous

The assets of the Trust shall not be subject to alienation, assignment, garnishment, attachment, execution, or levy of any kind, and any attempt to cause such benefits to be so subjected shall not be recognized by the Trustee.

This Trust Agreement shall be construed and administered in accordance with the laws of the state of domicile of the Employer, unless the Employer and Trustee otherwise agree in writing.

In the event of any conflict of the provisions of the Plan and the Agreement, an interpretation that would best suit the continued qualification of the Plan and Trust shall prevail.

Any notice from the Trustee to the Employer pursuant to this Agreement shall be effective if sent by first-class mail to the Employer at his or its address on the Application or such other address as the Employer most recently has furnished to the Trustee, calling attention to it as a change of address.

Any distribution to a Participant, his estate, or his designated beneficiary shall be considered to have been duly made if sent by the Trustee by first-class mail to the address specified by the Employer for the purpose; or, if none, either (i) in care of the Employer at the address of the Employer for purposes of notices hereunder, or (ii) the last address, if any, of the Participant on the Trustee's records, whichever the Trustee selects in its absolute discretion.

At no time shall it be possible for any part of the assets of the Trust to be used for or diverted to purposes other than for the exclusive benefit of Participants in the Plan and their beneficiaries.

SECTION 14   The Trust Fund

Amounts received by the Trustee from the Employer shall be invested in the name of the Trustee or its nominee. The Trustee shall obtain a Tax Identification Number for the Trust Fund. Property contained in the Trust Fund may not be combined with any other property owned by any other person or entity, nor may any property in the name of the Trust Fund return, under any circumstances, to the Employer.

It is contemplated that the Trust Fund will be a single indivisible fund. However, the Trustee, at its discretion, may adopt such book-keeping procedures as it considers necessary and desirable, depending upon the nature of the Retirement Plan and its reporting requirements.

Accordingly, where the contribution from the Employer is allocated to Participants on the basis of unit or dollar amounts, the Trustee shall keep such separate bookkeeping records as it deems desirable to show such separate portions. Any such treatment for bookkeeping purposes shall not, of course, affect the degree to which the rights of a Participant have been reduced through incomplete vesting.

Similarly, the Trustee may install bookkeeping procedures to control and identify contributions received from Employees. Any contributions received from Employees shall be maintained in a separate portion of the Trust Fund. In the event that Employees make both mandatory and voluntary contributions to the Trust, the Trustee may, within its discretion, establish separate procedures to distinguish the Mandatory Contribution portion from the Voluntary Contribution portion. Where Life Insurance contracts are purchased by the Trustee, it may adopt such bookkeeping procedures as it finds necessary to report the receipt of premiums, changes in reserve values, or other developments affecting such contracts.

Date: _____

Employer: _____

By: _____
       (Authorized Signature)

The named Trustee(s) acknowledges receipt of a copy of the Plan and Trust Agreement and hereby accepts its appointment as of this _____ day of _____, 19__.

Trustee(s):
_____
_____
_____

APPENDIX E

Adoption Agreement

1. INFORMATION ABOUT THE EMPLOYER

Name _____

Business Address _____

_____

Nature of Business _____

Tax Identification # _____

Employer's Fiscal Year _____

Subchapter S Corporation ☐ Yes ☐ No

Date of Incorporation _____

2. THE TRUSTEE

The Employer appoints the following Trustee(s) in accordance with the Trust Agreement, effective on the date that the Employer and Trustee execute said Agreement.

Name(s) _____

_____

Business Address _____

_____

3. PLAN MANAGER

The Employer appoints the following Plan Manager to perform the duties provided in the Plan and Trust Agreement.

Name(s) _____

_____

Business Address _____

_____

4. Plan Year

The Effective Date of the Plan shall be _____.
Plan Year shall mean the Employer's fiscal year unless a different Plan
Year is selected as follows: _____ to _____.
Anniversary date shall be the last day of the Plan Year unless a
different date is selected as follows: _____.

5. Plan Compensation

Plan Compensation shall mean all income paid the Participant.
  ☐ A. In the Plan Year
  ☐ B. In the Fiscal Year ending within the Plan Year
Unless the following item(s) would be excluded:
  ☐ C. Bonus
  ☐ D. Overtime
  ☐ E. Commission payments
  ☐ F. Other remuneration _____
      If integrated formula is selected (under option 15(c)), there
      shall be no exclusions.
No more than $100,000 of the earnings of a more than 5% share-
holder in a Subchapter S corporation may be considered.

6. Application of Forfeitures

In accordance with Section 4 of Article VIII, forfeitures under the
Plan shall be applied in the following manner:
  ☐ A. Be reallocated in the same proportion that the current year's
      contribution is allocated among Participants.
  ☐ B. Be used to reduce subsequent contributions by the Em-
      ployer.
  ☐ C. Be reallocated among all Participants except for those who
      have a greater than 5% stock interest in the corporation, in
      the proportion that the current year's contribution for such
      Participant bears to the total contribution for all such Partic-
      ipants.

7. Years of Service

In accordance with Section 5 of Article III, years of service shall
include previous service with _____
_____.

8. NORMAL RETIREMENT AGE

Normal Retirement Age under the Plan shall be the _____ birthday (no less than 60 nor more than 70). The Normal Retirement Age shall be 65 unless otherwise specified. If an integrated formula is selected, the Normal Retirement Age shall not be less than 65.

9. EARLY RETIREMENT

☐ A. There shall be no early retirement under the Plan.

☐ B. A Participant who has attained age _____ (no less than 50) with _____ years of participation shall be fully vested and shall be entitled to take an early retirement if he or she so desires.

10. ELIGIBILITY REQUIREMENTS

A. Employee Classification
   ☐ i. All Employees
   ☐ ii. Salaried Employees Only
   ☐ iii. Hourly Employees Only
   ☐ iv. All Employees except for those who are subject to a Collective Bargaining Agreement unless such agreement provides for their inclusion hereunder
   ☐ v. All Employees except for commission salesmen
   ☐ vi. All Employees at _____
      (specific site, department, or division)

B. An Employee is one who after commencing employment works 1,000 hours during the following 12 months.

C. Years of Service
   Immediate Vesting Requirement
   All present Employees who have completed three years of service.
   Employees hired after the effective date when they have completed three years of service.
   Otherwise, all present and future Employees after completing one year of service and reaching the minimum age.

D. Minimum Age
   ☐ i. Present Employees: _____ years of age (maximum of 21)
   ☐ ii. Future Employees: _____ years of age (maximum of 21)

All officers, shareholders, supervisors, and highly compensated employees must be able to meet the eligibility requirements for future employees on the Plan's effective date under options C and D above.

11. MANDATORY CONTRIBUTIONS

In accordance with Article IV of the Plan, a Participant must make contributions in accordance with the following formula:

☐ A. No Mandatory Contributions shall be required under the Plan.

☐ B. For an otherwise eligible Participant hereunder, he or she must contribute _____% of his compensation (percentage selected by Employer cannot exceed 6%).

☐ C. For an otherwise eligible Participant to participate hereunder, he must contribute _____% (not to exceed 6%) of his compensation in excess of his or her Social Security Wage Base (unless option A above is indicated, this formula must be used if the Plan is to be integrated with Social Security on an excess basis only).

12. VOLUNTARY CONTRIBUTIONS BY EMPLOYEES

☐ A. An Employee is permitted to contribute an amount not to exceed 10% of his or her Plan Compensation each year.

☐ B. _____% is to be read in place of 10% above.

☐ C. Participants shall not be permitted to make Voluntary Contributions hereunder.

13. VESTING

The Employee's interest in Employer contributions shall become nonforfeitable in accordance with the following schedule:

☐ A. 100% immediately upon becoming a Participant

☐ B. Six-Year Rule

Years of Service	Nonforfeitable Percentage
2	20
3	40
4	60
5	80
6	100

☐ C. Other _____

_____

_____

14. CONTRIBUTIONS BY THE EMPLOYER

In accordance with Article VI of the Plan, the Employer shall annually make contributions out of its Net Profits in accordance with the following:

☐ A. The Employer shall contribute such amount as annually determined by its Board of Directors.

☐ B. The Employer shall contribute such amount as annually determined by its Board of Directors; however, in the event that the Board of Directors does not act within its fiscal year, the company shall make a contribution in accordance with the following:

☐ i. The company shall contribute _____% of the compensation of the Participants.

☐ ii. The company shall contribute _____% of its Net Profits for such year.

☐ C. The Employer shall contribute _____% of the compensation of the Participants.

☐ D. The Employer shall make contributions in accordance with the level of its Net Profits as follows:

If the Annual Net Profit is:		The Employer's contribution as a percentage of the Participant's compensation shall be:
1. Less than $____		____%
2. $____	or more, but less than $____	____%
3. $____	or more, but less than $____	____%
4. $____	or more, but less than $____	____%
5. $____	or more	____%

☐ E. The Employer shall make a contribution of _____% (not more than 7.51%) of compensation in excess of the Social Security Wage Base (as defined hereunder). This option may be chosen by itself or in conjunction with any other contribution formula hereunder.

15. ALLOCATION OF THE EMPLOYER'S CONTRIBUTION

☐ A. In the proportion that each Participant's individual compensation bears to the total compensation of all Participants.

☐ B. In the proportion that each Participant's points bears to the total points of all Participants where each Participant is credited with _____ point(s) (no more than 2) for each full year of continuous service and _____ point(s) (no more than 2) for each full $100 of compensation.

☐ C. Allocated on the basis of _____% (not more than 7%) of the Participant's compensation in excess of Social Security Wage Base, the balance, if any, to be allocated in the proportion that each Participant's individual compensation bears to the total compensation of all Participants.

If contribution option 14E is chosen in conjunction with this allocation formula or if another contribution formula is chosen and contributions are made in a manner so that there are no participants other than those participating on an excess basis, then any forfeitures will be used to reduce the amount of Employer contributions for such year. Any balance remaining shall be allocated in the proportion that each Participant's compensation bears to the total compensation of all Participants. For purposes of allocating such remaining balance, a Participant shall include Employees who are otherwise eligible except for the fact that their compensation is below the maximum amount of wages subject to Social Security taxes.

If this option is chosen and there are Participants for whom an allocation is made other than on an excess basis only, then forfeiture will be allocated as follows:

☐ i. To reduce Employer contributions.

☐ ii. In proportion that each Participant's compensation bears to that total compensation of all Participants.

16. SOCIAL SECURITY WAGE BASE

For purposes of this Plan, Social Security Wage Base shall mean:

☐ A. The Social Security Wage Base in effect for the year in which the Plan Year begins.

☐ B. A stated dollar amount of $_____ (may not be more than the Social Security Wage Base as in effect when the Plan is adopted or amended).

The Employer (a) acknowledges receipt of the current Prospectus of the named fund or security, and represents that each Participant has received such Prospectus, (b) represents that each new Participant will receive the then-current Prospectus, (c) on behalf of himself and each Participant consents to the Plan and Trust Agreement, (d) represents that he will file such information with the Internal Revenue Service as the Service may require, and any other filings required by the State or Federal laws for any taxable year, (e) agrees to vote or instruct the voting of shares as requested by Participants concerning their Mandatory and Voluntary Contributions, (f) realizes that neither the Sponsor nor Broker-Dealer can furnish legal advice, and (g) acknowledges and agrees to the Fee Schedule listed under the investment instructions for the maintenance of Participant accounts, if applicable.

DATE: _____

EMPLOYER: _____

By: _____

(Authorized Signature)

The named Trustee(s) acknowledges receipt of a copy of the Plan and Trust Agreement and hereby accepts its appointment as of this _____ day of _____, 19____.

TRUSTEE(S):

_____

_____

_____

INDEX

255